'Rosen and Kasaab's *Crime, Violence and the State in Latin America* is essential reading for anyone who wants to understand how criminal organizations flourish in the power vacuums present in fragile states. Beyond merely illustrating how corruption impedes development in individual states, the authors demonstrate how the spread of illicit networks threaten regional security as well. It's a cogent, timely study that will benefit practitioners and undergraduates alike.'

Christine J. Wade, *Professor of Political Science and International Studies at Washington College*

"Rosen and Kassab prove again they are the go to authors when it comes to understanding the connections between organized crime, illicit markets, violence and weak states. *Crime, Violence and the State in Latin America* represents another masterful treatise on the salient issues that shape the developing world today. Rosen and Kassab link power, organized crime and weak institutions into a sophisticated and methodologically rigorous framework that explains the mechanism by which illicit non-state actors challenge state authority. Through well researched case studies Rosen and Kassab help to further our understanding of the consequences that crime and violence have on institutionalization and democratization in the developing world. This volume is a must read for anyone interested in the intersection of crime, violence and the development of state power.'

Orlando J. Pérez, *Dean of the School of Liberal Arts and Sciences and Professor of Political Science, University of North Texas at Dallas*

Crime, Violence and the State in Latin America

In this succinct text, Jonathan D. Rosen and Hanna Samir Kassab explore the linkage between weak institutions and government policies designed to combat drug trafficking, organized crime, and violence in Latin America.

Using quantitative analysis to examine criminal violence and publicly available survey data from the Latin American Public Opinion Project (LAPOP) to conduct regression analysis, individual case studies on Colombia, Mexico, El Salvador, and Nicaragua highlight the major challenges that governments face and how they have responded to various security issues. Rosen and Kassab later turn their attention to the role of external criminal actors in the region and offer policy recommendations and lessons learned. Questions explored include:

- What are the major trends in organized crime in this country?
- How has organized crime evolved over time?
- Who are the major criminal actors?
- How has state fragility contributed to organized crime and violence (and vice versa)?
- What has been the government's response to drug trafficking and organized crime?
- Have such policies contributed to violence?

Crime, Violence and the State in Latin America is suitable to both undergraduate and graduate courses in criminal justice, international relations, political science, comparative politics, international political economy, organized crime, drug trafficking, and violence.

Jonathan D. Rosen is Assistant Professor of Criminal Justice at Holy Family University, USA. His research interests include drug trafficking, organized crime, and violence.

Hanna Samir Kassab is Teaching Assistant Professor at East Carolina University, USA. His research interests include war, terrorism, and organized crime.

Routledge Studies in Latin American Politics

https://www.routledge.com/Routledge-Studies-in-Latin-American-Politics/book-series/RSLAP

Crime, Violence and the State in Latin America

Jonathan D. Rosen and
Hanna Samir Kassab

Routledge
Taylor & Francis Group

NEW YORK AND LONDON

First published 2021
by Routledge
52 Vanderbilt Avenue, New York, NY 10017

and by Routledge
2 Park Square, Milton Park, Abingdon, Oxon, OX14 4RN

Routledge is an imprint of the Taylor & Francis Group, an informa business

Library of Congress Cataloging-in-Publication Data
Names: Rosen, Jonathan D., author. | Kassab, Hanna Samir, 1984– author.
Title: Crime, violence and the state in Latin America / Jonathan D. Rosen &
    Hanna Samir Kassab.
Description: New York, NY : Routledge, 2020. | Includes bibliographical
    references and index.
Identifiers: LCCN 2020012614 (print) | LCCN 2020012615 (ebook) |
    ISBN 9780367529468 (hardback) | ISBN 9781003079910 (ebook) |
    ISBN 9781000164275 (adobe pdf) | ISBN 9781000164305 (mobi) |
    ISBN 9781000164336 (epub)
Subjects: LCSH: Organized crime—Latin America. | Violent crime—Latin
    America. | Drug control—Latin America. | Internal security—Latin
    America. | Failed states—Latin America. | Latin America—Politics and
    government—21st century.
Classification: LCC HV6453.L29 R67 2020 (print) | LCC HV6453.L29 (ebook) |
    DDC 364.10972—dc23
LC record available at https://lccn.loc.gov/2020012614
LC ebook record available at https://lccn.loc.gov/2020012615

ISBN: 978-0-367-52946-8 (hbk)
ISBN: 978-1-003-07991-0 (ebk)

Typeset in Times New Roman
by Apex CoVantage, LLC

To Karina Castillo Vargas and Noha Abou Jaoude

Contents

Figures and Tables

Figures

Tables

Acknowledgments

We would like to thank the wonderful staff at Routledge for this opportunity. It has been a pleasure working with the press and we hope our partnership will continue. Thanks to our editor at Routledge, Natalja Mortensen, for her dedication and support throughout the publication process.

In addition, we would like to thank the very helpful comments of the peer reviewers.

A special thanks to Mohsen Azadi for reviewing our statistical models. We really appreciate your patience and time.

A special thanks to our respective institutions: Holy Family University and East Carolina University.

Moreover, we would like to thank our families. A special thanks to Jonathan's wife, Karina Castillo Vargas, and Hanna's aunt, Noha Abou Jaoude, for their love and support. Jonathan would like to thank the Vargas family, Luz Amanda, Argentina, and Rosalina, for their love, support, and kindness.

1 Introduction and Theoretical Approach

Latin America has been the center of the US-led war on drugs for several decades.[1] The region is home to countries that cultivate, refine, and traffic drugs. Organized crime groups have evolved over time and diversified their business activities. Moreover, there have been intense theoretical discussions about how to define gangs, criminal bands, drug cartels, and organized crime groups. Scholars question whether some drug cartels should be considered narco-terrorists[2] and differ in terms of how to classify groups such as Mara Salvatrucha (MS-13). This work will examine a variety of different organized crime groups in Mexico, El Salvador, and Colombia and how they contribute to criminal violence. Some researchers believe that MS-13 is not a street gang due to the power of the organization and, therefore, should be treated like an urban guerrilla force.[3] Meanwhile, other scholars contend that MS-13 is a third-generation gang,[4] while the Supreme Court of El Salvador has categorized MS-13 as terrorists.[5] For the purpose of this research, MS-13 will be defined as a transnational organized crime group as this organization operates across several countries—El Salvador, Honduras, Guatemala, Southern Mexico, and the United States—and participates in a variety of illicit activities from extortion to serving as hired assassins.[6] Finally, the Barack Obama administration also classified MS-13 as a transnational organized crime group, and the US Treasury Department has subjected the organization to sanctions.[7]

Drug trafficking and organized crime as well as government policies have contributed to the high levels of violence plaguing the region.[8] Latin America is the most violent region in the world in terms of homicides. The region is also home to some of the most violent countries and cities on the planet. In 2016, for instance, El Salvador had a homicide rate of 81.2 per 100,000, followed by Venezuela and Honduras, which both had rates of 59 per 100,000.[9] In 2017, Venezuela had a homicide rate of 89 per 100,000, while El Salvador recorded a rate of 60 per 100,000 (see Figure 1.1).[10] Moreover, Latin America is home to 43 of the 50 most violent cities. Brazil had 19 of the most violent cities, while Mexico had eight, and Venezuela had seven. In addition, Colombia had four of the most violent cities, while Honduras had two.[11] In 2017, Caracas, Venezuela, ranked as the most violent city in the world with a homicide rate of 130.4 per 100,000. Acapulco, located in Guerrero, Mexico, had a homicide rate of 113.2

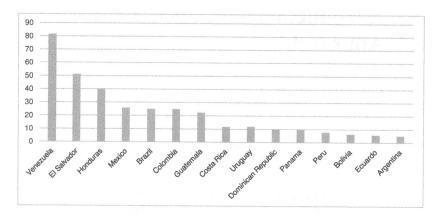

Figure 1.1 2018 Homicide Rate per 100,000

Source: Created by authors with data from Chris Dalby and Camilo Carranza, "InSight Crime's 2018 Homicide Round-Up," *InSight Crime*, January 22, 2019

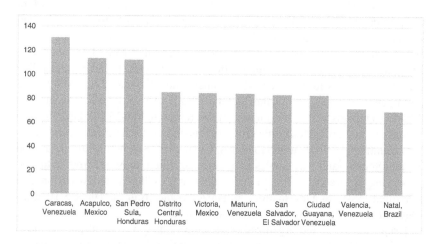

Figure 1.2 Most Violent Cities in Latin America

Source: Created by authors with data from Tristan Clavel, "Latin America Again Dominates World's 50 Deadliest Cities Ranking," *InSight Crime*, April 7, 2017; Citizen's Council for Public Security and Criminal Justice (Consejo Ciudadano para la Seguridad Pública y la Justicia Penal—CCSPJP)

per 100,000, while San Pedro Sula, Honduras and San Salvador, El Salvador, recorded rates of 112.1 and 83.4 per 100,000, respectively (see Figure 1.2).

This introductory chapter begins with a brief history of organized crime in Latin America. It then examines the concept of state fragility and how such factors can foster criminal activity, which represents one of the main theoretical arguments of this work. Organized crime groups have taken advantage of high levels of corruption to operate unabated. The chapter also examines the role of hardline government strategies and how they have contributed to criminal violence. State fragility alone, therefore, does not explain criminal violence, but rather state policies designed to combat criminal groups often have resulted in high levels of organized crime-related violence. Finally, the chapter concludes with an examination of the methodology utilized in this work and an overview of the book's organization.

A Brief History of Organized Crime in Latin America

The history of organized crime in Latin America is a history of state fragility underscored by poverty and corruption. Plagued by colonialism and the political instability of foreign decolonization, legacies of slavery, mass murder, and the exploitation of natural resources, the region's attempts at economic and political stability have been challenging.[12] This, combined with the discovery of cocaine in the nineteenth century, formed a pressure cooker of criminality that could very well be compared to a scientific laboratory leading to illicit markets. This section will briefly explore the development of organized crime in Latin America.

To begin, we must first explore the discovery of cocaine. First synthesized in 1860 in a German lab from the leaves of coca, cocaine took off as a miracle drug in Europe and the United States.[13] Coca comes from Latin America, specifically areas of what we know as Peru. Historically, coca leaves have been used by the people there, consumed by chewing and swallowing the juices.[14] Its traditional uses go beyond ceremonial and medicinal purposes.[15] This was thought to be repeated in its more potent, chemically extracted product, cocaine. Many celebrated the profound effects of cocaine, most notably Sigmund Freud.[16] However, this enthusiasm was short-lived. By the early 1900s, many scientists and physicians warned about the dangers of cocaine. Cocaine finally became a banned substance in 1917 with the onset of Prohibition.[17] Along with alcohol and marijuana, cocaine was illegal by law.[18] This marked the beginning of illicit markets for alcohol and cocaine.

After Prohibition, cocaine remained illegal. There was very little demand for the product except in certain social arenas like the emerging jazz scene in the United States and in Nazi Germany.[19] In Peru, people were discouraged to use coca leaves by international organizations touting it as an unhealthy substance.[20] Apart from these two facts, very little is documented on the subject of global cocaine use.[21] Marijuana was more on the radar, but this would all change by the 1970s. During the 1950s, cocaine use skyrocketed along with heroin and marijuana use.[22] Supply lines began in Mexico with production as well as trafficking. This led to the 1961 United Nations Single Convention on Narcotic Drugs designed to put pressure on states like Mexico that were producing illegal substances.[23] Economic as well as military aid was given to Mexico to clamp down on all illegal enterprises. This was successful in Mexico especially after the controversial Operation Condor in 1975 that helped combat illegal networks. Yet suppliers, feeling the heat of law enforcement from the United States, simply moved their enterprise to other states that had natural resources for producing drugs. This began the process described as the balloon effect, where if pressure is brought on one location, traffickers simply move to another.[24] Peru, Colombia, Bolivia, and the states of Central America were now the main benefactors of Richard Nixon's new "war on drugs" (1971).[25] During this time, these states were suffering the ravages of import substitution industrialization (ISI), a development strategy aimed at encouraging production of light to medium manufacturing goods in the agricultural economies of newly independent states of Latin America.[26] By 1970, the strategy proved unsuccessful due to corruption and inefficiency.[27] Unemployment and cost of living rose, leaving people unsatisfied.

In the new areas of cocaine development, specifically in Andean states and especially Colombia, traffickers worked closely with military and government officials through bribery. Governmental involvement in illegal business was not a new phenomenon. *Time Magazine*, in a 1949 edition, reported "Last week after he stepped off the plane from Lima, waiting detectives nabbed Rafael Menacho Vicente, 55, Cuban consul to Peru. In his diplomatic pouch was a package containing two pounds of cocaine, worth around $10,000 in the underworld."[28] As cocaine trafficking increased into the United States, the more traffickers profited, and the more corrupt states became. Corruption served to protect illicit supply chains, as states with corrupt bureaucracies would ensure the longevity of cocaine traffickers regardless of external pressure.

From this historical analysis, we can isolate two necessary components that lead to successful organized criminal networks. Both factors involve the state. The state must be able to deliver to the people alternatives to criminal life as well as maintain a certain level of justice and equality. The irony here is that prohibition of certain goods and services makes those alternatives, as well as justice and equality, less likely. Exploring these two factors is necessary to understand the inner workings of organized criminal networks.

Organized criminals pursue wealth through illicit means. They develop complex supply chains that link to global demand markets. Organized crime is the practice of selling goods or providing services in illegal goods. Its success is predicated on the use of violence and corruption to protect and prolong profits. Many hundreds of people may be dependent on the selling of illegal goods that are only profitable due to the enormous risk involved. The cost incurred by a country may be its institutions, as people in power fall prey to corrupt practices, giving organized criminals impunity (i.e., the ability to get away with crimes).[29] This book will argue that this dynamic leads to state fragility.

Organized crime competes with the state over the state's perception of morality. Certain commodities, such as narcotics, have been designated as societal evils and dangerous, and thus should not be provided to the public. This approach is a supply-side approach, meaning that if such commodities are made illegal, then people will refrain from selling, and therefore buying, them. The penalty for selling is prison time. This strategy is considered deterrence.[30]

A deterrence strategy was pursued regarding alcohol during a period known as Prohibition in the early twentieth century. A similar strategy continues today stemming from President Richard Nixon's "war on drugs."[31] The logic of this strategy is as follows:

> [n]o single law-enforcement problem has occupied more time, effort and money in the past four years than that of drug abuse and drug addiction. We have regarded drugs as "public enemy number one," destroying the most precious resource we have—our young people—and breeding lawlessness, violence and death.[32]

Said differently, to curb the supply of narcotics in the United States, the government increased efforts to destroy those supplying the drugs. Stopping these individuals and breaking up organized criminal groups were at the core of this strategy.

Drugs are more readily available and cheaper than in the 1970s, when the war on drugs began.[33] The problem with a supply-side approach is that illicit products fetch greater profits than licit ones. This is because of the risk people are taking to provide illicit goods. Prohibition cuts the supply of the goods and drives up the price.[34] In other words, risk is factored into the cost of narcotics and, as a result, provides an incentive to those seeking wealth fast.[35] What makes matters worse is that illicit goods are usually those commodities people desire due to addiction and cannot be found at the corner store. As a result, suppliers can make the price as high as they want. This is known as demand inelasticity, which measures how quantity demanded may change with increases in price. For instance, if a good is elastic, the higher the price results in less of the good demanded. Inelastic demand means that no matter how high the price, demand stays almost constant. Thus, one can extract higher profit for goods that are demand inelastic, as the costs remain the same.[36] Three factors, namely, price inelasticity, risk, and addiction create the perfect storm for the organization of criminal networks for the accumulation of wealth.

Furthermore, corruption is a tool that traffickers utilize to protect themselves and is part of the transaction costs. Transaction cost is an investment made, or a price one pays, to conduct business. These include:

> the costs of political activity, bargaining, legal action, and so on involved in deliberate efforts to create new rules, the costs of inefficiency resulting from commitment problems and other forms of political transaction costs, as well as all the costs involved in setting up, maintaining and changing the structure of rules and organizations, and monitoring the actions of the agents governed by those rules.[37]

Illicit transaction costs are qualitatively different from licit transaction costs and include costs of concealment, evasion, and corruption.[38] These costs are used to protect an illicit supply chain from law enforcement. The function of such costs is therefore twofold: to survive and to maximize wealth.

Thus, illicit markets can grow and succeed in places where individuals take extraordinary risks to make money and where it is possible to corrupt governments. This is the definition of weak and fragile states. States that suffer from organized crime tend to be those with extractive political institutions, those that take wealth away from one set of people in society to redistribute it to another.[39] In such an environment, people tend to move away from legitimate enterprises and embrace the black market. Under these circumstances, underdevelopment is sewn into a state and economy, leaving it to stagnate. In corrupt states, organized crime can flourish, as institutions are not equipped with the tools to hold corrupt police officers and members of government accountable for their actions. During Prohibition, the United States found itself in this position, facing not only increasing corruption, but also crime.[40] Law enforcement eventually boosted its ability to punish those who broke the law.

From this analysis, the profitability of illegal markets forces criminals to use corruption to protect themselves and their supply chains. This contributes to state fragility and weakness. High levels of corruption are associated with high levels of impunity, which makes the state weak and ineffective in bringing criminals to justice.[41] Strong, effective states are necessary to clamp down on corruption and protect the administration of justice.[42] The theoretical section will later expand on this argument.

Literature Review

This book addresses a need for a comprehensive book on criminal violence and state fragility in Latin America. Currently, there are many works that address drug trafficking and organized crime in one country. Scholars such as Russell Crandall, Jennifer S. Holmes, Bruce Bagley, and Arlene Tickner have focused on drug trafficking and organized crime in Colombia.[43] Moreover, Jorge Chabat, David Shirk, Peter Watt, John Bailey, Wil G. Pansters, and Roberto Zepeda[44] have written books and articles about organized crime in Mexico. These scholarly works address not only the history of drug trafficking and violence in Mexico, but also the failures of counternarcotic policies.

There are also various single-author books on gangs in Central America. First, Sonja Wolf's *Mano Dura: The Politics of Gang Control in El Salvador* is an ethnographic study that analyzes how non-governmental organizations (NGOs) have attempted to change the gang laws implemented by the Salvadoran government.[45] Wolf's work relies on interviews with activists and analyzes various Salvadoran newspapers.[46] Second, Robert Brenneman's *Homies and Hermanos: God and Gangs in Central America* explores the role of the Evangelical church in helping gang members exit the gang life. This book focuses on the role of the church in gang life and does not address the relationship between the state and the *maras* (gangs). Third, T.W. Ward's *Gangsters Without Borders: An Ethnography of a Salvadoran Street Gang* is a qualitative study that examines the lives of gang members.[47] While these studies are rich in detail, they do not analyze how gangs collaborate with other organized crime actors in Honduras and El Salvador and fail to examine the relationship between the state and organized crime. Finally, these ethnographic research projects do not have quantitative information about the maras, but instead rely on in-depth interviews with a small number of gang members.

Single-author case studies are rich in detail,[48] and the aforementioned works provide excellent information on gangs in El Salvador and Honduras as well as drug trafficking and organized crime in Colombia and Mexico. However, there are limitations with such studies. While these works are rich in breadth, one is not able to generalize with a single-case study. Instead, single-case studies help generate future research questions and hypotheses.

There are several books that address drug trafficking and criminal violence in various Latin American countries. *Making Peace in Drug Wars: Crackdowns and Cartels in Latin America* by Benjamin Lessing, a political scientist at the University of Chicago, employs the use of game theory to understand state strategies to combat drug-related violence in Brazil, Colombia, and Mexico. Lessing focuses on the concept of "condition repression" to decrease the levels of violence of drug cartels. This book, however, does not focus on institutions and fragile states. Instead, the work examines the war on drugs and the responses of the state.[49] Another book that explores drug trafficking in Colombia and Mexico is Victor J. Hinojosa's *Domestic Politics and International Narcotics Control: U.S. Relations with Mexico and Colombia, 1989–2000.* Hinojosa's work provides interesting information about double standards in US drug policy toward Mexico and Colombia. This work relies on historical examples, but it fails to address many of the current events in drug trafficking, organized crime, and violence as it was published in 2007. Finally, the goal of Hinojosa's book is not to understand the nature of organized crime, but rather to focus on US foreign policy and drug certification practices.[50]

In addition to single- and coauthored works, there are various edited volumes that analyze issues of drug trafficking, organized crime, state fragility, and violence. First, Bruce M. Bagley and his colleagues published a volume titled *Drug Trafficking, Organized Crime, and Violence in the Americas Today.*[51] While this book is a comprehensive study of the trends in drug trafficking, it does not concentrate on the relationship between the state and organized crime and lacks a coherent theoretical framework given the diverse group of authors from a variety of different disciplines, including epidemiology, political science, international relations, sociology, and anthropology. This book also concentrates on drug trafficking, but it fails to examine the role of gangs in Central America. Second, Jonathan D. Rosen and Hanna Samir Kassab and their contributors in *Fragile States in the Americas* analyze state fragility in the Americas. This volume includes case studies from around the region. While the authors focus on the concept of state fragility, the cases examine the nature and causes of state fragility and do not concentrate solely on drug trafficking and organized crime.[52]

Theoretical Approach: State Fragility, Corruption, and Government Policies

A democratic country that has a strong state apparatus must combat corruption and impunity and implement the rule of law.[53] People who break laws must be arrested and have their chance in court to prove their innocence. If a person is convicted of the crime, then this individual must be sentenced to jail or prison. Fragile states, on the other hand, are plagued by high levels of corruption.[54] In fragile states, individuals can avoid being arrested because they can bribe police officers. Countries that do not have an efficient and functioning judiciary system do not prosecute the guilty. States that are plagued by fragility in the judicial system are prone to having judges bribed, extorted, or even killed. In summary, corruption and the inability to implement the rule of law is a key trend impacting countries defined by state weakness. As a result, fragile states are rife with impunity.

Transparency is kryptonite for corrupt politicians and criminal actors. States that are fragile are often characterized by low levels of transparency, which enables criminal groups to penetrate the state apparatus. Journalists play a fundamental role in any democratic state because they help hold government officials and society accountable for their actions. Criminal groups do not want individuals to know about deals made with corrupt politicians, police officers, or judges. Increasing transparency, therefore, requires a functioning and independent media.[55]

Criminal groups take advantage of state fragility and corruption. Organized crime involves a conspiracy to sell illegal goods. A group of individuals come together to make profits, protecting themselves through corruption and violence.[56] The latter part of this definition emphasizes the survival and enrichment of organized criminal groups. Without corruption, illegal enterprises would find it difficult to survive, having to rely on assassination and violence to protect themselves from law enforcement. If weak and fragile states suffer from corrupt institutions, then it must be expected that powerful organized crime networks will begin to spread across the state. Extractive political institutions are often at the core of weak and fragile states, contributing to underdevelopment and further economic, political, and social instability. This section will thus explore the connection between organized crime and corruption, with the link being weak political institutions.

What constitutes a weak or fragile state? These terms designate worsening conditions for a state as it lacks the capability to solve threats to its sovereignty. These threats can be from state and non-state actors. Non-state threats may include social, political, economic, environmental, and health issues.[57] Effective functioning democratic states implement the rule of law and combat corruption and impunity. Impunity is the reason for persistently high rates of criminal activity, specifically homicides, in Latin America. For instance, in North America and Europe, around 80 percent of homicides result in conviction. Compare that to Latin American states like Brazil, Colombia, Honduras, and Venezuela, where the figure is closer to 10 percent.[58]

The weaker the state, the more fragile it becomes in administering its sovereign territory. Failed states "provide opportunities for actors outside the government—whether religious fundamentalists, disaffected citizens, or merely opportunists seeking power—to attempt to seize the state apparatus by violent means."[59] Organized criminal networks are placed in this category as well. The cases explored in the following chapters will demonstrate how law enforcement simply cannot act in an effective manner due to the power, in terms of both violence and corruption, of criminal enterprises.

Regarding weak and fragile states, Peter Lupsha, an organized crime expert, describes three stages of organized crime and its penetration into the state and its institutions. These are predatory, parasitical, and symbiotic. The predatory stage designates the relative weakness of the criminal groups to state institutions. The state can effectively deal with criminal networks through its judicial institutions.[60] The more powerful the criminal network becomes, the more it will begin to compete with the state. The parasitical stage, the second stage, illustrates the growing dominance of the criminal group over the state itself, when organized criminal networks begin controlling large swaths of territory making it as powerful as the state.[61] Finally, the symbiotic stage describes a situation where the state has become part of the criminal network itself.[62] From this point, criminal networks are now part of the state itself. The idea of state-sponsored organized crime can be an accurate descriptor. Gautam Basu further describes the relationship between weak states and organized criminal networks through the mechanism of corruption.[63] It can be concluded from this that organized criminal networks rely on corrupt fragile states to expedite their own success.[64] Corruption is a major mechanism for the growth of organized crime.

Organized criminal networks fill political vacuums created by state fragility. Latin America serves as an ideal case study as organized crime spreads from producing/supplier states to demand/consumption states. Power must be established by the state. Without an effective state to exercise control and justice within its borders, state authorities will eventually face serious challenges to their authority. Fragile states are defined by inherent structural weakness. Fragile states are those that suffer from corruption defined by extractive institutions. Extractive institutions have a negative impact on underdevelopment, leading to corruption and the inevitable success of organized crime. Weak states can be taken over by violent non-state actors, as their weakness and fragility contribute to their becoming prey. Hence, there is a connection between fragile states, power vacuums, and organized crime. From this, it can be concluded that power vacuums allow for the development of illicit markets given the freedom to operate.

Corrupt fragile states foster the growth of organized crime networks.[65] As these enterprises become more and more profitable, we begin to see external proliferation into bordering states. This is because of the need to expand and export into other states. As illegal markets expand, we may begin to see worsening fragility and the creation of vacuums. The postulations of Lupsha and Basu corroborate findings, and further studies show that drug trafficking and organized crime can foster different forms of conflict and criminal violence.[66] Hence, the theoretical framework of this book is as follows: fragile and corrupt states form the perfect environment for illicit trafficking, which further aggravates state fragility. Power vacuums are created when fragile states are hindered by corruption due to the nature of political institutions as well as underdevelopment. These factors hinder the state from being able to tackle organized crime and other non-state threats.[67] Power vacuums must be understood within the concept of the state. This book uses a traditional conception formulated by Max Weber. Weber defines the state as a unit of governance that enjoys a "monopoly on the legitimate use of physical force within a given territory."[68] Power vacuums are usually filled quickly by an opportunistic actor waiting to take advantage of the void. For a state to be effective, it must control its territory. Challenges to the state and its laws must be punished to retain territorial integrity. In relation to this starting point, there are three major factors a state must possess to be considered effective. First, a state and its use of force must be seen as legitimate. Second, a state must be capable of successfully achieving its aim when it uses violence. Third, it must be the only authority within that territory with the ability to use force. Fragile states lack all three factors.

This book conceptualizes fragile states as those that are corrupt and, as a result, whose dispensation of violence and justice is no longer seen as legitimate. These factors contribute to the second quality: because of inherent weakness brought on by corruption and underdevelopment, their capability is significantly reduced. In other words, they lack the ability to combat challenges (threats, whether internal or external) to their authority and power. As a result, fragile states surrender parts of their territory to other actors. This then creates the vacuum of power. For this reason, power vacuums are areas of competition created by a void left by a fragile state actor.

State failure occurs when a state becomes ungovernable, overrun by warring organized criminal networks and other competing non-state actors (e.g., gangs and drug trafficking organizations). Surrounding states then become victims, especially if they themselves are already weak and vulnerable.[69] Failed states "provide opportunities for actors outside the government—whether religious fundamentalists, disaffected citizens, or merely opportunists seeking power—to attempt to seize the state apparatus by violent means."[70] As in Lebanon after 1975 and contemporary Somalia and Afghanistan, non-state actors have the strength to organize and compete directly with a state's monopoly on the use of violence and implementation of the rule of law. When states succumb to these actors, it is likely that they will become a center for organized crime, terrorism, and other illicit activities.[71] As a result, failed and fragile states present a real danger for all states within the international system.

Even more serious is the contagion effect that weak, fragile, and failed states have on other already fragile states. Fragile states are unable to neutralize competitors to their sovereignty and autonomy. Consequently, criminal actors enjoy a greater degree of freedom than they do in stronger states with functioning institutions. This allows non-state actors of any variety to carry out production, trafficking, and, if they are terrorist networks, political governance without fear of punishment. One significant example occurred in 2000 in Lebanon. When Israeli forces unilaterally evacuated South Lebanon, Hezbollah, a criminal and terrorist organization, quickly filled the void. Lebanon, already weakened by the civil war as well as Syrian occupation, could not act quickly to defend its territorial integrity.[72] Today, Lebanon exists as a state with two armies, a hindrance to its development, locking it in fragility. In summary, fragile states provide the illicit infrastructure for safe operation of criminal actors.

This book argues that at its core, extractive political institutions grounded in institutionalized corruption are at the center of illicit markets:

> Extractive political institutions concentrate power in the hands of a narrow elite and place few constraints on the exercise of this power. Economic institutions are then often structured by this elite to extract resources from the rest of the society. Extractive economic institutions thus naturally accompany extractive political institutions. In fact, they must inherently depend on extractive political institutions for their survival.[73]

These institutions contribute to poverty since people no longer have faith in the legitimate economy as elites and government officials simply flow tax revenues and other methods of bribery into personal coffers. This reduces investment opportunities, leading to unemployment. This fact leaves citizens with very little, forcing them into the production of illegal commodities. One former drug trafficker noted the difficulty of living in a developing state with very little opportunity:

> A guy, a peasant in Colombia, if he grows oranges, he can't sell the oranges because they rot . . . but if somebody comes and asks him. . . . "Can you grow some coca leaves for us, and we pay you for whatever you produce," well the guy is going to do it. So why don't you pay $5 for each orange . . .? He doesn't care what it is, what he's growing.[74]

Hence, corrupt institutions foster the development of highly sophisticated illicit supply chains.[75] This book understands institutions to be:

> political mechanisms that increase political accountability, either by encouraging punishment of corrupt individuals or by reducing the informational problem related to government activities, [and thus] tend to reduce the incidence of corruption.[76]

Institutions, therefore, reproduce either corruption or development based on whether they themselves are corrupt or not. If corrupt institutions foster the development of illicit supply chains, the answer may be institutional reform. In other words, the remedy suggested in this book is the development of strong politically inclusive institutions that encourage development through reinvestment. Strong, democratically inclusive institutions increase investor confidence for three reasons determined by their characteristics:

> enforcement of property rights for a broad cross section of the society, so that a variety of individuals have incentives to invest and take part in economic life; constraints on the actions of elites, politicians, and other powerful groups, so that these people cannot expropriate the incomes and investments of others or create a highly uneven playing field; and some degree of equal opportunity for broad segments of society, so that individuals can make investments, especially in human capital, and participate in productive activities.[77]

Said differently, strong, politically democratic and inclusive institutions produce states with the ability to fight and neutralize illegal actors because they promote development. These institutions produce effective states that possess increased ability to neutralize competitors of sovereignty (e.g., organized crime groups). By encouraging legitimate businesses to grow and hire workers independent of the pressure of making bribery payments, the state and its people are more likely to enjoy the fruits of their labor. With increased confidence in the economy, the state will move further away from its fragile category toward being classified as an effective apparatus. Respect for private property, contracts, laws, and justice helps bolster investor confidence, creating a path for economic development in the long term.[78]

The theoretical framework developed here will be applied across several states in Latin America. The hypothesis of this book is as follows: if the state apparatus is weak and fragile (i.e., unable to neutralize threats to sovereignty) then the state may become prey to organized criminal actors, and this can lead to organized crime-related violence. Fragile states are easier to corrupt than effective ones. In addition, they are less likely to challenge entrenched and powerful networks that have sizable militias and gangs at their disposal. Underdeveloped states pose a unique opportunity for organized criminal networks. Those weak and fragile states with already corrupt political institutions further hinder the viability of these states. With few opportunities to provide for their families, it may be easier to seduce people away from illegal lifestyles. This book's framework thus makes a direct correlation between organized crime and weak states. Without dealing with these factors, namely, corruption and underdevelopment (factors that contribute to state weakness), any attempt at iron-fist policing furthers the already difficult situation. This may be occurring in El Salvador where heavy state policing is contributing to further recruitment by gangs. Hence, the state must understand the factors that contribute to organized crime, that is, state fragility, when clamping down on organized criminal networks.

This book seeks to show that there is a link between weak institutions and government policies designed to combat drug trafficking, organized crime, and violence. The countries examined in the case studies throughout this book are plagued by high levels of corruption, impunity, and weak institutions. As will be discussed further in the specific chapters, experts have calculated impunity in countries like Mexico to be over 90 percent. Organized crime groups flourish in states that are characterized by a weak state apparatus. Criminals seek to partake in illicit activities without being caught. For example, Central American countries have been plagued by institutional weakness. Honduras, for instance, witnessed connections between organized crime groups and elites, demonstrating the power and reach of criminal enterprises.[79]

What has been the response of governments seeking to combat organized-crime related violence? In various cases such as Mexico, Colombia, Honduras, and El Salvador governments have taken a tough on crime approach, often referred to as *mano dura*. The idea is that the government must respond to gangs, organized crime groups, and other illicit actors by arresting people who violate the law. Steven Dudley, an organized crime expert, contends:

> In El Salvador, this included rounding up thousands of youth based on their appearance, associations or address. Most of these arrests did not hold up in Salvadoran courts but served to further stigmatize already marginal communities and may have accelerated recruitment for the gangs themselves. Far more troubling, from a criminology standpoint was the effect Mano Dura had on the prison system, the mara leadership and its operational structures.[80]

Thus, *mano dura* strategies have resulted in thousands of young people in places like El Salvador being caught up in the prisons system. Being labeled as a gang member and a criminal can be hard to overcome and can contribute—along with other factors—to the prison system becoming a revolving door for youth.

The military has played an integral part in such iron-fist policies and the war on drugs. The police forces in many Latin American countries are riddled with high levels of corruption because of a variety of factors, including low pay and lack of professionalism.[81] Polling data demonstrate that civilians have higher levels of trust in the military. Experts note that this could be because citizens do not have daily interactions with the military, while people have more interaction with the police.[82] Felipe Calderón, the president of Mexico from 2006 to 2012, launched the war on drugs using the military because he did not have confidence in the ability of the police forces given the high levels of corruption permeating the institution.[83] In December 2017, the Mexican Congress passed a law granting the military a bigger role and more power in internal security efforts to combat drug trafficking and organized crime. According to Alejandro Madrazo Lajous, a professor at the Center for Research and Teaching in Economics (Centro de Investigación y Docencia Económicas—CIDE), "This bill effectively displaces the Constitution." In addition, he noted: "It allows the president to unilaterally militarize any part of the country for any time he considers necessary or adequate without any control either by congress or the judiciary."[84] Critics have also contended that the increasing role of the military does not focus on the need to reform the police and separate the functions of the police and military in internal security functions.[85] Even some members of the military have been critical of the institutions role. Jesus Estrada Bustamante, a retired Army General, contended in an interview: "We don't want to perform the functions of the police."[86] In sum, the use of the military in counter-drug and counter-gang strategies has been controversial. There is a correlation between corruption and institutional weakness and the use of the military. The case of Mexico, for instance, shows that the president used the armed forces in the drug war because of high levels of distrust in the ability of the police forces.

The chapters in this book will examine the consequences of tough on crime policies. Citizens want politicians to ensure their safety. People want to be able to live their lives, walk in their neighborhoods, take their kids to school, and go to work without the fear of being killed, extorted, or kidnapped. *Mano dura* policies are used by politicians to demonstrate to the public that the government is taking crime seriously and is attempting to reduce it. The subsequent chapters in the book will show that the militarization of the drug war in places like Mexico and anti-gang policies in Central America have been criticized by many experts because of the increasing levels of violence.[87] In addition, there have been major concerns about human rights abuses conducted by the security forces in Colombia, Mexico, and the Central American countries examined in this volume.

Finally, this book will examine how tough on crime policies have placed a strain on not only the security forces and judicial system but also prisons.[88] Research conducted on the prison system in Latin American countries show that many prisons operate as schools of crime. As will be explored in the chapter on El Salvador, prisons play an integral part in the organization of gangs like MS-13. Gang members are expected to be arrested and have used the prison system as a method to organize with different cliques from around the country.[89] *Mano dura* strategies have had many unintended consequences that will be analyzed more extensively throughout this work.

Case Selection and Methodology

This book focuses on criminal violence and state fragility in the cases of Colombia, Mexico, El Salvador, and Nicaragua. The first three countries have been plagued by drug trafficking, organized crime, and violence. Today, El Salvador is home to some of the most powerful gangs in the Western Hemisphere, MS-13 and the 18th Street gang. While both Mexico and Colombia have lower homicide rates than El Salvador, both countries have been epicenters of criminal violence. In addition, Colombia had the most powerful criminal organization in the Americas in the 1980s and 1990s, the Medellín cartel. The demise of the Medellín cartel and its rival Cali cartel led to a fragmentation of organized crime. There are hundreds of criminal actors that exist in Colombia today that have contributed to criminal violence. Finally, Mexico has had more than 120,000 drug-related deaths over the past 12 years and is home to some of the most violent cities in the world as well as the most powerful transnational organized crime groups in the Western Hemisphere.[90]

Each of the countries examined in this book are characterized by high levels of state fragility and corruption. How does one calculate state fragility? The Fund for Peace publishes the Fragile State Index (FSI), which utilizes the conflict assessment framework, or "CAST." This index incorporates both quantitative and qualitative methods and uses 12 factors. The first indicator is referred to as cohesion and includes three variables: security apparatus, factionalized elites, and group grievance. The second indicator is political and includes the following subcategories: state legitimacy, public services, and human rights. The FSI also incorporates economic indicators, which are calculated based on economic decline, uneven development, and human flight. Finally, the FSI has social indicators based on demographics, refugees and internally displaced persons, and external intervention.[91]

The FSI score has a maximum of 120. In 2019, Mexico had a 69.7 FSI score and ranked 98th. El Salvador scored a 69.8 in 2019 and ranked 96th out of 128 countries. Meanwhile, Colombia had an FSI of 75.7 and ranked 70th out of 178 countries.[92] Furthermore, the NGO Transparency International publishes the Corruption Perceptions Index (CPI), which provides a score and rank for countries in the world. According to the 2018 index, Mexico received a score of 28 out of 100, with the lower the number the more corruption. It also ranked 138 out of 100, with Somalia, the most corrupt country, ranking 180, while El Salvador scored 35 out of 100. Finally, Colombia scored 36 out of 100 on the CPI.[93]

Nicaragua is included in this study because it does not have high levels of criminal violence and represents an anomaly. Nicaragua, for example, had a homicide rate of seven per 100,000 in 2017, which is substantially less than its Northern Triangle neighbors. This book examines why Nicaragua, which is one of the poorest countries in Central America, does not have criminal violence. In addition, Nicaragua does not have a large presence of gangs and organized crime, which is not the same for its Northern Triangle neighbors.[94]

Furthermore, each of these countries examined have been at the center of various US interventions. The United States government, for instance, has invested billions in counternarcotic operations in Colombia and Mexico, including Plan Colombia and the Mérida Initiative. El Salvador also has received large amounts of foreign aid through various security plans, including the Central American Regional Security Initiative (CARSI). El Salvador also has been elevated on the security agenda of the United States, as it has been plagued by gangs and gang-related violence.[95] Finally, Nicaragua has had a long history of US intervention since the Cold War. Yet this country represents a scholarly puzzle, as it does not have high levels of criminal violence.

In terms of methodology, this book uses quantitative analysis to examine criminal violence. We seek to operationalize perceptions of insecurity, trust in government institutions, and state fragility. We utilize publicly available survey data from the Latin American Public Opinion Project (LAPOP) to conduct regression analysis. The individual country surveys conducted by LAPOP use a multi-stage cluster sampling. Each country survey has a sample size of more than 1,500. Regression analysis helps determine the factors that influence perceptions of insecurity, violence, and trust in the institutions. In summary, the use of regression analysis helps us quantify different phenomenon and strengthens our arguments made about factors that contribute to criminal violence and perceptions of insecurity and trust in institutions.[96]

Book Overview

The book is divided into various case studies. The chapters seek to examine the following questions: 1) What are the major trends in organized crime in this country? 2) How has organized crime evolved over time? 3) Who are the major criminal actors (e.g., gangs, cartels, criminal bands)? 4) How has state fragility contributed to organized crime and violence (and vice versa)? 5) What has been the government's response to drug trafficking and organized crime? 6) Have such policies contributed to violence?

Chapter 2 focuses on the case of Colombia, which has been at the center of drug trafficking and organized crime in Latin America for decades. The chapter explores the evolution of criminal violence from the days of Pablo Escobar and his Medellín cartel in the 1980s and early 1990s to the collapse of the two major drug cartels and the fragmentation of organized crime. The United States government invested $10 billion in Plan Colombia, a counternarcotics strategy that sought to decrease drug production and trafficking. The chapter explores the results of the counternarcotics strategies and the impact on organized crime and criminal violence. It explains how organized crime has evolved and how new actors, such as the criminal bands, have emerged. In addition, the chapter explores the current and potential future trends in organized crime as the country moves into the implementation phase of the peace process with the largest guerrilla organization, the Revolutionary Armed Forces of Colombia (FARC). The peace process and the election of the new president have created significant shifts in the security strategy, and the nature of organized crime and criminal violence is transforming.

Chapter 3 examines the case of Mexico. It begins by exploring the country's transition to democracy and the impact on organized crime and criminal violence. The chapter then examines President Felipe Calderón's drug war, which began in 2006. It then turns to an analysis of the different types of cartels that operate in the country and the impact of the administration's security strategy on organized crime, drug trafficking, and violence. The chapter then explores trends in drug-related violence in the country. Next, it highlights the need to reform different security institutions.

Chapter 4 focuses on El Salvador and Nicaragua. It starts with an examination of Salvadoran street gangs. The chapter then turns to the Salvadoran government's *mano dura* strategies designed to combat gangs and gang-related violence. It focuses on the consequences of such policies and highlights recent trends in criminal violence. The chapter also explains the linkages between state fragility and institutional corruption. Next, it analyzes why Nicaragua did not see such high levels of violence until April 2018. The chapter explores the role of the Nicaraguan police and the political system in preventing gangs from entering the country and controlling levels of violence, demonstrating the need to understand the nature of the political system.

Chapter 5 analyzes the behavior of the external organized criminal networks of China and Russia and their penetration into Latin America. The chapter considers the depth of Russian and Chinese state fragility required for success and focuses on the Triads, their history, development, and major practices. The Triads work with already established gangs and bring value to the narcotics trade by profiting on poorly regulated Chinese chemical and drug standards. They can bring in precursor methamphetamine chemicals as well as fentanyl for processing in Latin America. By doing so, the Triads formulate an excellent strategy of self-preservation and profit. Further, an unstable Chinese economy is pushing unskilled labor away from China and into the hands of the Triads for human trafficking into Latin America.

Chapter 6 concludes by summarizing the importance of state fragility and the proliferation of organized criminal networks. Variables of consideration include economic underdevelopment and corruption, and we specifically assess their interactions to understand the resilience of organized criminal networks. The chapter addresses the issue of institutional reform, focusing on the judiciary, police, and penitentiary system. It stresses the need to combat the demand for illicit products, such as narcotics.

Conclusion

Countries in Latin America have suffered from high levels of state fragility. This chapter has examined the relationship between fragile states and organized crime. In the subsequent chapters, this book will focus on case studies and analyze the trends in organized crime and violence. The individual case studies highlight the major challenges that governments have faced as well as how they have responded to the various security issues. The second to last chapter explores the role external criminal actors play in certain countries in the region. The final chapter concludes with some policy recommendations and lessons learned from the cases examined in this book.

Notes

1. Bruce Michael Bagley, "The new hundred years war? US national security and the war on drugs in Latin America," *Journal of Interamerican Studies and World Affairs* 30, no. 1 (1988): pp. 161–182; Bruce M. Bagley, "Colombia and the war on drugs," *Foreign Affairs* 67, no. 1 (1988): pp. 70–92.
2. Fernando Celaya Pacheco, "Narcofearance: How has narcoterrorism settled in Mexico?" *Studies in Conflict & Terrorism* 32, no. 12 (2009): pp. 1021–1048; Gregg S. Etter and Erica L. Lehmuth, "The Mexican drug wars: Organized crime, narcoterrorism, insurgency or asymmetric warfare?" *Journal of Gang Research* 20, no. 4

(2013): pp. 1–33; Rensselaer W. Lee, "Colombia's cocaine syndicates," *Crime, Law and Social Change* 16, no. 1 (1991): pp. 3–39.

3. John P. Sullivan, "Maras morphing: Revisiting third generation gangs," *Global Crime* 7, no. 3–4 (2006): pp. 487–504.

4. Ibid.

5. Arron Daugherty, "El Salvador Supreme Court labels street gangs as terrorist groups," *InSight Crime*, August 26, 2015, www.insightcrime.org/news-briefs/el-salvador-supreme-court-labels-street-gangs-as-terrorist-groups, accessed February 7, 2019.

6. For more, see José Miguel Cruz, "Central American maras: From youth street gangs to transnational protection rackets," *Global Crime* 11, no. 4 (2010): pp. 379–398.

7. "Executive Order 13581 – Blocking property of transnational criminal organizations," *The White House*, July 25, 2011, https://obamawhitehouse.archives.gov/the-press-office/2011/07/25/executive-order-13581-blocking-property-transnational-criminal-organizat, accessed May 5, 2019, p. 2.

8. For more on violence in the Americas, see Hanna S. Kassab and Jonathan D. Rosen, eds., *Violence in the Americas* (Lanham, MD: Lexington Books, 2018).

9. David Gagne, "InSight Crime's 2016 homicide round-up," *InSight Crime*, January 16, 2017, www.insightcrime.org/news/analysis/insight-crime-2016-homicide-round-up/, accessed June 19, 2018.

10. Tristan Clavel, "InSight Crime's 2017 homicide round-up," *InSight Crime*, January 19, 2018, www.insightcrime.org/news/analysis/2017-homicide-round-up/, accessed June 19, 2018.

11. Tristan Clavel, "Latin America again dominates world's 50 deadliest cities ranking," *InSight Crime*, April 7, 2017, www.insightcrime.org/news/brief/latin-america-dominates-world-50-deadliest-cities/, accessed June 19, 2018; Seguridad, Justicia y Paz, *Metodología del ranking (2017) de las 50 ciudades más violentas del mundo* (Mexico: Seguridad, Justicia y Paz, 2018).

12. For more, see Jeremy Adelman, *Colonial Legacies: The Problem of Persistence in Latin American History* (New York, NY: Routledge, 1999); Anibal Quijano, "Coloniality of power and Eurocentrism in Latin America," *International Sociology* 15, no. 2 (2000): pp. 215–232; J. Jorge Klor de Alva, "Colonialism and postcolonialism as (Latin) American mirages," *Colonial Latin American Review* 1, no. 1–2 (1992): pp. 3–23; Daron Acemoglu, Simon Johnson, and James A. Robinson, "The colonial origins of comparative development: An empirical investigation," *American Economic Review* 91, no. 5 (2001): pp. 1369–1401.

13. For more on the history of cocaine, see Fiedrich Wöhler, "Ueber eine organische Base in der Coca," *Archiv der Pharmazie* 152, no. 1 (1860): pp. 29–32; Jessica Gold, Kimberly Frost-Pineda, and Mark S. Gold, "A brief history of cocaine," *JAMA* 295, no. 22 (2006): pp. 2665–2666.

14. Amy Sue Biondich and Jeremy David Joslin, "Coca: The history and medical significance of an ancient Andean tradition," *Emergency Medicine International* (2016): p. 1.

15. For more on the uses of coca, see Father Bernabe, *History of the Inca Empire: An Account of the Indian's Customs and their Origin, Together with a Treatise on Inca Legend* (Austin, TX: University of Texas Press, 1979).

16. Paul Gootenberg, *Cocaine: Global Histories* (New York, NY: Routledge, 1999), p. 3.

17. Margaret P. Battin, Erik Luna, Arthur G. Lipman, Paul M. Gahlinger, Douglas E. Rollins, Jeanette C. Roberts, and Troy L. Booher, *Drugs and Justice: Seeking a Consistent, Coherent and Comprehensive View* (New York, NY: Oxford University Press, 2008), p. 34.

18. For an in-depth look into the subject of Prohibition, please refer to Lisa McGirr, *The War on Alcohol: Prohibition and the Rise of the American State* (New York, NY: W.W. Norton & Company, Inc., 2015).

19. Paul Gootenberg, *Cocaine: Global Histories*, p. 3.
20. Ibid.
21. Ibid.
22. William L. Marcy, *Politics of Cocaine: How U.S. Foreign Policy Has Created a Thriving Drug Industry in Central and South America* (Chicago: Chicago Review Press, 2010), p. 8.
23. Ibid., p. 10.
24. See Bruce Bagley, *Drug Trafficking and Organized Crime in the Americas* (Washington, DC: Woodrow Wilson Center, 2012).
25. Karst J. Besteman, "Alternative perspectives on the drug policy debate," in *The Drug Legalization Debate*, ed. James Inciardi (London: Sage, 1999), p. 151.
26. Howard J. Wiarda, *Political Development in Emerging Nations: Is There Still a Third World?* (Belmont, CA: Thompson-Wadsworth, 2004), p. 117.
27. Ibid.
28. "The White Goddess," *Time Magazine*, April 11, 1949.
29. Oyster Bay Conference on Organized Crime (1965), quoted in Norman W. Philcox, *An Introduction to Organized Crime* (Springfield: Charles C. Thomas Publisher, 1978), p. 4.
30. James A. Inciardi, "American drug policy: The continuing debate," in *Drug War: The Policy Battle Continues*, ed. Laura E. Huggins (Stanford: Hoover Institution Press, 2005), p. 7.
31. Margaret P. Battin, Erik Luna, Arthur G. Lipman, Paul M. Gahlinger, Douglas E. Rollins, Jeanette C. Roberts, and Troy L. Booher, *Drugs and Justice: Seeking a Consistent, Coherent and Comprehensive View*, p. 34.
32. Karst J. Besteman, "Alternative perspectives on the drug policy debate," in *The Drug Legalization Debate*, ed. James Inciardi.
33. Bruce M. Bagley and Jonathan D. Rosen, eds., *Drug Trafficking, Organized Crime, and Violence in the Americas Today* (Gainesville, FL: University Press of Florida, 2015).
34. Mark Thornton, *The Economics of Prohibition* (Salt Lake City, UT: University of Utah Press, 1991), p. 91.
35. Scott H. Decker and Margaret Townsend Chapman, *Drug Smugglers on Drug Smuggling: Lessons from the Inside* (Philadelphia, PA: Temple University Press, 2008), p. 52.
36. N. Gregory Mankiw, *Principles of Macroeconomics* (Mason: South-Western Cengage Learning, 2009), p. 90.
37. Avner Greif and Christopher Kingston, "Institutions: Rules and equilibrium," in *Political Economy of Institutions, Democracy and Voting*, eds. Norman Schofield and Gonzalo Caballero (New York, NY: Springer, 2011), p. 17.
38. Gautam Basu, "Concealment, corruption, and evasion: A transaction cost and case analysis of illicit supply chain activity," *Journal of Transportation Security* 7, no. 3 (2014): pp. 209–226.
39. Ibid.
40. "Committee on the Judiciary, House of Representatives, Sixtieth Congress: Argument of Hon. Richard Bartholdt, Representative from Missouri, in Opposition to the Several Bills to Restrict Interstate Commerce in Certain Cases," Libertarianism.org, April 10, 1908, 2017, www.libertarianism.org/publications/essays/wet-dry-richard-bartholdt-against-prohibition, accessed June 20, 2017; The Congressman had the foresight to see how the eventual 'war on drugs' would fail as well.
41. Edward Lemon, "Tajikistan," *Freedom House 2016 Report* (2016): p. 2.
42. Bruce Bagley, *Drug Trafficking and Organized Crime in the Americas: Major Trends in the Twenty-First Century*; for more on corruption, see Joseph S. Tulchin and Ralph H. Espach, *Combating Corruption in Latin America* (Washington, DC:

Woodrow Wilson Center Press, 2000); Kurt Gerhard Weyland, "The politics of corruption in Latin America," *Journal of Democracy* 9, no. 2 (1998): pp. 108–121.

43. Arlene B. Tickner, "Colombia and the United States: From counter-narcotics to counterterrorism," *Current History* 102, no. 661 (2003): p. 77; Russell Crandall, *Driven by Drugs: US Policy Toward Colombia* (Boulder, CO: Lynne Rienner, 2008, second edition); Jennifer S. Holmes, Kevin M. Curtin, and Sheila Amin Gutiérrez de Piñeres, *Guns, Drugs, and Development in Colombia* (Austin, TX: University of Texas Press, 2008); Bruce Michael Bagley, "The new hundred years war? US national security and the war on drugs in Latin America," *Journal of Interamerican Studies and World Affairs* 30, no. 1 (1988): pp. 161–182.

44. Peter Watt and Roberto Zepeda, *Drug War Mexico: Politics, Neoliberalism and Violence in the New Narcoeconomy* (London, UK: Zed Books, 2012); David A. Shirk, *Mexico's New Politics: The Pan and Democratic Change* (Boulder, CO: Lynne Rienner Publishers, 2005); John Bailey, *The Politics of Crime in Mexico: Democratic Governance in a Security Trap* (Boulder, CO: Lynne Rienner Publishers, 2014); Jonathan D. Rosen and Roberto Zepeda, *Organized Crime, Drug Trafficking, and Violence in Mexico: The Transition from Felipe Calderón to Enrique Peña Nieto* (Lanham, MD: Lexington Books, 2016); Jorge Chabat, "Mexico's war on drugs: No margin for maneuver," *The ANNALS of the American Academy of Political and Social Science* 582, no. 1 (2002): pp. 134–148; David A. Shirk, "Drug violence in Mexico: Data and analysis from 2001–2009," *Trends in Organized Crime* 13, no. 2–3 (2010): pp. 167–174; Wil G. Pansters, "Drug trafficking, the informal order, and caciques. Reflections on the crime-governance nexus in Mexico," *Global Crime* 19, no. 3–4 (2018): pp. 315–338.

45. Carlos Ponce, "Book review of 'Mano Dura. The politics of gang control in El Salvador'," *Trends in Organized Crime* 18, no. 3 (2017): pp. 322–324.

46. Some scholars have criticized Wolf for not providing a clear methodology of her interview techniques. For example, see Carlos Ponce, "Book review of 'Mano Dura. The politics of gang control in El Salvador'," pp. 322–324.

47. Sonja Wolf, *Mano Dura: The Politics of Gang Control in El Salvador* (Austin, TX: University of Texas Press, 2017); Robert Brenneman, *Homies and Hermanos: God and Gangs in Central America* (New York, NY: Oxford University Press, 2012); T. W. Ward, *Gangsters Without Borders: An Ethnography of a Salvadoran Street Gang* (New York, NY: Oxford University Press, 2013).

48. For more, see Khairul Baharein Mohd Noor, "Case study: A strategic research methodology," *American Journal of Applied Sciences* 5, no. 11 (2008): pp. 1602–1604.

49. Benjamin Lessing, *Making Peace in Drug Wars: Crackdowns and Cartels in Latin America* (New York, NY: Cambridge University Press, 2018).

50. Victor J. Hinojosa, *Domestic Politics and International Narcotics Control: U.S. Relations with Mexico and Colombia, 1989–2000* (New York, NY: Routledge, 2007).

51. Bruce M. Bagley and Jonathan D. Rosen, eds., *Drug Trafficking, Organized Crime, and Violence in the Americas Today.*

52. Jonathan D. Rosen and Hanna S. Kassab, eds., *Fragile States in the Americas* (Lanham, MD: Lexington Books, 2016).

53. For more, see Scott Mainwaring and Timothy Scully, eds., *Building Democratic Institutions: Party Systems in Latin America* (Stanford, CA: Stanford University Press, 1995); Andreas Schedler, "What is democratic consolidation?" *Journal of Democracy* 9, no. 2 (1998): pp. 91–107.

54. Jonathan D. Rosen and Hanna S. Kassab, eds., *Fragile States in the Americas*; Kees Koonings and Dirk Kruijt, *Armed Actors: Organised Violence and State Failure in Latin America* (London, UK: Zed Books, 2004).

55. For more, see Celeste González de Bustamante and Jeannine E. Relly, "Journalism in times of violence: Social media use by US and Mexican journalists working in

northern Mexico," *Digital Journalism* 2, no. 4 (2014): pp. 507–523; Jeannine E. Relly and Celeste González de Bustamante, "Silencing Mexico: A study of influences on journalists in the Northern states," *The International Journal of Press/ Politics* 19, no. 1 (2014): pp. 108–131.

56. Center for Strategic & International Studies (CSIS), *Russian Organised Crime* (Washington DC: CSIS, 1997), pp. 23–24.

57. Hanna Samir Kassab, *Weak States in International Relations Theory: The Cases of Armenia, St. Kitts and Nevis, Lebanon and Cambodia* (Palgrave: New York, 2015), p. 12.

58. Robert Muggah and Ilona Szabó de Carvalho, "There's a cure for Latin America's murder epidemic—and it doesn't involve more police or prisons," *World Economic Forum*, April 4, 2017, www.weforum.org/agenda/2017/04/there-s-a-cure-for-latin-america-s-murder-epidemic-and-it-doesn-t-involve-more-police-or-prisons/, accessed June 18, 2018, p. 3.

59. Monika François and Inder Sud, "Promoting stability and development in fragile and failed states," *Development Policy Review* 24, no. 2 (2006): pp. 141–160.

60. Peter Lupsha, "Transnational organized crime versus the nation-state," *Transnational Organized Crime* 2, no. 1 (1996): p. 31; for more, see Jonathan D. Rosen, Bruce Bagley, and Jorge Chabat, eds., *The Criminalization of States: The Relationship Between States and Organized Crime* (Lanham, MD: Lexington Books, 2019).

61. Peter Lupsha, "Transnational organized crime versus the nation-state," p. 32.

62. Ibid.

63. Gautam Basu, "Concealment, corruption, and evasion: A transaction cost and case analysis of illicit supply chain activity," p. 219.

64. Peter Lupsha, "Transnational organized crime versus the nation-state," p. 31.

65. For more, see Bruce Bagley, *Drug Trafficking and Organized Crime in the Americas*.

66. Mark A. R. Kleiman, Jonathan P. Caulkins, and Angela Hawken, *Drugs and Drug Policy: What Everyone Needs to Know* (New York, NY: Oxford University Press, 2011), p. 16.

67. Hanna Samir Kassab, *Weak States in International Relations Theory: The Cases of Armenia, St. Kitts and Nevis, Lebanon and Cambodia*, p. 12.

68. Max Weber, *The Vocation Lectures*, eds. David Owen and Traci B. Strong (Indianapolis: Hackett Publishing, 2004), p. 33.

69. Monika François and Inder Sud, "Promoting stability and development in fragile and failed states."

70. Ibid.

71. Quoted in Mujib Mashal, "Afghan Taliban awash in heroin cash, a troubling turn for war," *The New York Times*, October 29, 2017.

72. Boaz Atzili, "State weakness and 'vacuum of power' in Lebanon," *Studies in Conflict & Terrorism* 33, no. 8 (2010): p. 765.

73. Daron Acemoglu and James Robinson, *Why Nations Fail: The Origins of Power, Prosperity and Poverty* (New York, NY: Crown Publishers, 2012), p. 54.

74. Quoted in Scott H. Decker and Margaret Townsend Chapman, *Drug Smugglers on Drug Smuggling: Lessons from the Inside*, p. 37.

75. Gautam Basu, "Concealment, corruption, and evasion: A transaction cost and case analysis of illicit supply chain activity," p. 210.

76. Daniel Lederman, Norman V. Loayza, and Rodrigo R. Soares, "Accountability and corruption: Political institutions matter," *Economics & Politics* 17, no. 1 (2005): pp. 1–2.

77. Daron Acemoglu, "Root causes: A historical approach to assessing the role of institutions in economic development," *Finance and Development* (June Issue, 2003), p. 27.

78. Daron Acemoglu and James A. Robinson, *Why Nations Fail: The Origins of Power, Prosperity and Poverty* (New York, NY: Crown Publishers, 2012), p. 51.

79. Steven Dudley, "Honduras elites and organized crime: Introduction," *InSight Crime*, April 9, 2016, www.insightcrime.org/investigations/honduras-elites-and-organized-crime-introduction/, accessed June 25, 2018.

80. Steven Dudley, "How 'Mano Dura' is strengthening gangs," *InSight Crime*, November 22, 2010, www.insightcrime.org/investigations/how-mano-dura-is-strengthening-gangs/, accessed June 25, 2018, p. 2.

81. For more, see Diane E. Davis, "Undermining the rule of law: Democratization and the dark side of police reform in Mexico," *Latin American Politics and Society* 48, no. 1 (2006): pp. 55–86; Liqun Cao and Jihong Solomon Zhao, "Confidence in the police in Latin America," *Journal of Criminal Justice* 33, no. 5 (2005): pp. 403–412; Peter Andreas, "The political economy of narco-corruption in Mexico," *Current History* 97 (1998): p. 160.

82. Brian Fonseca and Eduardo A. Gamarra, *Culture and National Security in the Americas* (Lanham, MD: Lexington Books, 2017); Mitchell A. Seligson, "The impact of corruption on regime legitimacy: A comparative study of four Latin American countries," *The Journal of Politics* 64, no. 2 (2002): pp. 408–433; Mark Ungar, "The privatization of citizen security in Latin America: From elite guards to neighborhood vigilantes," *Social Justice* 34, no. 3–4 (2007): pp. 20–37.

83. Bruce M. Bagley and Jonathan D. Rosen, eds., *Drug Trafficking, Organized Crime, and Violence in the Americas Today*.

84. Quoted in Elisabeth Malkin, "Mexico strengthens military's role in drug war, outraging critics," *The New York Times*, December 15, 2017.

85. Quoted in Ibid.

86. Quoted in Steve Fisher and Patrick J. McDonnell, "Mexico sent in the army to fight the drug war. Many question the toll on society and the army itself," *Los Angeles Times*, June 18, 2018.

87. Sonja Wolf, "El Salvador's pandilleros calmados: The challenges of contesting mano dura through peer rehabilitation and empowerment," *Bulletin of Latin American Research* 31, no. 2 (2012): pp. 190–205; Mo Hume, "Mano dura: El Salvador responds to gangs," *Development in Practice* 17, no. 6 (2007): pp. 739–751.

88. Jonathan D. Rosen and Marten W. Brienen, eds., *Prisons in the Americas in the Twenty-First Century: A Human Dumping Ground* (Lanham, MD: Lexington Books, 2015).

89. José Miguel Cruz, "Central American maras: From youth street gangs to transnational protection rackets."

90. Elyssa Pachico, "Latin America dominates list of world's most violent cities," *InSight Crime*, January 22, 2015, www.insightcrime.org/news-analysis/latin-america-dominates-list-of-worlds-most-violent-cities, accessed February 7, 2019; Jonathan D. Rosen and Roberto Zepeda, *Organized Crime, Drug Trafficking, and Violence in Mexico: The Transition from Felipe Calderón to Enrique Peña Nieto*; Bruce Michael Bagley, "The new hundred years war? US national security and the war on drugs in Latin America;" Russell Crandall, *Driven by Drugs: US Policy Toward Colombia*; José Miguel Cruz, "Criminal violence and democratization in Central America: The survival of the violent state," *Latin American Politics and Society* 53, no. 4 (2011): pp. 1–33.

91. The Fund for Peace, "Fragile states index," *FFP*, https://fragilestatesindex.org/indicators/, accessed July 11, 2019.

92. For more, see https://fragilestatesindex.org/country-data/, accessed July 11, 2019.

93. Transparency International, "Corruption Perceptions Index 2018," *TI*, www.transparency.org/cpi2018, accessed July 11, 2019.

94. José Miguel Cruz, "Criminal violence and democratization in Central America: The survival of the violent state," *Latin American Politics and Society* 53, no. 4 (2011): pp. 1–33.

95. For more, see Jonathan D. Rosen and Roberto Zepeda, *Organized Crime, Drug Trafficking, and Violence in Mexico: The Transition from Felipe Calderón to Enrique Peña Nieto*; Russell Crandall, *Driven by Drugs: US Policy Toward Colombia* (Boulder, CO: Lynne Rienner, 2008, second edition); José Miguel Cruz, "Criminal violence and democratization in Central America: The survival of the violent state."
96. For links to the studies conducted by LAPOP, see www.vanderbilt.edu/lapop/, accessed February 10, 2020 and March 9, 2020.

Works Cited

Acemoglu, Daron. "Root causes: A historical approach to assessing the role of institutions in economic development," *Finance and Development* (June Issue, 2003): p. 27.

Acemoglu, Daron, Simon Johnson, and James A. Robinson. "The colonial origins of comparative development: An empirical investigation," *American Economic Review* 91, no. 5 (2001): pp. 1369–1401.

Acemoglu, Daron and James Robinson. *Why Nations Fail: The Origins of Power, Prosperity and Poverty*. New York, NY: Crown Publishers, 2012.

Adelman, Jeremy. *Colonial Legacies: The Problem of Persistence in Latin American History*. New York, NY: Routledge, 1999.

Andreas, Peter. "The political economy of narco-corruption in Mexico," *Current History* 97 (1998): p. 160.

Atzili, Boaz. "State weakness and 'Vacuum of power' in Lebanon," *Studies in Conflict & Terrorism* 33, no. 8 (2010): p. 765.

Baharein Mohd Noor, Khairul. "Case study: A strategic research methodology," *American Journal of Applied Sciences* 5, no. 11 (2008): pp. 1602–1604.

Bagley, Bruce Michael. "Colombia and the war on drugs," *Foreign Affairs* 67, no. 1 (1988): 70–92.

Bagley, Bruce Michael. "The new hundred years war? US national security and the war on drugs in Latin America," *Journal of Interamerican Studies and World Affairs* 30, no. 1 (1988): pp. 161–182.

Bagley, Bruce Michael. *Drug Trafficking and Organized Crime in the Americas*. Washington, DC: Woodrow Wilson Center, 2012.

Bagley, Bruce Michael and Jonathan D. Rosen, eds. *Drug Trafficking, Organized Crime, and Violence in the Americas Today*. Gainesville, FL: University Press of Florida, 2015.

Bailey, John. *The Politics of Crime in Mexico: Democratic Governance in a Security Trap*. Boulder, CO: Lynne Rienner Publishers, 2014.

Basu, Gautam. "Concealment, corruption, and evasion: A transaction cost and case analysis of illicit supply chain activity," *Journal of Transportation Security* 7, no. 3 (2014): pp. 209–226.

Battin, Margaret P., Erik Luna, Arthur G. Lipman, Paul M. Gahlinger, Douglas E. Rollins, Jeanette C. Roberts, and Troy L. Booher. *Drugs and Justice: Seeking a Consistent, Coherent and Comprehensive View*. New York, NY: Oxford University Press, 2008.

Bernabe, Father. *History of the Inca Empire: An Account of the Indian's Customs and Their Origin, Together with a Treatise on Inca Legend*. Austin, TX: University of Texas Press, 1979.

Besteman, Karst J. "Alternative perspectives on the drug policy debate," in *The Drug Legalization Debate*, ed. James Inciardi. London, UK: Sage, 1999, p. 151.

Biondich, Amy Sue and Jeremy David Joslin. "Coca: The history and medical significance of an ancient andean tradition," *Emergency Medicine International* (2016): p. 1.

Brenneman, Robert. *Homies and Hermanos: God and Gangs in Central America*. New
York, NY: Oxford University Press, 2012.

Cao, Liqun and Jihong Solomon Zhao. "Confidence in the police in Latin America,"
Journal of Criminal Justice 33, no. 5 (2005): pp. 403–412.

Center for Strategic & International Studies (CSIS). *Russian Organised Crime*. Washington, DC: CSIS, 1997, pp. 23–24.

Chabat, Jorge. "Mexico's war on drugs: No margin for maneuver," *The ANNALS of the
American Academy of Political and Social Science* 582, no. 1 (2002): pp. 134–148.

Clavel, Tristan. "Latin America again dominates world's 50 deadliest cities ranking,"
InSight Crime, April 7, 2017, www.insightcrime.org/news/brief/latin-america-domi-
nates-world-50-deadliest-cities/, accessed June 19, 2018.

Clavel, Tristan. "InSight Crime's 2017 homicide round-up," *InSight Crime*, January 19,
2018, www.insightcrime.org/news/analysis/2017-homicide-round-up/, accessed June
19, 2018.

"Committee on the Judiciary, House of Representatives, Sixtieth Congress: Argument
of Hon. Richard Bartholdt, Representative from Missouri, in Opposition to the Several Bills to Restrict Interstate Commerce in Certain Cases." *Libertarianism.org*,
April 10, 1908, 2017, www.libertarianism.org/publications/essays/wet-dry-richard-
bartholdt-against-prohibition, accessed June 20, 2017

Crandall, Russell. *Driven by Drugs: US Policy Toward Colombia*. Boulder, CO: Lynne
Rienner, 2008, second edition.

Cruz, José Miguel. "Central American maras: From youth street gangs to transnational
protection rackets," *Global Crime* 11, no. 4 (2010): pp. 379–398.

Cruz, José Miguel. "Criminal violence and democratization in Central America: The
survival of the violent state," *Latin American Politics and Society* 53, no. 4 (2011):
pp. 1–33.

Daugherty, Arron. "El Salvador Supreme Court labels street gangs as terrorist groups,"
InSight Crime, August 26, 2015, www.insightcrime.org/news-briefs/el-salvador-
supreme-court-labels-street-gangs-as-terrorist-groups, accessed February 7, 2019.

Davis, Diane E. "Undermining the rule of law: Democratization and the dark side of
police reform in Mexico," *Latin American Politics and Society* 48, no. 1 (2006):
pp. 55–86.

Decker, Scott H. and Margaret Townsend Chapman. *Drug Smugglers on Drug Smuggling: Lessons from the Inside*. Philadelphia, PA: Temple University Press, 2008.

Dudley, Steven. "How 'Mano Dura' is strengthening gangs," *InSight Crime*, November
22, 2010, www.insightcrime.org/investigations/how-mano-dura-is-strengthening-
gangs/, accessed June 25, 2018.

Dudley, Steven. "Honduras elites and organized crime: Introduction," *InSight Crime*,
April 9, 2016, www.insightcrime.org/investigations/honduras-elites-and-organized-
crime-introduction/, accessed June 25, 2018.

Etter, Gregg S. and Erica L. Lehmuth. "The Mexican drug wars: Organized crime,
narco-terrorism, insurgency or asymmetric warfare?" *Journal of Gang Research* 20,
no. 4 (2013): pp. 1–33.

"Executive Order 13581—Blocking property of transnational criminal organizations,"
The White House, July 25, 2011, https://obamawhitehouse.archives.gov/the-press-
office/2011/07/25/executive-order-13581-blocking-property-transnational-criminal-
organizat, accessed May 5, 2019, p. 2.

Fisher, Steve and Patrick J. McDonnell. "Mexico sent in the army to fight the drug war. Many question the toll on society and the army itself," *Los Angeles Times*, June 18, 2018.

Fonseca, Brian and Eduardo A. Gamarra, *Culture and National Security in the Americas*. Lanham, MD: Lexington Books, 2017.

François, Monika and Inder Sud. "Promoting stability and development in fragile and failed states," *Development Policy Review* 24, no. 2 (2006): pp. 141–160.

The Fund for Peace. "Fragile states index," *FFP*, https://fragilestatesindex.org/indicators/, accessed July 11, 2019.

Gagne, David. "InSight Crime's 2016 homicide round-up," *InSight Crime*, January 16, 2017, www.insightcrime.org/news/analysis/insight-crime-2016-homicide-round-up/, accessed June 19, 2018.

Gold, Jessica, Kimberly Frost-Pineda, and Mark S. Gold. "A brief history of cocaine," *JAMA* 295, no. 22 (2006): pp. 2665–2666.

González de Bustamante, Celeste and Jeannine E. Relly. "Journalism in times of violence: Social media use by US and Mexican journalists working in northern Mexico," *Digital Journalism* 2, no. 4 (2014): pp. 507–523.

Gootenberg, Paul. *Cocaine: Global Histories*. New York, NY: Routledge, 1999.

Greif, Avner and Christopher Kingston. "Institutions: Rules and equilibrium," in *Political Economy of Institutions, Democracy and Voting*, eds. Norman Schofield and Gonzalo Caballero. New York, NY: Springer, 2011, p. 17.

Hinojosa, Victor J. *Domestic Politics and International Narcotics Control: U.S. Relations with Mexico and Colombia, 1989–2000*. New York, NY: Routledge, 2007.

Holmes, Jennifer S., Kevin M. Curtin, and Sheila Amin Gutiérrez de Piñeres. *Guns, Drugs, and Development in Colombia*. Austin, TX: University of Texas Press, 2008.

Hume, Mo. "Mano dura: El Salvador responds to gangs," *Development in Practice* 17, no. 6 (2007): pp. 739–751.

Inciardi, James A. "American drug policy: The continuing debate," in *Drug War: The Policy Battle Continues*, ed. Laura E. Huggins. Stanford: Hoover Institution Press, 2005.

Kassab, Hanna Samir. *Weak States in International Relations Theory: The Cases of Armenia, St. Kitts and Nevis, Lebanon and Cambodia*. New York, NY: Palgrave, 2015.

Kassab, Hanna Samir and Jonathan D. Rosen, eds. *Violence in the Americas*. Lanham, MD: Lexington Books, 2018.

Kleiman, Mark A. R., Jonathan P. Caulkins, and Angela Hawken. *Drugs and Drug Policy: What Everyone Needs to Know*. New York, NY: Oxford University Press, 2011.

Klor de Alva, J. Jorge. "Colonialism and postcolonialism as (Latin) American mirages," *Colonial Latin American Review* 1, no. 1–2 (1992): pp. 3–23.

Kruijt, Dirk. *Armed Actors: Organised Violence and State Failure in Latin America*. London, UK: Zed Books, 2004.

LAPOP, see: www.vanderbilt.edu/lapop/, accessed February 10, 2020, accessed March 9, 2020.

Lederman, Daniel. Norman V. Loayza, and Rodrigo R. Soares. "Accountability and corruption: Political institutions matter," *Economics & Politics* 17, no. 1 (2005): pp. 1–2.

Lee, Rensselaer W. "Colombia's cocaine syndicates," *Crime, Law and Social Change* 16, no. 1 (1991): pp. 3–39.

Lemon, Edward. "Tajikistan," *Freedom House 2016 Report*, 2016.

Lessing, Benjamin. *Making Peace in Drug Wars: Crackdowns and Cartels in Latin America*. New York, NY: Cambridge University Press, 2018.

Lupsha, Peter. "Trasnational organized crime versus the nation-state," *Transnational Organized Crime* 2, no. 1 (1996): p. 31.

Mainwaring, Scott and Timothy Scully, eds. *Building Democratic Institutions: Party Systems in Latin America*. Stanford: Stanford University Press, 1995.

Malkin, Elisabeth. "Mexico strengthens military's role in drug war, outraging critics," *The New York Times*, December 15, 2017.

Mankiw, N. Gregory. *Principles of Macroeconomics*. Mason: South-Western Cengage Learning, 2009.

Marcy, William L. *Politics of Cocaine: How U.S. Foreign Policy Has Created a Thriving Drug Industry in Central and South America*. Chicago: Chicago Review Press, 2010.

Mashal, Mujib. "Afghan Taliban awash in heroin cash, a troubling turn for war," *The New York Times*, October 29, 2017.

McGirr, Lisa. *The War on Alcohol: Prohibition and the Rise of the American State*. New York, NY: W.W. Norton & Company, Inc., 2015.

Muggah, Robert and Ilona Szabó de Carvalho. "There's a cure for Latin America's murder epidemic—and it doesn't involve more police or prisons," *World Economic Forum*, April 4, 2017, www.weforum.org/agenda/2017/04/there-s-a-cure-for-latin-america-s-murder-epidemic-and-it-doesn-t-involve-more-police-or-prisons/, accessed June 18, 2018.

Oyster Bay Conference on Organized Crime (1965), quoted in N. W. Philcox. *An Introduction to Organized Crime*. Springfield: Charles C. Thomas Publisher, 1978, p. 4.

Pacheco, Fernando Celaya. "Narcofearance: How has narcoterrorism settled in Mexico?" *Studies in Conflict & Terrorism* 32, no. 12 (2009): pp. 1021–1048.

Pachico, Elyssa. "Latin America dominates list of world's most violent cities," *InSight Crime*, January 22, 2015, www.insightcrime.org/news-analysis/latin-america-dominates-list-of-worlds-most-violent-cities, accessed February 7, 2019.

Pansters, Wil G. "Drug trafficking, the informal order, and caciques. Reflections on the crime-governance nexus in Mexico," *Global Crime* 19, no. 3–4 (2018): pp. 315–338.

Ponce, Carlos. Book Review of "Mano Dura. The politics of gang control in El Salvador," *Trends in Organized Crime* 18, no. 3 (2017): pp. 322–324.

Quijano, Anibal. "Coloniality of power and Eurocentrism in Latin America," *International Sociology* 15, no. 2 (2000): pp. 215–232.

Relly, Jeannine E. and Celeste González de Bustamante. "Silencing Mexico: A study of influences on journalists in the Northern states," *The International Journal of Press/Politics* 19, no. 1 (2014): pp. 108–131.

Rosen, Jonathan D., Bruce Bagley, and Jorge Chabat, eds. *The Criminalization of States: The Relationship Between States and Organized Crime*. Lanham, MD: Lexington Books, 2019.

Rosen, Jonathan D. and Marten W. Brienen, eds. *Prisons in the Americas in the Twenty-First Century: A Human Dumping Ground*. Lanham, MD: Lexington Books, 2015.

Rosen, Jonathan D. and Hanna S. Kassab, eds. *Fragile States in the Americas*. Lanham, MD: Lexington Books, 2016.

Rosen, Jonathan D. and Roberto Zepeda. *Organized Crime, Drug Trafficking, and Violence in Mexico: The Transition from Felipe Calderón to Enrique Peña Nieto*. Lanham, MD: Lexington Books, 2016.

Schedler, Andreas. "What is democratic consolidation?" *Journal of Democracy* 9, no. 2 (1998): pp. 91–107.

Seguridad, Justicia y Paz. *Metodología del ranking (2017) de las 50 ciudades más violentas del mundo*. Mexico: Seguridad, Justicia y Paz, 2018.

Seligson, Mitchell A. "The impact of corruption on regime legitimacy: A comparative study of four Latin American countries," *The Journal of Politics* 64, no. 2 (2002): pp. 408–433.

Shirk, David A. "Drug violence in Mexico: Data and analysis from 2001–2009," *Trends in Organized Crime* 13, no. 2–3 (2010): pp. 167–174.

Shirk, David A. *Mexico's New Politics: The Pan and Democratic Change*. Boulder, CO: Lynne Rienner Publishers, 2005.

Sullivan, John P. "Maras morphing: Revisiting third generation gangs," *Global Crime* 7, no. 3–4 (2006): pp. 487–504.

Thornton, Mark. *The Economics of Prohibition*. Salt Lake City, UT: University of Utah Press, 1991.

Tickner, Arlene B. "Colombia and the United States: From counternarcotics to counterterrorism," *Current History* 102, no. 661 (2003): p. 77.

Transparency International. "Corruption perceptions index 2018," *TI*, www.transparency.org/cpi2018, accessed July 11, 2019.

Tulchin, Joseph S. and Ralph H. Espach. *Combating Corruption in Latin America*. Washington, DC: Woodrow Wilson Center Press, 2000.

Ungar, Mark. "The privatization of citizen security in Latin America: From elite guards to neighborhood vigilantes," *Social Justice* 34, no. 3/4 (109–110) (2007): pp. 20–37.

Ward, T.W. *Gangsters Without Borders: An Ethnography of a Salvadoran Street Gang*. New York, NY: Oxford University Press, 2013.

Watt, Peter and Roberto Zepeda. *Drug War Mexico: Politics, Neoliberalism and Violence in the New Narcoeconomy*. London, UK: Zed Books, 2012.

Weber, Max. *The Vocation Lectures*. Ed. David Owen and Traci B. Strong. Indianapolis: Hackett Publishing, 2004, p. 33.

Weyland, Kurt Gerhard. "The politics of corruption in Latin America," *Journal of Democracy* 9, no. 2 (1998): pp. 108–121.

Wiarda, Howard J. *Political Development in Emerging nations: Is There Still a Third World?* Belmont: Thompson-Wadsworth, 2004.

Wöhler, Fiedrich. "Ueber eine organische Base in der Coca," *Archiv der Pharmazie* 152, no. 1 (1860): pp. 29–32.

Wolf, Sonja. "El Salvador's pandilleros calmados: The challenges of contesting mano dura through peer rehabilitation and empowerment," *Bulletin of Latin American Research* 31, no. 2 (2012): pp. 190–205.

Wolf, Sonja. *Mano Dura: The Politics of Gang Control in El Salvador*. Austin, TX: University of Texas Press, 2017.

2   Colombia

This chapter examines the evolution of drug trafficking, organized crime, and drug-related violence in Colombia. It analyzes how different strategies have resulted in changes in the dynamics of criminal actors. The chapter focuses on the peace process and the challenges that exist. It also utilizes regression models to explore the perceptions of Colombians regarding levels of insecurity and the different criminal actors, such as the FARC. The chapter explores how Colombia has witnessed an evolution in the actors involved in drug trafficking and organized crime. During the 1980s, the country had two major cartels that dominated the criminal landscape: the Medellín and Cali cartels.[1] The Colombian government recognized the need to bring down the major kingpins. They believed that capturing the leaders of these cartels would result in the demise of these criminal organizations. This strategy, which has been referred to by experts as the kingpin strategy, contends that the capture of a major leader will result in the dismantling of the cartel, as the organizations will not survive without the top boss.[2]

The Colombian government cooperated closely with the US Drug Enforcement Administration (DEA). Pablo Escobar was killed in Medellín, Colombia in 1993 as Colombian authorities intercepted a phone call that he made to his son.[3] The death of Escobar led to the collapse of the Medellín cartel, which dominated organized crime and contributed to the high levels of criminal violence in Colombia. Yet the rival Cali cartel increased in power—albeit for a short period of time. Jeremy McDermott, an expert on organized crime, maintains: "For two years after Escobar's death, the Cali Cartel was able to continue operating with the same model, until the leaders, the Rodriguez Orejuela brothers, were captured in 1995."[4] Yet the end of the two major cartels responsible for drug trafficking, organized crime, and high levels of drug-related violence did not mean that drug trafficking would cease in the country. The dismantling of Cali and Medellín, the cartels that dominated the industry, left an opportunity for people involved in the criminal underworld. Colombia experienced the emergence of several hundred small drug cartels that moved in to fill the void left by the end of the major cartels.[5]

The Evolution of Plan Colombia

The Bill Clinton administration decided to support the Colombian government to combat drug trafficking and organized crime, which presented security challenges for the country. However, the Clinton government had a different conceptualization of Plan Colombia than the original plan developed by Andrés Pastrana (1998–2002).[6] Individuals, such as drug czar Barry McCaffrey, helped change the goals of Plan Colombia to focus less on the internal armed conflict and peace and more on combating the production and trafficking of drugs, particularly cocaine. The US government invested more resources to help improve the military and strengthen the police than to bolster programs designed to strengthen institutions.[7]

The objectives of Plan Colombia[8] shifted over time with the election of Álvaro Uribe, who served as the president from 2002 to 2010. Uribe understood that he needed to modify the objectives of Plan Colombia for the Bush administration to view this country as a priority and provide more resources. President Uribe shifted the discourse of the problem and argued that Colombia had narco-terrorists. The change in the vision of Plan Colombia better aligned with the George W. Bush administration's global war on terrorism.[9]

President Uribe became the closest ally of the Bush administration in the region. President Bush, however, not only supported the Colombian government in terms of rhetoric but also increased the amount of resources designated to go to Plan Colombia. In fact, the United States government invested $10 billion between 2002 and 2015. The Bush administration continued to invest in the military and "hard" components as opposed to strengthening institutions.[10]

While the Uribe administration hailed Plan Colombia as a success, critics contend that coca cultivation, drug production, and trafficking have continued unabated.[11] Moreover, Plan Colombia had many negative consequences because of aerial spraying initiatives. The United States government allocated significant resources to spraying herbicides to combat the cultivation of coca. First, spraying herbicides from aircraft can cause serious environmental and health damages as pilots can miss targets because of wind. Colombia, which has an estimated 10 percent of the world's biodiversity, has experienced high levels of environmental damage because of the aerial spraying programs. Second, peasant farmers can acquire more money cultivating coca than other products. Coca farmers can plant coca with other legal crops to make it harder for pilots to identify while airborne. In summary, coca cultivation has shifted between different departments within Colombia.[12]

While President Uribe claimed a victory in combating coca cultivation, the reality is that it simply ballooned to other departments. The Uribe administration did not design an effective, safe, and environmentally friendly strategy to decrease the major sources of revenue for transnational organized crime groups operating in the country. The vast number of organized crime groups competed for control of coca as well as the production and trafficking of cocaine as the profits remained steady over time.

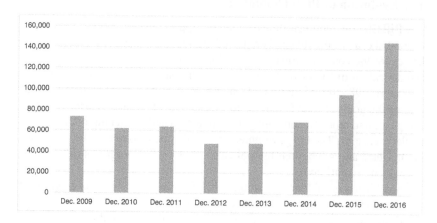

Figure 2.1 Colombian Coca Cultivation (Hectares)

Source: Created by authors with data from United Nations Office on Drugs and Crime (UNODC), *Colombia: Monitoreo de territorios afectados por cultivos ilícitos 2016* (Bogotá, CO: UNODC, 2017)

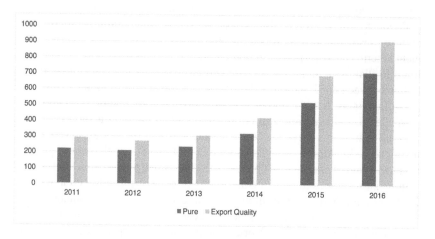

Figure 2.2 Potential Cocaine Production in Colombia

Source: Created by authors with data from Drug Enforcement Administration (DEA), *Colombian Cocaine Production Expansion Contributes to Rise in Supply in the United States* (Springfield. VA: DEA, 2017); estimates are from the US government and the Colombian Observatory on Drugs

Despite the resources allocated to combat drug trafficking, Colombia remains the leading producer of cocaine (see Figures 2.1 and 2.2). Nick Miroff argues:

> This surge in consumption can be traced directly to Colombia's bumper harvest. The country's illegal coca crop doubled between 2013 and 2015, reaching nearly 400,000 acres. That's almost twice as much as the combined output of Peru and Bolivia, the world's second- and third-largest producers.[13]

The increase in cocaine production results in more earning potential for drug trafficking organizations. In addition, the United States has experienced an increase in the number of cocaine consumers in recent years. As a result, drug trafficking organizations are responding to the demand for cocaine in the United States.[14]

Operationalizing Perceptions of Insecurity

The Uribe administration witnessed improvements in security. For example, Colombia saw a significant decrease in the number of homicides (see Figure 2.3). Colombia had 28,837 homicides in 2002. By 2006, the number of homicides had decrease to 17,479. By the end of the Uribe administration in 2010, Colombia's homicides decreased to 15,459. Yet Colombians still feel unsafe today. According to the 2016/2017 Colombia survey data by Vanderbilt University's Latin American Public Opinion Project (LAPOP), 21.92 percent of the interviewees responded "Very Unsafe" when asked about their perceptions of neighborhood insecurity, while 27.51 percent contended that they felt "Somewhat Unsafe."

What factors influence the perceptions of neighborhood insecurity?[15] The independent variables controlled for were age, sex, urban, and monthly household income. The age variable was recoded into six categories.[16] The dependent variable is coded "Very Safe," "Somewhat Safe," "Somewhat Unsafe," and "Very Unsafe."[17] The model indicates that sex, urban, and monthly household income are statistically significant at the 95-percent confidence level. The

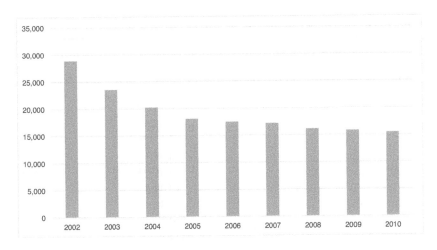

Figure 2.3 Homicides in Colombia (2002–2010)

Source: Created by authors with data from "15th Anniversary of Plan Colombia: Learning from Its Successes and Failures," *Washington Office on Latin America*, February 1, 2016; data from Ministry of Defense of Colombia

interpretation of the results reveals that a one-unit increase in age (i.e., male to female) leads to a 0.132 shift in the dependent variable. This means that on average females are more likely to perceive the neighborhood as more unsafe. Moreover, a one-unit shift in the urban variable (i.e., urban to rural) leads to a −0.311 change in the dependent variable. Thus, people living in rural areas, on average, are more likely to perceive their neighborhoods as safe. Finally, a one-unit shift in monthly household income results in a −0.013 shift in the dependent variable. In other words, people with higher monthly household incomes, on average, perceive their neighborhoods to be safer (see Table 2.1).

How do Colombians feel in terms of level of victimization? Using 2016/2017 Colombia LAPOP survey data, we created a regression model to determine the variables that influence the frequency of someone being a victim of crime. The dependent variable, victim of crime in the last 12 months according to frequency, is coded from 1 to 20. The independent variables are age, sex, skin color, monthly household income, and urban.[18] The independent variables controlled for are the same as above. Skin color is coded one for very light and 11 for very dark.

The only variable that is statistically significant in the new model is skin color. This suggests that racism and marginalization impact victimization. The results are interesting because one would think that monthly household income as well as where one lives could impact the frequency of victimization. In addition, one might think that age could impact whether one is a victim of crime, as youth could be more likely to be targeted by gangs and other criminal organizations. In summary, the model reveals that a one-unit change in skin color leads to a −0.188 change in the dependent variable (see Table 2.2).

Table 2.1 Factors Influencing Perceptions in Neighborhood Security

Variables	Coeff (SE)	t-test
Age	−0.026	−1.19
	(0.022)	
Sex	0.132**	2.29
	(0.058)	
Urban	−0.311***	−3.67
	(0.085)	
Monthly Household Income	−0.013**	−2.35
	(0.006)	
Constant	2.880***	16.94
	(0.170)	
Observations	1,344	
R-Squared	0.022	
Standard Errors in Parentheses		

*** p<0.01, ** p<0.05, * p<0.1

Source: Created by authors with data from the 2016/2017 LAPOP survey

Table 2.2 Factors Influencing the Frequency of Being the Victim of Crime in the Last 12 Months

Variable	Income Coeff (SE)	t-test
Age	−0.075	−0.93
	(0.081)	
Sex	−0.046	−0.19
	(0.242)	
Skin Color	−0.188*	−2.89
	(0.065)	
Monthly Household Income	−0.021	−0.84
	(0.025)	
Urban	0.072	0.21
	(0.334)	
Constant	3.042*	3.70
	(0.822)	
Observations	341	
R-Squared	0.025	
Robust Standard Errors in Parentheses		

* $p < 0.05$

Source: Created by authors with data from the 2016/2017 LAPOP survey

The BACRIM: Transforming the Criminal Underworld

In addition to the FARC, Colombia has also had a lengthy history of right-wing paramilitary groups that have been responsible for high levels of violence and human rights abuses. The largest group, the United Self-Defense Forces of Colombia (Autodefensas Unidas de Colombia, AUC), demobilized during the Uribe administration.[19] However, the critics of the demobilization process contend that the paramilitaries have demobilized into different criminal bands that are involved in a diverse array of criminal activities, including drug trafficking, illegal mining, and extortion.[20]

The evolution of the paramilitaries into criminal bands has been referred to by some experts as the "third generation" of drug cartels in Colombia. The BACRIM are not shrouded in ideology, but rather the different organizations compete for markets and territory and use the skills that they have acquired over the decades. The BACRIM have been involved in serious human rights abuses in Colombia and represent a major threat to security.[21]

The Peace Process: Negotiating with the FARC

Juan Manuel Santos, the President of Colombia between 2010 and 2018, assumed office as an ally of President Uribe.[22] It is important to remember that Santos served as the Minister of Defense during the Uribe administration and led many of the initiatives designed to combat the FARC and increase security in Colombia. Upon assuming office, Santos made a calculated decision that the government needed to negotiate with the FARC to end the more than 50 years of internal armed conflict[23] that has impacted the lives of generations of Colombians. President Santos held secret negotiations with the largest guerrilla group for two years. The Colombian government began formal negotiations with the FARC that lasted for four years in Cuba.[24]

Colombia has faced major obstacles regarding the implementation of the peace accord. The Santos administration believed that it would pay for the peace process with revenues from the booming oil industry.[25] Yet the decline in oil prices in 2014 made this option less viable. Furthermore, the Santos administration sought financial support from the international community. The Obama administration agreed to provide the Colombian government with $450 million through a program known as Paz Colombia (Peace Colombia). Yet the Trump administration appears to be unwilling to support Colombia during the peace process implementation phase. This is likely because President Trump is more interested in combating cocaine production and trafficking and is focused on his "America First" platform.[26]

While the signing of the peace accord is a historic moment in the country, many Colombians remain very critical of the peace process. This often revolves around distrust in the FARC. For example, 64.48 percent of respondents in the LAPOP survey contended "Not at All" when asked if they trust the FARC. This is likely because the FARC has been involved in drug trafficking, kidnapping, extortion, and violence, which has created high levels of distrust among society.

What factors determine one's levels of trust in the FARC? A regression model controlling for age, urban, education, skin color, and monthly household income can help determine the factors that influence trust in the FARC. The age variable is from 18 to 88, but it has been recoded into six categories. The sex variable is divided into male and female, while urban is coded urban and rural. In addition, the education variable is years of schooling and ranges from no schooling to 18 or more. The skin color variable gives one for very light and 11 for very dark. Monthly household income is from no income to more than 3,250,000 pesos. Finally, the dependent variable, trust in the FARC, is coded 1 for "Not at All" and 7 for "A Lot."[27]

The model indicates that age, urban, and education are statistically significant at the 95-percent confidence level. The interpretation of the model is that a one-unit increase in age leads to a 0.116 shift in the dependent variable. This means that the older one is, the more trust in the FARC. Furthermore, a one-unit shift in urban (i.e., urban to rural) leads to a 0.181 shift in the dependent variable. Therefore, people living in rural areas have higher levels of trust in the FARC. Finally, the education variable indicates that a one-unit shift in education leads to a 0.027 shift in the dependent variable. In other words, people with more education have higher levels of trust in the FARC. In summary, age, urban, and education impact the levels of trust in the FARC (see Table 2.3). Yet it is important to recognize that there are some limitations when conducting survey

Table 2.3 Factors Influencing Trust in the FARC

Variable	Coeff (SE)	t-test
Age	0.116***	3.28
	(0.035)	
Urban	0.181*	1.82
	(0.100)	
Education	0.027**	2.30
	(0.012)	
Skin Color	−0.033	−1.62
	(0.020)	
Monthly Household Income	−0.006	−0.67
	(0.009)	
Constant	1.210***	5.08
	(0.238)	
Observations	1,309	
R-Squared	0.015	
Robust Standard Errors in Parentheses		

*** p<0.01, ** p<0.05, * p<0.1

Source: Created by authors with data from the 2016/2017 LAPOP survey

analysis. The survey is a closed-ended question and does not enable the respondent to define trust or explain such answers. Perhaps people who are older, more educated, and live in rural areas believe that the FARC can be trusted to honor their commitments.

Colombians also remain skeptical that the FARC will demobilize: 40.18 percent of the respondents in the LAPOP survey contended that it is unlikely that the FARC will demobilize after the agreement. Meanwhile, 27.37 contended that it is very unlikely that the FARC will demobilize. Regression analysis can help explain the factors that influence how one feels about the possibility of the FARC demobilizing. The dependent variable of the model, likelihood of the FARC demobilizing after a peace agreement, is divided into "Very Likely," "Likely," "Unlikely," and "Very Unlikely." The independent variables are age, urban, and education. The education variable is coded as zero to 18 or more years of school.[28]

The regression analysis indicates that age, urban, and education are statistically significant at the 95-percent confidence level. The model reveals that a one-unit shift in age leads to a −0.121 change in the dependent variable. This means that older people are more likely to believe that the FARC can demobilize after the agreement. Meanwhile, a one-unit shift in urban (i.e., urban to rural), leads to a −0.135 change in the dependent variable. People living in rural areas are more likely to believe that the FARC can demobilize after a peace accord. This could be because older people have lived through decades of the internal armed conflict and might be more likely to believe that the FARC can change. People living in rural areas have been most impacted by the conflict, and there are many people in rural areas who have a great desire for Colombia to end the more than five decades of internal armed conflict. Finally, a one-unit shift in education leads to a –0.023 shift in the dependent variable. In other words, this means that people who are more educated are more likely to believe that the FARC can demobilize after a peace accord (see Table 2.4). The results might also be impacted by the desire of Colombians for peace and the hope that the FARC will demobilize to end the more than 50-year internal armed conflict.

There, however, are many individuals who are skeptical that the FARC will stop partaking in criminal activities even after a peace agreement. When asked what is the likelihood that the FARC will stop partaking in drug trafficking after a peace agreement, 41.42 percent of survey respondents in the 2016 LAPOP study contended that it is "Very Unlikely," while 41.62 percent maintained that it is "Unlikely." Thus, most Colombians are highly skeptical that the FARC will stop trafficking drugs even after the peace accord.

What factors influence someone's response to whether the FARC will stop drug trafficking after the peace agreement. Our regression model controls for age, urban, skin color, and education. The age variable is recoded into six categories. The other variables are coded the same as mentioned above in the other regression models. The dependent variable is coded as follows: "Very Likely," "Likely," "Unlikely," and "Very Unlikely."[29]

The model indicates that age, urban, and education are statistically significant at the 95-percent confidence level. The interpretation of the model

Table 2.4 Factors Influencing Perceptions About FARC Demobilization After a Peace Accord

Variable	Coeff (SE)	t-test
Age	−0.121***	−5.83
	(0.021)	
Urban	−0.135**	−2.16
	(0.062)	
Education	−0.023***	−3.18
	(0.007)	
Constant	3.497***	24.66
	(0.142)	
Observations	1,524	
R-Squared	0.024	
Robust Standard Errors in Parentheses		

*** p<0.01, ** p<0.05, * p<0.1

Source: Created by authors with data from the 2016/2017 LAPOP survey

Table 2.5 Factors Influencing Perceptions About Whether the FARC Will Stop Drug Trafficking After an Accord

Variable	Coeff (SE)	t-test
Age	−0.051***	−2.63
	(0.019)	
Urban	−0.146**	−2.50
	(0.058)	
Skin Color	−0.008	−0.69
	(0.012)	
Education	−0.013**	−2.00
	(0.006)	
Constant	3.643***	26.22
	(0.139)	
Observations	1,499	
R-Squared	0.010	
Robust Standard Errors in Parentheses		

*** p<0.01, ** p<0.05, * p<0.1

Source: Created by authors with data from the 2016/2017 LAPOP survey

reveals that a one unit increase in age leads to a −0.051 shift in the dependent variable. This means that people who are older believe that it is more likely that the FARC will stop trafficking drugs after the demobilization. Furthermore, a one-unit shift in urban (i.e., urban to rural) results in a −0.146 shift in the dependent variable. Thus, people living in rural areas a more likely to believe that the FARC will stop partaking in drug trafficking after the peace agreement (see Table 2.5). Finally, a one-unit shift in education results in a −0.013 shift in the dependent variable. In other words, people who are more educated are more likely to believe that the FARC will stop drug trafficking after the accord.

The demobilization of the FARC[30] presents serious obstacles as the former combatants seek to reinsert themselves into Colombian society. It is highly likely that Colombian society will not accept former combatants given the harm that the FARC has caused to so many Colombians over the decades-long conflict. What happens to former members of the FARC who do not have the necessary skills to compete in the highly competitive globalized world of the twenty-first century? It is highly possible that former combatants could be forced to return to a life of crime. Many former FARC soldiers have a particular "skill set" that can be utilized by other criminal actors (e.g., extortion, drug trafficking, kidnapping). Thus, former FARC soldiers could join other criminal groups, such as the BACRIM.[31]

President Iván Duque and the Future of Drug Trafficking and Organized Crime

Iván Duque Márquez of the Democratic Center (Centro Democrático) beat Gustavo Petro in the June 2018 election. Petro received 42 percent of the votes, while Duque received 54 percent. Many Colombians had never heard of Duque as he worked at the Inter-American Development bank in Washington, DC. Duque, however, had the support of Álvaro Uribe and represented a change to Juan Manuel Santos' policies. His conservative policies and opposition to the peace deal enabled him to gain support within Colombia. Many Colombians did not support the peace deal with the FARC, and President Santos became less popular over time as many citizens disapproved of him and the direction of the country. According to June S. Beittel:

> He [Duque] was the handpicked candidate of former president Uribe, who vocally opposed many of Santos's policies. Disgruntled Colombians perceived Santos as an aloof president whose energy and political capital were expended accommodating an often-despised criminal group, the FARC. President Duque appeared to be technically oriented and interested in economic reform, presenting himself as a modernizer.[32]

President Duque, therefore, represented a rejection of the Santos administration's policies as he stressed the need to focus on economic modernization.

There are significant shifts in Colombia's security policy under Duque. One of the major changes is that Duque is revamping the war on drugs to combat criminal activity, as cocaine trafficking is the most lucrative endeavor for transnational organized crime groups. In 2017, Colombia witnessed a record of 171,000 hectares cultivated, which means that organized crime groups will continue to battle for control of the cocaine industry—an industry that is thriving and is more profitable than ever. Parker Asmann, an organized crime expert, maintains:

> Colombia continues to be the world's principal producer of cocaine with the Pacific region accounting for nearly 40 percent of the country's coca crops, followed by the Central region with a little more than 30 percent, according to the UNODC. The number of hectares under coca cultivation in the country has steadily increased each year since 2013.[33]

In March 2019, the Colombian Constitutional Court began to debate the possibility of removing the ban on using glyphosate during aerial fumigation to combat the rising levels of coca cultivation. The Duque administration sought to use glyphosate to reduce the number of hectares of coca being cultivated. The Colombian Constitutional Court made rulings in 2015 and 2017 that placed restrictions on methods of aerial spraying.[34]

Coca cultivation spiked for several reasons. The main cause of the proliferation in coca production is that the Santos government stopped aerial fumigation as the World Health Organization noted that this product could cause cancer.[35] However, the US government has disagreed about this herbicide causing cancer. According to a 2018 Government Accountability Report (GAO):

> The debate over the purported negative health effects of glyphosate has made aerial spraying efforts in Colombia controversial. In March 2015, the World Health Organization's International Agency for Research on Cancer identified glyphosate as "probably" able to cause cancer in humans. However, two U.S. agencies dispute these findings. From 2002 through 2011, State formally certified to Congress that the glyphosate spraying program posed no unreasonable health risks to humans. The Environmental Protection Agency has also generally concluded that glyphosate exposure from aerial eradication in Colombia has not been linked to adverse health effects. Several other studies we reviewed discussed the potential health effects of glyphosate.[36]

Yet academics have been critical of the fumigation programs and questioned the potential health and environmental side effects.

Coca cultivation also increased because the manual eradication of coca also declined. Experts note that the drop in the price of other illicit commodities, such as gold, led Colombian peasant farmers to return to coca.[37] Farmers will continue to grow the crops if they can make more money.[38] Coca farmers also can face threats from organized crime groups if they grow other licit products.

President Duque has received pressure from the United States to reduce coca cultivation, drug trafficking, and organized crime. Donald Trump has been vocal about Colombia's increasing level of drug production:

> I'll tell you something: Colombia, you have your new president of Colombia, really good guy. I've met him, we had him at the White House. He said how he was going to stop drugs. More drugs are coming out of Colombia right now than before he was president, so he has done nothing for us.[39]

While President Trump looks at the problem in Colombia as an issue of supply, the US government should analyze the problem from a holistic perspective as opposed to focusing on meeting particular metrics: the number of hectares sprayed or the amount of cocaine seized per month.[40] Ultimately, it is unlikely that the Trump administration will move away from the old metrics as it is ramping up the war on drugs and focusing on supply-side strategies in an effort to combat drug trafficking and organized crime.

The Trump administration is placing the responsibility on Colombia and is less interested in cooperating through programs designed to reduce coca cultivation, decrease corruption, and address the underlying structural issues in Colombia. USAID and other programs that have addressed the rule of law, police reform, and combating violence will not receive increases in funding. The Trump administration is placing the burden on the Duque government to address the increases in production in cocaine as well as cocaine trafficking. The current organized crime landscape reveals that various groups will compete for control of the lucrative cocaine industry, meaning that the violence could increase as groups battle for control of territory.

Operationalizing Corruption, State Fragility, and Trust in Institutions

The LAPOP 2016/2017 Colombia survey data reveals that 12.88 percent of the population has been asked for a bribe by a police officer. What variables determine whether someone is asked to pay a bribe to a police officer? This variable is coded as no and yes. The independent variables for this model are age and monthly household income.[41] The age variable is 18 to 88, but it has been recoded into six categories.[42] The skin color variable is coded one for very light and 11 for very dark. Finally, monthly household income is from no income to more than 3,250,000 pesos.[43]

The logistic regression model reveals that age, sex, and monthly household income are statistically significant at a 95-percent confidence level. The interpretation of the model is as follows: a one-unit change in age results in a −0.339 shift in the log-odds of the dependent variable. Moreover, a one-unit change in sex (i.e., male to female) leads to a −0.912 shift in the log-odds of the dependent variable. Finally, a one-unit shift in household monthly income results in a 0.071 change in the log-odds of the dependent variable. This means that people who are wealthier, on average, are more likely to have been asked by a police officer for a bribe (see Table 2.6).

Given the high level of corruption and impunity in Colombia, this could create an incentive to bribe government officials, police officers, and members

Table 2.6 Factors Associated With Whether a Police Officer Asked for a Bribe in Colombia

Variables	Coeff (SE)	t-test
Age	−0.339***	−4.76
	(0.071)	
Sex	−0.912***	−4.81
	(0.189)	
Monthly Household Income	0.071***	3.69
	(0.019)	
Constant	−0.462	−1.24
	(0.373)	
Observations	1,346	
Standard Errors in Parentheses		

*** p<0.01, ** p<0.05, * p<0.1

Source: Created by authors with data from the 2016/2017 LAPOP survey

of the court to avoid the bureaucracy or avoid penalties (e.g., jail time). In fact, 18.28 percent of the LAPOP 2016/2017 survey population contended that paying a bribe is justified in Colombia, while 81.72 percent said that it is not. A regression model helps determine the variables that impact whether someone believes paying a bribe is justified. The dependent variable, that paying a bribe is justified, is coded into no and yes. The independent variables are age, sex, and whether a police officer has asked for a bribe (coded into no and yes).[44]

The logistic regression model reveals that age, sex, and a police officer asking for a bribe are statistically significant at the 95-percent confidence level.[45] The interpretation of the model is that a one-unit increase in age leads to a −0.156 shift in the log-odds of the dependent variable. This means, on average, that older people are less likely than younger people to believe that a bribe is justified. Furthermore, a unit change in sex (i.e., male to female) results in a −0.492 change in the log-odds of the dependent variable. Therefore, women, on average, are less likely than men to believe that paying a bribe is justified (see Table 2.7). Finally, a one-unit shift in whether a police officer has asked for a bribe (i.e., shift from no to yes) results in a 0.889 change in the log-odds of the dependent variable.

Organized crime groups have taken advantage of state fragility in Colombia. Given the vast geography of Colombia, local governments have had a difficult time governing territory and implementing the rule of law. Local governments are often underfunded and have major issues with transparency and accountability. The countless scandals and state weaknesses contribute to the lack of trust in local governments. High levels of distrust can exacerbate the problem because citizens will be less likely to report crimes and seek assistance from the government if they are distrustful of the institution. Vanderbilt University's LAPOP 2016/2017 Colombia survey data demonstrates that local governments face

Table 2.7 Factors Influencing Whether Paying a Bribe is Justified

Variable	Coeff (SE)	t-test
Age	−0.156***	−2.70
	(0.058)	
Sex	−0.492***	−3.77
	(0.131)	
Police Officer Asked for Bribe	0.889***	5.73
	(0.155)	
Constant	−0.560**	−2.07
	(0.270)	
Observations	1,540	
Standard Errors in Parentheses		

*** p<0.01, ** p<0.05, * p<0.1

Source: Created by authors with data from the 2016/2017 LAPOP survey

major issues with lack of trust. In fact, 18.23 percent of respondents answered "Not at All" when asked if they had trust in local governments.

What variables influence levels of trust in the local government? A regression model can help determine the influence of different independent variables on the dependent variable, trust in local government, which is coded 1 for "Not at All" and 7 for "A Lot." The independent variables are age, sex, ideology, urban, and monthly household income. The age variable includes a range from 18 to 88 years old. This variable is recoded into six categories. Sex is divided into male and female, while ideology is coded 1 for left and 10 for right. Finally, urban is divided into urban and rural, and monthly household income is from no income to more than 3,250,000 pesos.[46]

The regression results indicate that age, sex, ideology, and urban are all statistically significant at a 95-percent confidence level. The interpretation of the model is as follows: a one-unit change in age results in a 0.143 change in trust in local government. This means, on average, that older people have more trust in the local government than do younger people. Furthermore, a one-unit shift in sex (i.e., male to female) leads to a 0.232 change in the dependent variable. In other words, females, on average, have more trust in the local government than do males. The ideology variable indicates that a one-unit change in ideology leads to a 0.107 shift in trust in the local government. Thus, on average, people who are more conservative have higher levels of trust in the local government (see Table 2.8). Finally, the model indicates that a one-unit change in the urban variable (i.e., urban to rural) leads to a 0.532 shift in trust in the local government. This suggests

Table 2.8 Factors Influencing Trust in Local Government

Variables	Coeff (SE)	t-test
Age	0.143***	3.22
	(0.043)	
Sex	0.232**	2.35
	(0.099)	
Ideology	0.107***	5.50
	(0.019)	
Urban	0.532***	3.07
	(0.173)	
Monthly Household Income	0.012	0.75
	(0.016)	
Constant	1.681***	4.61
	(0.364)	
Observations	1,271	
R-Squared	0.055	
Standard Errors in Parentheses		

*** $p<0.01$, ** $p<0.05$, * $p<0.1$

Source: Created by authors with data from the 2016/2017 LAPOP survey

that people living in rural areas, on average, have higher levels of trust in the local government than do individuals living in urban areas.

Colombia faces major issues with corruption and impunity in its institutions, which have impacted trust in other institutions.[47] Colombians have low levels of trust in politicians, the judicial system, and police forces—among other institutions (see Figures 2.4 and 2.5). The high levels of impunity

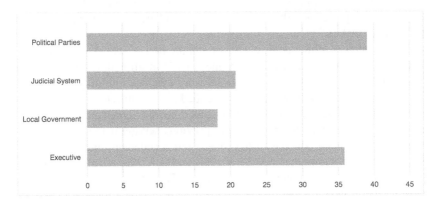

Figure 2.4 Percentage Who Responded "Not At All" for Levels of Trust in Political Parties, Judicial System, Local Government, and Executive

Source: Created by authors with 2016/2017 LAPOP data

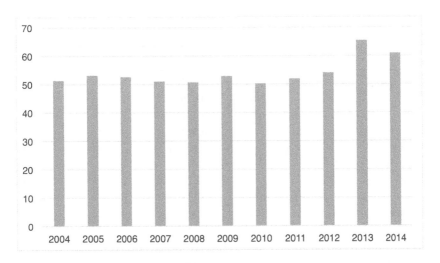

Figure 2.5 The Percentage of Colombians Who Have Little or No Confidence That the Judicial System Will Punish Offenders for Robbery or Assault

Source: Created by authors with data from Miguel García Sánchez. Jorge Daniel Montalvo, Mitchell A. Seligson, *Cultura política de la democracia en Colombia*, 2015 (Nashville, TN: LAPOP, 2015)

Note: The question asks the respondent if they believe that the Colombian judiciary would punish the offenders if the respondent was a victim of assault or robbery

present in the country have resulted in skepticism among many citizens who question the rule of law.[48] There is a perception that well-connected people, such as politicians, can commit crimes without being punished for their transgressions.

While the Uribe government hailed Colombia's police reform as a model for other countries, the reality is that the institution remains highly distrusted by Colombians. According to the 2016/2017 LAPOP data, 17.30 percent of Colombians responded "Not at All" when asked about their level of trust in the police. On the other hand, only 8.68 percent of the population responded "A Lot."

What variables influence levels of trust in the police? The dependent variable, trust in the police, was coded one for not at all and seven for a lot. The independent variables in the model were age, sex, monthly household income, urban, and skin color. Age was coded into six different categories as the variable includes ages between 18 and 88. The other independent variables remained the same as described in the previous section using a regression model. However, we added ideology, where left is coded one and ten is coded right. The model shows that monthly income and skin color are not statistically significant at the 95-percent confidence level. Thus, we ran the model again without these two variables.[49]

The regression model reveals that sex, ideology, and urban are statistically significant at the 95-percent confidence level. The results of the model reveal that a one-unit change in age results in a 0.062 change in the dependent variable.

Table 2.9 Factors Influencing Trust in the National Police

Variables	Coeff (SE)	t-test
Age	0.062	1.72
	(0.036)	
Sex	0.371*	3.30
	(0.112)	
Ideology	0.103*	4.26
	(0.024)	
Urban	0.329*	2.36
	(0.139)	
Constant	2.047*	8.22
	(0.249)	
Observations	1,465	
R-Squared	0.040	
Standard Errors in Parentheses		

*** $p<0.01$, ** $p<0.05$, * $p<0.1$

Source: Created by authors with data from the 2016/2017 LAPOP survey

A one-unit change in sex (i.e., male to female) leads to a 0.371 shift in the dependent variable. Furthermore, a one-unit shift in the ideology variable results in a 0.103 unit change in levels of trust in the national police. Finally, a one-unit change in the urban variable (i.e., a shift from urban to rural) causes a 0.329-unit shift in the dependent variable. In other words, people living in rural areas have higher levels of trust in the police than do people living in urban areas (see Table 2.9).

Conclusion

Colombia has a long history of drug trafficking, organized crime, and violence. The nature of organized crime has shifted in Colombia in part because of the government's policies to combat the leading criminal organizations. While the United States government has supported various Colombian administrations with billions of dollars through initiatives such as Plan Colombia, drug trafficking and organized crime continue. Today, Colombia is the leading cocaine producer in the world. The criminal dynamics in Colombia will continue to evolve over time. As new actors, such as the BACRIM, emerge on the criminal scene, there is a need to learn from the lessons of the past. The Colombian government must make serious efforts to combat corruption by increasing accountability. There is a need for serious institutional reforms in Colombia to address the high levels of impunity. Unless these issues are resolved, organized crime and drug trafficking will continue to thrive and new criminal actors will fill the power vacuums in certain zones of the country, which, in turn could lead to human rights abuses and decreased levels of citizen security.

Notes

1. Bruce Michael Bagley, "US foreign policy and the war on drugs: Analysis of a policy failure," *Journal of Interamerican Studies and World Affairs* 30, no. 2–3 (1988): pp. 189–212; Bruce Michael Bagley, "The new hundred years war? US national security and the war on drugs in Latin America," *Journal of Interamerican Studies and World Affairs* 30, no. 1 (1988): pp. 161–182.
2. For more, see Bruce M. Bagley, "Colombia and the war on drugs," *Foreign Affairs* 67, no. 1 (1988): pp. 70–92; Robert Filippone, "The Medellin Cartel: Why we can't win the drug war," *Studies in Conflict & Terrorism* 17, no. 4 (1994): pp. 323–344.
3. For more, see Jorge Giraldo Ramírez and Juan Pablo Mesa, "Reintegración sin desmovilización: el caso de las milicias populares de Medellín," *Colombia Internacional* 77 (2013): pp. 217–239; Francisco Gutiérrez Sanín and Ana María Jaramillo, "Crime, (counter-) insurgency and the privatization of security: The case of Medellín, Colombia," *Environment and Urbanization* 16, no. 2 (2004): pp. 17–30.
4. Jeremy McDermott, "20 years after Pablo: The evolution of Colombia's drug trade," *InSight Crime*, December 3, 2013, www.insightcrime.org/news-analysis/20-years-after-pablo-the-evolution-of-colombias-drug-trade, accessed September 2017, p. 1.
5. Jonathan D. Rosen and Bruce M. Bagley, "Is Plan Colombia a model? An analysis of counternarcotics strategies in Colombia," *Global Security Review* 1 (2017): pp. 8–14.

6. Ibid.; Jonathan Daniel Rosen, "Lecciones y resultados del Plan Colombia (2000–2012)," *Contextualizaciones Lat.*, Año 6, número 10 (enero–julio 2014): pp. 1–12.

7. For more, see June S. Beittel, *Colombia: Background, U.S. Relations, and Congressional Interest* (Washington, DC: Congressional Research Service, 2012); for more on Plan Colombia: see: Jonathan Daniel Rosen and Roberto Zepeda Martínez, "La guerra contra las drogas en Colombia y México: estrategias fracasadas," *Ánfora* 21, no. 38 (2014): pp. 179–200; Jonathan Daniel Rosen, "Lecciones y resultados del Plan Colombia (2000–2012)," *Contextualizaciones Lat.*, pp. 1–12.

8. For more, see Michael Shifter, "Plan Colombia: A retrospective," *Americas Quarterly* 6, no. 3 (2012): p. 36.

9. Jonathan D. Rosen, *The Losing War: Plan Colombia and Beyond* (Albany, NY: SUNY Press, 2014); for more, see Winifred Tate, "Repeating past mistakes: Aiding counterinsurgency in Colombia," *NACLA Report on the Americas* 34, no. 2 (2000): pp. 16–19; Jonathan Daniel Rosen and Roberto Zepeda Martínez, "La guerra contra las drogas en Colombia y México: estrategias fracasadas," *Ánfora* 21, no. 38 (2014): pp. 179–200; Adam Isacson, "Failing grades: Evaluating the results of Plan Colombia," *Yale Journal International Affairs* 1 (2005): p. 138.

10. Washington Office on Latin America, "15th anniversary of Plan Colombia: Learning from its successes and failures," *Washington Office on Latin America*, February 1, 2016. www.wola.org/files/1602_plancol/, accessed September 2017.

11. Coletta Youngers and Eileen Rosin, eds., *Drugs and Democracy in Latin America: The Impact of US Policy* (Boulder, CO: Lynne Rienner Publishers, 2005); Michael Kenney, "The architecture of drug trafficking: Network forms of organisation in the Colombian cocaine trade," *Global Crime* 8, no. 3 (2007): pp. 233–259.

12. Coletta Youngers and Eileen Rosin, eds., *Drugs and Democracy in Latin America: The Impact of US Policy.*

13. Nick Miroff, "American cocaine use is way up. Colombia's coca boom might be why," *The Washington Post*, March 4, 2017, p. 1.

14. Bruce Michael Bagley, "Dateline drug wars: Colombia: The wrong strategy," *Foreign Policy*, no. 77 (Winter 1989–90): pp. 154–171; Christopher Woody, "In the world's biggest cocaine producer, cultivation reportedly surged again in 2016," *Business Insider*, March 13, 2017; Michelle L. Dion and Catherine Russler, "Eradication efforts, the state, displacement and poverty: Explaining coca cultivation in Colombia during Plan Colombia," *Journal of Latin American Studies* 40, no. 3 (2008): pp. 399–421.

15. The LAPOP survey team indicates that the following command for weighting the data: svyset upm [pw=wt], strata(estratopri)

16. Recode q2 (18/28=1) (29/39=2) (40/50=3) (51/61=4) (62/72=5) (73/88=6), gen (age)

17. The model is tested for multicollinearity. The model has a mean VIF of 1.09, indicating that it does not have issues with multicollinearity. The linktest produces a hatsq that is not statistically significant, indicating that the model does not have specification issues. The Breusch-Pagan/Cook-Weisberg test for heteroskedasticity results in a Prob > chi2 of 0.584, indicating that the model does not have issues with heteroskedasticity.

18. We ran a regression and tested for multicollinearity. The model has a Mean Variance Inflation Factor (VIF) of 1.07. A VIF of 10 requires further examines. Thus, the model does not suffer from multicollinearity. The linktest produces a hatsq that is not statistically significant, indicating that the model is properly specified. Furthermore, the Breusch-Pagan/Cook-Weisberg test for heteroskedasticity results in a Prob > chi2 of 0.00, suggesting that the model has heteroskedasticity. We adjusted this by running the vce (robust) command in Stata 15.1.

19. Marc Chernick, "The paramilitarization of the war in Colombia," *NACLA Report on the Americas* 31, no. 5 (1998): pp. 28–33; Winifred Tate, "Paramilitaries in Colombia," *The Brown Journal of World Affairs* 8, no. 1 (2001): pp. 163–175.

20. Tristan Clavel, "Colombia's Urabeños recruiting dissidents from FARC Peace Process," *InSight Crime*, January 26, 2017, www.insightcrime.org/news-briefs/

colombia-urabenos-recruiting-dissidents-farc-peace-process, accessed April 23, 2018; Elvira Maria Retrepo y Bruce Michael Bagley, eds, *La desmovilización de los paramilitares en Colombia entre el escepticismo y la esperanza* (Bogotá, CO: Universidad de los Andes, 2011); Winifred Tate, "Paramilitaries in Colombia," *Brown Journal World Affairs* 8 (2001): p. 163.

21. Jeremy McDermott, "The BACRIM and their position in Colombia's underworld," *InSight Crime*, www.insightcrime.org/investigations/bacrim-and-their-position-in-colombia-underworld/ May 2, 2014, accessed March 9, 2020, p. 6.

22. Hanna Samir Kassab and Jonathan D. Rosen, *Corruption, Institutions, and Fragile States* (New York, NY: Palgrave Macmillan, 2018).

23. For more on the history of the internal armed conflict, see Marc W. Chernick, "Negotiated settlement to armed conflict: Lessons from the Colombian peace process," *Journal of Interamerican Studies and World Affairs* 30, no. 4 (1988): pp. 53–88; Lawrence Boudon, "Guerrillas and the state: The role of the state in the Colombian peace process," *Journal of Latin American Studies* 28, no. 2 (1996): pp. 279–297.

24. Bruce M. Bagley and Jonathan D. Rosen, eds., *Colombia's Political Economy at the Outset of the Twenty-First Century: From Uribe to Santos and Beyond* (Lanham, MD: Lexington Books, 2015); Caitlyn Davis and Harold Trinkunas, "Has Colombia achieved peace? 5 things you should know," *Brookings*, August 25, 2016, www.brookings.edu/blog/order-from-chaos/2016/08/25/has-colombia-achieved-peace-5-things-you-should-know/, April 2018.

25. Bruce M. Bagley and Jonathan D. Rosen, eds., *Colombia's Political Economy at the Outset of the Twenty-First Century: From Uribe to Santos and Beyond.*

26. Jonathan D. Rosen and Roberot Zepeda, "Crimen Organizado, Narcotráfico y Conflicto Interno en Colombia: Tendencias y Desafíos," 2018, Working Paper.

27. We tested the model for multicollinearity and model specification. The model has a mean VIF of 1.26, indicating that the model does not have issues with multicollinearity. The linktest indicates that the model is properly specified. In addition, the Breusch-Pagan/Cook-Weisberg test for heteroskedasticity produces a Prob > chi2 of 0.00, which means that the model has to be corrected for heteroskedasticity. The model is corrected using the vce (robust) command in Stata 15.1. We controlled for skin color as the FARC have targeted underrepresented minority groups that have suffered from discrimination.

28. The model is tested for multicollinearity, model specification, and heteroskedasticity. The model has a mean VIF of 1.19, indicating that it does not have issues with multicollinearity. The linktest produces a hatsq that is not statistically significant, indicating that the model is properly specified. The Breusch-Pagan/Cook-Weisberg test for heteroskedasticity produces a Prob > Ch2 of 0.00, indicating that the model needs to be readjusted for heteroskedasticity. The model is adjusted using the vce (robust) command in Stata 15.1.

29. We tested multicollinearity, model specification, and heteroskedasticity in the regression model. The model has a mean VIF of 1.14, which means that the model does not have issues with multicollinearity. The linktest produces at hatsq that is not statistically significant, indicating that the model is properly specified. The Breusch-Pagan/Cook-Weisberg test for heteroskedasticity results in a Prob > ch2 of 0.00, indicating that the model needs to be corrected for heteroskedasticity. The model is corrected using the vce (robust) command in Stata 15.1. We control for skin color to account for the impact of racism.

30. For more on the FARC, see Bilal Y. Saab and Alexandra W. Taylor, "Criminality and armed groups: A comparative study of FARC and paramilitary groups in Colombia," *Studies in Conflict & Terrorism* 32, no. 6 (2009): pp. 455–475; Jim Rochlin, "Plan Colombia and the revolution in military affairs: The demise of the FARC," *Review of International Studies* 37, no. 2 (2011): pp. 715–740.

31. Mike LaSusa, "FARC dissidents forming criminal groups in Ecuador: Reports," *InSight Crime*, August 9, 2016, www.insightcrime.org/news/brief/farc-dissidents-forming-criminal-groups-in-ecuador-reports/, accessed April 26, 2018, pp. 1–2.

32. June S. Beittel, *Colombia: Background and U.S. Relations*, p. 9.
33. Parker Asmann, "Colombia cocaine production breaks new record levels: UNODC report," *InSight Crime*, September 19, 2018, www.insightcrime.org/news/analysis/colombia-cocaine-production-breaks-new-record-levels-unodc-report/; www.insightcrime.org/news/brief/colombia-coca-production-hits-new-record-high-us-figures-say/, accessed May 15, 2019; for more, see United Nations Office on Drugs and Crime (UNODC), *Colombia Coca Cultivation Survey 2017* (Bogotá, CO: UNODC, 2018).
34. Direct quote from Adam Isacson, "Restarting aerial fumigation of drug crops in Colombia is a mistake," *WOLA*, March 7, 2019, www.wola.org/analysis/restarting-aerial-fumigation-of-drug-crops-in-colombia-is-a-mistake/, accessed May 15, 2019.
35. Adam Isacson, "Confronting Colombia's coca boom requires patience and a commitment to the peace accords," *WOLA*, March 13, 2017, www.wola.org/analysis/confronting-colombias-coca-boom-requires-patience-commitment-peace-accords/, accessed May 15, 2019.
36. Government Accountability Office (GAO), *COLOMBIA: U.S. Counternarcotics Assistance Achieved Some Positive Results, but State Needs to Review the Overall U.S. Approach* (Washington, DC: GAO, 2018), p. 40.
37. Adam Isacson, "Restarting aerial fumigation of drug crops in Colombia is a mistake"; Adam Isacson, "Confronting Colombia's coca boom requires patience and a commitment to the peace accords."
38. Laura Alejandra Alonso and Parker Asmann, "Glyphosate alone won't fix Colombia's complex coca woes," *InSight Crime*, March 14, 2019, www.insightcrime.org/news/analysis/glyphosate-alone-wont-fix-colombia-complex-coca-woes/, accessed May 15, 2019, p. 7.
39. Jack Norman, "Drug trafficking from Colombia up since Duque took office: Trump," *Colombia Reports*, March 30, 2019.
40. Jeremy McDermott, "Op-Ed: Duque 'has done nothing for us,' says Trump," *InSight Crime*, April 6, 2019, www.insightcrime.org/news/analysis/duque-done-nothing-trump-us-colombia/, accessed May 15, 2019, p. 3.
41. I first ran the model controlling for skin color. However, the Box-Tidwell model reveals that skin color made the model non-linear, which violates the assumption that there is a linear relationship between the odds ratio and the independent variables. I removed skin color and ran the model again. The new model does not have issues with linearity.
42. The recode is as follows: recode q2 (18/28=1) (29/39=2) (40/50=3) (51/61=4) (62/72=5) (73/88=6), gen (age)
43. The model is tested for multicollinearity and specification issues. The results reveal that the model does not have issues with multicollinearity, as the mean VIF is 1.04. The linktest indicates that the model is properly specified. Moreover, the svy command produces linearized coefficients and standard errors.
44. After running the regression, I tested to see if the model had any issues with specification or multicollinearity. The logit model does not have issues with model specification at the linktest results is not statistically significant at the 95-percent confidence level. The model also does not have issues with multicollinearity, as the mean VIF is 1.04, which is well below 10.
45. The Box-Tidwell model indicates that this model does not have issues with non-linearity.
46. The linktest indicates that the model is properly specified. After running the regression, it is also important to test for multicollinearity and heteroskedasticity. The Mean Variance Inflation Factor (VIF) is 1.09. A score of 10 or above suggest that the model has issues with multicollinearity. Moreover, the Breusch-Pagan/

Cook-Weisberg test for heteroskedasticity results in Prob > chi2 of 0.139, indicating that the model does not have problems with heteroskedasticity.

47. For more, see Laura Langbein and Pablo Sanabria, "The shape of corruption: Colombia as a case study," *Journal of Development Studies* 49, no. 11 (2013): pp. 1500–1513.
48. Adriaan Alsema, "Colombia's impunity rate at virtually 99%: Incoming chief prosecutor," *Colombia Reports*, August 2, 2016.
49. After running the regression, we tested for multicollinearity, model specification, and heteroskedasticity. The model has Mean Variance Inflation Factor (VIF) of 1.03, suggesting that it does not have issues with multicollinearity. The linktest indicates that the model does not have issues with specification. Finally, the Breusch-Pagan/ Cook-Weisberg test for heteroskedasticity results in Prob > chi2 of 0.404, indicating that the model does not have problems with heteroskedasticity.

Works Cited

Alonso, Laura Alejandra and Parker Asmann. "Glyphosate alone won't fix Colombia's complex coca woes," *InSight Crime*, March 14, 2019, www.insightcrime.org/news/ analysis/glyphosate-alone-wont-fix-colombia-complex-coca-woes/, accessed May 15, 2019, p. 7.

Alsema, Adriaan. "Colombia's impunity rate at virtually 99%: Incoming chief prosecutor," *Colombia Reports*, August 2, 2016.

Asmann, Parker. "Colombia cocaine production breaks new record levels: UNODC report," *InSight Crime*, September 19, 2018, www.insightcrime.org/news/analysis/ colombia-cocaine-production-breaks-new-record-levels-unodc-report/; www. insightcrime.org/news/brief/colombia-coca-production-hits-new-record-high-us-figures-say/, accessed May 15, 2019.

Bagley, Bruce Michael. "Colombia and the war on drugs," *Foreign Affairs* 67, no. 1 (1988): pp. 70–92.

Bagley, Bruce Michael. "The new hundred years war? US national security and the war on drugs in Latin America," *Journal of Interamerican Studies and World Affairs* 30, no. 1 (1988): pp. 161–182.

Bagley, Bruce Michael. "US foreign policy and the war on drugs: Analysis of a policy failure," *Journal of Interamerican Studies and World Affairs* 30, no. 2–3 (1988): pp. 189–212.

Bagley, Bruce Michael. "Dateline drug wars: Colombia: The wrong strategy," *Foreign Policy*, no. 77 (Winter 1989–90): pp. 154–171.

Bagley, Bruce Michael and Jonathan D. Rosen, eds. *Colombia's Political Economy at the Outset of the Twenty-First Century: From Uribe to Santos and Beyond*. Lanham, MD: Lexington Books, 2015.

Beittel, June S. *Colombia: Background, U.S. Relations, and Congressional Interest*. Washington, DC: Congressional Research Service, 2012.

Boudon, Lawrence. "Guerrillas and the state: The role of the state in the Colombian peace process," *Journal of Latin American Studies* 28, no. 2 (1996): pp. 279–297.

Chernick, Marc W. "Negotiated settlement to armed conflict: Lessons from the Colombian peace process," *Journal of Interamerican Studies and World Affairs* 30, no. 4 (1988): pp. 53–88.

Chernick, Marc W. "The paramilitarization of the war in Colombia," *NACLA Report on the Americas* 31, no. 5 (1998): pp. 28–33.

Clavel, Tristan. "Colombia's Urabeños recruiting dissidents from FARC Peace Process," *InSight Crime*, January 26, 2017, www.insightcrime.org/news-briefs/colombia-urabenos-recruiting-dissidents-farc-peace-process, accessed April 23, 2018.

Davis, Caitlyn and Harold Trinkunas. "Has Colombia achieved peace? 5 things you should know," *Brookings*, August 25, 2016, www.brookings.edu/blog/order-from-chaos/2016/08/25/has-colombia-achieved-peace-5-things-you-should-know/, April 2018.

Dion, Michelle L. and Catherine Russler. "Eradication efforts, the state, displacement and poverty: Explaining coca cultivation in Colombia during Plan Colombia," *Journal of Latin American Studies* 40, no. 3 (2008): pp. 399–421.

Filippone, Robert. "The Medellin Cartel: Why we can't win the drug war," *Studies in Conflict & Terrorism* 17, no. 4 (1994): pp. 323–344.

Government Accountability Office (GAO). *COLOMBIA: U.S. Counternarcotics Assistance Achieved Some Positive Results, But State Needs to Review the Overall U.S. Approach*. Washington, DC: GAO, 2018, p. 40.

Gutiérrez Sanín, Francisco and Ana María Jaramillo. "Crime, (counter-) insurgency and the privatization of security-the case of Medellín, Colombia," *Environment and Urbanization* 16, no. 2 (2004): pp. 17–30.

Isacson, Adam. "Failing grades: Evaluating the results of plan Colombia," *Yale Journal International Affairs* 1 (2005): p. 138.

Isacson, Adam. "Confronting Colombia's coca boom requires patience and a commitment to the peace accords," *WOLA*, March 13, 2017, www.wola.org/analysis/confronting-colombias-coca-boom-requires-patience-commitment-peace-accords/, accessed May 15, 2019.

Isacson, Adam. "Restarting aerial fumigation of drug crops in Colombia is a mistake," *WOLA*, March 7, 2019, www.wola.org/analysis/restarting-aerial-fumigation-of-drug-crops-in-colombia-is-a-mistake/, accessed May 15, 2019.

Kassab Hanna, Samir and Jonathan D. Rosen. *Corruption, Institutions, and Fragile States*. New York, NY: Palgrave Macmillan, 2018.

Kenney, Michael. "The architecture of drug trafficking: Network forms of organisation in the Colombian cocaine trade," *Global Crime* 8, no. 3 (2007): pp. 233–259.

Langbein, Laura and Pablo Sanabria. "The shape of corruption: Colombia as a case study," *Journal of Development Studies* 49, no. 11 (2013): pp. 1500–1513.

LaSusa, Mike. "FARC dissidents forming criminal groups in Ecuador: Reports," *InSight Crime*, August 9, 2016, www.insightcrime.org/news/brief/farc-dissidents-forming-criminal-groups-in-ecuador-reports/, accessed April 26, 2018, pp. 1–2.

McDermott, Jeremy. "20 years after Pablo: The evolution of Colombia's drug trade," *InSight Crime*, December 3, 2013, www.insightcrime.org/news-analysis/20-years-after-pablo-the-evolution-of-colombias-drug-trade, accessed September 2017, p. 1.

McDermott, Jeremy. "The BACRIM and Their Position in Colombia's Underworld," *InSight Crime*, May 2, 2014, www.insightcrime.org/investigations/bacrim-and-their-position-in-colombia-underworld/, accessed March 9, 2020, p. 6.

McDermott, Jeremy. "Op-Ed: Duque 'has done nothing for us,' says Trump," *InSight Crime*, April 6, 2019, www.insightcrime.org/news/analysis/duque-done-nothing-trump-us-colombia/, accessed May 15, 2019, p. 3.

Norman, Jack. "Drug trafficking from Colombia up since Duque took office: Trump," *Colombia Reports*, March 30, 2019.

Ramírez, Jorge Giraldo and Juan Pablo Mesa. "Reintegración sin desmovilización: el caso de las milicias populares de Medellín," *Colombia Internacional* 77 (2013): pp. 217–239.

Retrepo, Elvira Maria y Bruce Michael Bagley, eds. *La desmovilización de los paramilitares en Colombia entre el escepticismo y la esperanza*. Bogotá, CO: Universidad de los Andes, 2011.

Rochlin, Jim. "Plan Colombia and the revolution in military affairs: The demise of the FARC," *Review of International Studies* 37, no. 2 (2011): pp. 715–740.

Rosen, Jonathan Daniel. "Lecciones y resultados del Plan Colombia (2000–2012)," *Contextualizaciones Lat*, Año 6, número 10 (enero–julio 2014): pp. 1–12.

Rosen, Jonathan Daniel. *The Losing War: Plan Colombia and Beyond*. Albany, NY: SUNY Press, 2014.

Rosen, Jonathan Daniel and Bruce M. Bagley. "Is Plan Colombia a model? An analysis of counternarcotics strategies in Colombia," *Global Security Review* 1 (2017): pp. 8–14.

Rosen, Jonathan Daniel and Roberto Zepeda Martínez. "La guerra contra las drogas en Colombia y México: estrategias fracasadas," *Ánfora* 21, no. 38 (2014): pp. 179–200.

Rosen, Jonathan Daniel and Roberot Zepeda Martínez. "Crimen Organizado, Narcotráfico y Conflicto Interno en Colombia: Tendencias y Desafíos," 2018, Working Paper.

Saab, Bilal Y. and Alexandra W. Taylor. "Criminality and armed groups: A comparative study of FARC and paramilitary groups in Colombia," *Studies in Conflict & Terrorism* 32, no. 6 (2009): pp. 455–475.

Shifter, Michael. "Plan Colombia: A retrospective," *Americas Quarterly* 6, no. 3 (2012): p. 36.

Tate, Winifred. "Repeating past mistakes: Aiding counterinsurgency in Colombia," *NACLA Report on the Americas* 34, no. 2 (2000): pp. 16–19.

Tate, Winifred. "Paramilitaries in Colombia," *The Brown Journal of World Affairs* 8, no. 1 (2001): pp. 163–175.

United Nations Office on Drugs and Crime (UNODC). *Colombia Coca Cultivation Survey 2017*. Bogotá, CO: UNODC, 2018.

Washington Office on Latin America. "15th anniversary of Plan Colombia: Learning from its successes and failures," *Washington Office on Latin America*, February 1, 2016. www.wola.org/files/1602_plancol/, accessed September 2017.

Woody, Christopher. "In the world's biggest cocaine producer, cultivation reportedly surged again in 2016," *Business Insider*, March 13, 2017.

Youngers, Coletta and Eileen Rosin, eds. *Drugs and Democracy in Latin America: The Impact of US Policy*. Boulder, CO: Lynne Rienner Publishers, 2005.

3   Mexico

Mexico is experiencing major challenges with organized crime, drug trafficking, and violence.[1] This chapter seeks to understand the recent trends in organized crime, focusing on the major players involved in such criminal activities. Criminal actors fight among each other for control of territory, which has contributed to high levels of criminal violence. Moreover, the chapter's main argument is that the government's drug war policies have led to a fragmentation of criminal organizations. In addition, the militarization of the drug war has resulted in hundreds of thousands of drug-related deaths. The chapter begins by analyzing Mexico's transition to democracy. It then turns to President Felipe Calderón's drug war, focusing on the government's counternarcotics strategies. The chapter then analyzes the nature of organized crime in Mexico, concentrating on the different types of cartels. It then turns to trends in violence. It concludes with an emphasis on the need to reform various institutions beset by corruption.

From Single-Party Rule to Democracy

Mexico had 71 years of single-party rule by the Institutional Revolutionary Party (Partido Revolucionario Institucional, PRI). The PRI can best be characterized as a political machine that sought to control all levels of government in the country's federal system (i.e., municipal, state, and federal).[2] The PRI dominated the elections, winning the majority of all the votes in all presidential elections until 1982. Victory, however, often came at a price as the political system can be characterized by high levels of corruption and fraud.[3]

While Mexico during this period could not be classified as a democracy, as by definition this requires the alternation of power, the government had fewer drug-related homicides than today.[4] This is because the Mexican government, which was plagued by high levels of corruption, controlled organized crime.[5] The government had what some may refer to as party "discipline" and tight control of all activities that occurred across Mexico's 31 states and the Federal District—Mexico City recently became the 32nd state. Christy Thornton and Adam Goodman contend, "The PRI's tight-fisted rule and near absolute political power ensured the complicity of law enforcement and the local business community. In turn, unchecked corruption allowed the trade to thrive, creating a Mexican 'pax mafiosa.'"[6] While negotiations between drug trafficking organizations and politicians and other government entities may not be the key to a thriving democracy, such activities helped reduce the levels of violence.

Mexico's political system, which had remained intact for seven decades, broke down with the election of Vicente Fox of the National Action Party (Partido Acción Nacional, PAN) in 2000.[7] The election of Fox represented a transition to democracy, but it turned Mexico's political system upside down, breaking the government's control on organized crime. According to Luis Gómez Romero of the University of Wollongong:

> both Mexicans and their newly elected government soon learned how deeply institutionalised corruption was in Mexico. In May 2001, Fox's secretary of foreign affairs, Jorge G. Castañeda, confessed to the Spanish newspaper El País that the democratic transition was proving harder than he and the president had foreseen.[8]

Reforming institutions that are built on corruption and clientelist relationships is a slow and difficult process.

Corruption and impunity have continued to plague Mexico despite the transition to democracy. According to Transparency International's CPI, Mexico scored a 29 out of 100 in 2017, where the lower the number means the more corruption there is. It ranked 135 out of 180, with the higher the number, the more corruption.[9] In addition, impunity is estimated to be as high as 99 percent.[10] The high levels of state fragility and weakness present an ideal place for organized crime groups to operate. These organizations seek to infiltrate the state apparatus by bribing politicians, judges, and police officers. Organized crime groups want to participate in criminal activities to make money.[11] Corrupt government officials can help them avoid prison time and continue their illicit activities.

Counternarcotic Strategies: Calderón's Drug War

In 2006, the PAN won again as President Felipe Calderón assumed the presidency during a highly contested election against Andrés Manuel López Obrador of the Party of the Democratic Revolution (Partido de la Revolución Democrática, PRD).[12] López Obrador argued that "[w]e cannot accept these results." He continued: "We are going to ask for clarity. We are going to ask for a vote count, polling place by polling place."[13] Many critics contended that the election was fraudulent. Voters took to the streets in protest, occupying the Zócalo Plaza in Mexico City.[14] Despite the claims of fraud, Calderón assumed the presidency with a large percentage of the Mexican public displeased given the allegations of voter fraud.

Some critics contend that Calderón launched the war on drugs in Mexico not only to combat drug trafficking and organized crime, but also to demonstrate his power and control over the country.[15] According to Bruce Bagley, an expert on drug trafficking and organized crime, "Calderón came in as a law-and-order president and wants to show he is capable of reasserting state authority to convince the Mexican people, as well as the US, that he is, in fact, in charge."[16] Jorge Castañeda echoes this point, contending that:

> Calderón decided for political reasons that what he was going to do was send the army into Michoacán and a couple of other states, do the job, and then get out. It did not work out that way. The war against the cartels was declared for political reasons, not for drug-related reasons. This is important because it means that if the premises were false then, they are still false now.[17]

The Calderón administration began by sending 7,000 troops to his home state of Michoacán.[18]

Why did Calderón deploy the military as opposed to utilizing the police forces to combat organized crime? The public has higher levels of confidence in the Mexican military, as the armed forces are perceived to be more professional, less corrupt, and better trained than the police. Castañeda, a former Mexican government official and security expert, contends that the Mexican military faces—and has faced—different obstacles. He maintains that:

> Mexican society knows full well that the corruption scandals in the military do not just belong to the past (Zedillo's drug czar, General Gutiérrez Rebollo, was arrested in 1998 for drug trafficking). Moreover, the modern Mexican military, founded after the Revolution in the twenties, has always been held on a short leash by the civilian leadership of the country.[19]

Castañeda has also questioned the readiness of the Mexican military.[20]

Critics have questioned whether Calderón made the right policy decision to send the military to combat drug trafficking and organized crime.[21] John Ackerman, a professor at the National Autonomous University of Mexico (Universidad Nacional Autónoma de México, UNAM), disagreed with Calderón's strategy, highlighting that Mexico is different from other countries in the region because of the limitations on the power of the armed forces.[22] Experts also have questioned whether such strategies would lead to higher levels of violence. Deploying the military on the streets could lead to clashes between drug traffickers and the armed forces.[23] There are also concerns over the potential—and existing—human rights abuses. Such fears increased over time as the Mexican military became involved in various human rights scandals during the drug war. Yet other scholars contend that the Calderón administration did not have many other choices besides using the military. Jorge Chabat, a Mexican security expert, said: "I agree that the Army may be corrupted in the fight against drug trafficking . . . but what option do you have?"[24] Another option would be not to declare the drug war and focus on addressing the underlying structural issues in Mexico (i.e., impunity and corruption). Deploying the military on the streets does not address the underlying problem: the demand for drugs.

The militarization of the drug war resulted in a fragmentation of organized crime groups, as organizations are at war with the government. According to Bagley, Mexico had six major drug trafficking organizations in 2006: Pacific cartel, Milenio cartel, La Familia Michoacana, Gulf cartel, Tijuana cartel, and Juárez cartel. The numbers of cartels have increased over time. By 2010, he estimates that Mexico had 12 major drug trafficking organizations.[25] Yet some experts debate the level of fragmentation. Beittel, an analyst in Latin American Affairs at the Congressional Research Service, contends that experts disagree about the nature of the fragmentation, but she maintains that the criminal landscape in Mexico has evolved over time.[26] In 2012, Mexico's Attorney General argued that there were 80 cartels, demonstrating the proliferation of organized crime groups.[27]

The Different Types of Cartels in Mexico

Eduardo Guerrero, a Mexican security expert, categorizes the drug trafficking landscape in Mexico into four types of cartels. First, he argues that there are three major national cartels: Los Zetas, Sinaloa, and Jalisco New Generation Cartel. These organizations control many of the international drug trafficking routes and are the most powerful players in the criminal landscape. The Sinaloa cartel has a long history of drug trafficking and violence. Some experts estimate that the cartel controls between 40 to 60 percent of drug trafficking.[28] The cartel is often considered to be the most powerful and largest organization operating in the Americas. Experts maintain that the cartel operates in more than half of the Mexican states and in around 50 countries.[29] The cartel has operations as far south as Argentina and as far north as Chicago and New York. Joaquín Guzmán Loera, known as "El Chapo," led the organization until his capture in 2016. Guzmán's Sinaloa cartel sought to operate and sell drugs in Chicago due to the strategic location of this city in the center of the country, which enables the cartel to distribute drugs to other parts of the United States. In 2013, Guzmán was named Chicago's public enemy number one, even though he never set foot in the city.[30] Jack Riley, the head of the DEA's office in Chicago, contended: "In my opinion, Guzman is the new Al Capone of Chicago. His ability to corrupt and enforce his sanctions with his endless supply of revenue is more powerful than Chicago's Italian organized crime gang."[31]

Yet the 2016 capture of Guzmán does not mean that the cartel will implode. Experts contend that the organization will continue to thrive. There is always another leader ready to take control of the organization. Ismael El Mayo Zambada has been running the Sinaloa cartel since the capture of Guzmán. Moreover, the cartel is less vertically structured than some individuals may think. Instead, the organization has subsidiaries, or franchises, throughout the world.[32]

Los Zetas

This group originated with defectors from the Mexican military who worked as hired guns and enforcers for the Mexican Gulf cartel.[33] In 2010, the enforcers formed their own cartel. The Zetas' presence extends into both Central and South America. Within Mexico, the cartel has expanded its operations into various states along the Pacific coast as well as Chihuahua, one of the largest states in the country, and various states located near the Gulf.[34] The organization operates in more than 400 municipalities in Mexico.[35] The cartel has also expanded its involvement in Guadalajara, a major metropolitan city in Jalisco.[36] The cartel is known for its ruthless tactics and violence.

However, the Zetas have lost ground in recent years, particularly with the rise of the Jalisco New Generation Cartel. The cartel has decreased in power not only because of the arrest of several leaders, but also due to fragmentation. According to George Mason University's Guadalupe Correa-Cabrera, an expert on drug trafficking and organized crime in Mexico:

> the Zetas are not what they used to be. The fragmentation of the Zetas has been enormous. The Zetas Old School (Zetas Vieja Escuela) and the Northeast Cartel are now the most important factions of the Zetas. But it's hard to identify, due to this severe fragmentation, whether or not some elements of these groups were even part of the original Zetas. It's difficult to link them to the personnel of the initial members because most of them are dead or in jail now.[37]

This demonstrates that power and dominance are not guaranteed. It is important to note that the Zetas are still a major player in Mexico's criminal landscape, but they are not the same cartel as they were several years ago.

The cartel has decreased in power because of the government's strategy. The extremely violent tactics of the Zetas warranted a response by the government, who utilized its security forces to try to strike back and combat the cartel. History demonstrates (e.g., Pablo Escobar and the Medellín cartel) that cartels that use indiscriminate violence and force in attempt to intimidate rivals, the government, and citizens will become a central focus of the security forces, who will attempt to dismantle the cartel by capturing key leaders and seizing its resources.[38] In sum, these bold tactics of using extreme public spectacles of violence resulted in the government responding and help explain why the cartel has decreased in power in recent years.

The Rise of Jalisco New Generation Cartel

This cartel emerged is a result of the deaths of key leaders and cartel infighting. The Jalisco New Generation Cartel (Cartel Jalisco Nueva Generación—CJNG) began after the death of Ignacio Coronel, a major leader in the Sinaloa cartel, who died in 2010. Experts note that Coronel gave instructions to the leader of the Milenio cartel, Óscar Orlando Nava Valencia, who was later captured.[39] The Milenio cartel fragmented into two groups, which clashed for control of routes and territory in Jalisco, a major battleground for drug trafficking and organized crime. One of the factions of the Milenio cartel, known as "The Twisted Ones" ("*Torcidos*"), morphed into what has become the Jalisco New Generation Cartel. Currently, the leader of the organization is Nemesio Oseguera Ramos.[40]

The group has expanded in power. While experts note that the cartel originally was more low profile in its actions, this has changed over time. In 2015, for instance, members of the cartel used a rocket launcher to shoot down an army helicopter,[41] demonstrating their ruthless tactics and willingness to use violence to send a message to the security forces attempting to capture leaders of the cartel. On May 1, 2015, the cartel set up various roadblocks throughout Jalisco to show its power.[42] Jalisco New Generation Cartel (Cartel Jalisco Nueva Generación—CJNG) has continued to expand its influence, not only in Jalisco, but throughout the country. Experts have noted the different strategies that the cartel has used to expand its territory and power. In Michoacán, the cartel has made various alliances with security forces. In addition, this organization has become involved in conflicts between different groups. In the southern state of Guerrero, the cartel has been gaining strength, and it has relied upon its social networks as well as "citizen networks." In Oaxaca, the cartel has started to combat the Zetas.[43] Thus, this cartel is on the rise and has become a major player in the criminal underworld.

Regional Cartels, "Toll-Collector Cartels," and "Cells"

In addition to the three major cartels mentioned above, there are four regional cartels: La Familia Michoacana, the Gulf cartel, the Knights Templar, and the Pacífico Sur (Beltrán Leyva). These cartels are described as playing a "secondary role in the drug-trading business because they receive relatively smaller profits from it."[44] The regional cartels, which are not the leaders in the drug trade, have made attempts to diversify their criminal portfolio. These organizations have moved into vehicle theft, kidnapping, extortion, and smuggling.

Furthermore, Guerrero identifies two "toll-collector cartels": Juárez (Carillo Fuentes) and Tijuana (Arellano Félix).[45] These organizations have strongholds in the border region and, as the name implies, earn their revenue stream through taxing illicit activities that move through territories. These cartels do not have a vast presence throughout Mexico and have not diversified into other criminal activities. In fact, it is possible that these organizations will cease to exist if they are unable to maintain control of their territory. It is not unfathomable that a larger and more violent drug trafficking organization could move into these controlled areas and displace these cartels.

There are also drug trafficking cells. Experts estimate that there are an estimated 202 mafia cells. Tamaulipas and Guerrero have 42 and 25 cells, respectively. These groups are based at the local levels. The primary source of revenue for these cells is the distribution of drugs. Yet experts note that there have been cases of some cells seeking to diversify their business activities, particularly through extortion and kidnapping.[46]

In summary, the Calderón administration sought to combat the leaders of the major drug trafficking organizations. The administration had some successes in capturing some cartel leaders. The Calderón administration published lists of the kingpins who had been captured or killed.[47] Yet the kingpin strategy has led to more violence as cartel leaders fight among each other for control of territory.[48]

Violence in Mexico

The Calderón administration ended with more than 70,000 drug-related deaths. In addition, another 26,000 people disappeared during his government. Thus, the government ended its six years in office with more than 100,000 deaths (see Figures 3.1 and 3.2).[49] Violence initially dropped during the Peña Nieto administration.[50] However, it then increased as the Peña Nieto government witnessed spikes in violence in 2016 and 2017. The data indicate that his administration finished with more drug-related deaths than the previous government.[51] In 2017, the country recorded 29,168 homicides.[52] The data also reveal nearly all states—27 out of 32—in the country experienced increases in homicides, when comparing the data from the previous year.[53]

Violence has shifted over time throughout the country (see Figure 3.3). Ciudad Juárez became the most dangerous city in the world during the Calderón administration.[54] Violence declined in this area, but it has spiked in recent years,

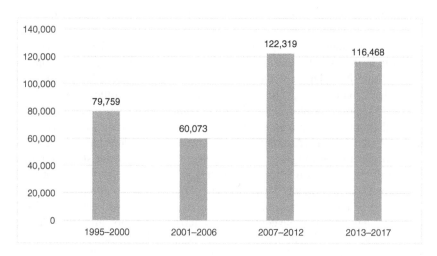

Figure 3.1 Homicides in Mexico (1995–2017)

Source: Created by authors with data from Laura Calderón, Octavio Rodríguez Ferreira, and David A. Shirk, *Drug Violence in Mexico: Data and Analysis Through 2017* (San Diego CA: University of San Diego, 2018); the National Institute of Statistics and Geography (Instituto Nacional de Estadística y Geografía-INEGI)

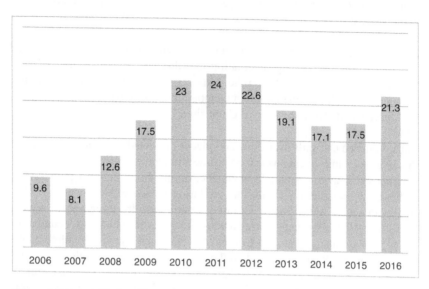

Figure 3.2 Homicide Rate in Mexico (per 100,000)

Source: "Mexico's Drug War," *Council on Foreign Relations*, May 25, 2017; data from the University of San Diego

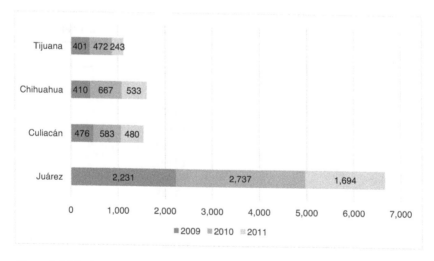

Figure 3.3 Mexican Municipalities With Most Organized Crime-Related Killings

Source: Created by authors with data from Eduardo Guerrero-Gutiérrez, *Security, Drugs, and Violence in Mexico: A Survey* (Mexico City: Lantia Consultores, S.C, 2011)

Note: Data for 2011 are based on estimates from January–July data

bringing stark reminders of the violent days of 2012. Luis Fernando Alonso contends that:

> Juárez and the state of Chihuahua have seen rising levels of violence in recent months, raising speculation that the dark days of brutal killings that the city saw in between the years 2008 and 2012 could be making a comeback. Just in the month of October, there have been 90 homicides in Juárez, and 183 in the state of Chihuahua.[55]

Thus, violence can shift over time, and places previously plagued by violence that have seen improvements can backslide and witness spikes in violence.[56]

Other states have seen upticks in violence during the Peña Nieto government. Colima, for example, is a small state bordering Jalisco and Michoacán.[57] This state with access to the Pacific Ocean has witnessed drastic increases in violence. In 2016, Colima experienced a 900-percent surge in homicides compared to 2015.[58] Tecomán, located in Colima, saw violence increase by almost 300 percent.[59] Some experts contend that the violence is a result of fighting for turf between the powerful Jalisco New Generation Cartel and the Sinaloa cartel.[60]

Using the LAPOP 2016/2017 data[61] on Mexico,[62] we conducted a regression analysis to determine what variables impact the frequency of murders in one's neighborhood, which is divided into once a week, once or twice a month, and one or twice a year. The independent variables were age, sex, urban, skin color,

Table 3.1 Factors Associated With Frequency of Murders in the Neighborhood

Variable	Coeff (SE)	t-test
Age	0.029	1.56
	(0.018)	
Sex	−0.076	−1.33
	(0.057)	
Urban	0.163*	2.02
	(0.081)	
Skin Color	−0.051*	−2.82
	(0.018)	
Monthly Household Income	0.008	1.44
	(0.006)	
Constant	2.430*	12.25
	(0.198)	
Observations	666	
R-Squared	0.025	
Robust Standard Errors in Parentheses		

*** $p<0.01$, ** $p<0.05$, * $p<0.1$

Source: Created by authors with data from the 2016/2017 LAPOP survey

and monthly household income. The age variable ranged from 18 to 88,[63] but we recoded age into six categories using Stata 15.1. We also used the variable skin color, which ranges from one through nine, with 1 being very light to control for potential racism. Finally, the last independent variable that we control for is monthly household income—this variable ranges from no income to more than $11,050.[64]

The regression results reveal that urban and skin color are statistically significant (see Table 3.1). A one-unit change in urban (i.e., urban to rural) leads to a 0.163 change in the frequency of murders in the neighborhood. In addition, a one-unit change in skin color results in a –0.051 change in the dependent variable, frequency of murders in the neighborhood.

Reforming Security Institutions

Many scholars have been critical of the government's policies designed to combat organized crime. Some experts have stressed the underlying factors in Mexico, such as corruption. According to Chabat, "if you don't make reforms at all levels at the same time, it won't work." Chabat continues:

> You can be very efficient capturing one criminal, and then he goes free because some judge was given some money. Or maybe you can capture the criminal, the judiciary works well, and then a drug lord escapes from a high security prison.[65]

As a result, Mexico faces many challenges implementing the rule of law.

Because of the high levels of impunity, Mexicans are extremely distrusting of security institutions, particularly the police. Mexicans have higher levels of distrust in the municipal and state police than in the federal police. In fact, 68.1 percent of the population believes that the municipal police are corrupt compared to 65.1 for the state police. On the other hand, 57.2 percent of the population thinks that the federal police are corrupt. The transit police are perceived as the most corrupt institution: 77.7 percent of the population believes that the transit police are corrupt (see Figure 3.4). There are several reasons that explain the high levels of distrust in the police. The transit police have the most interaction with the population, as they are on the streets every day. Higher levels of interaction with the population, particularly negative encounters (e.g., asking for bribes), can impact the perception of the police. The municipal police are less popular than the state as well as the federal police for several reasons. The local police forces are not as well trained and are less professional than the federal police. They also operate at the local level, which is characterized by less transparency and accountability.[66] On the other hand, the federal police are better trained and better educated than the municipal police forces.

The police forces are in need of systematic reforms. Working as a police officer in Mexico is a dangerous job. In addition, the salaries are low, which makes the police forces more susceptible to partaking in corruption. The Calderón and the Peña Nieto administrations have made various reforms to the police.

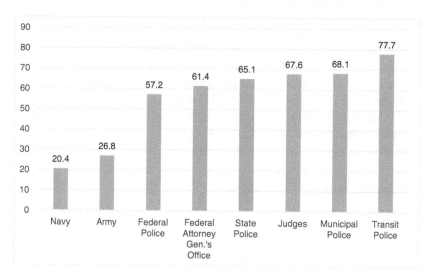

Figure 3.4 Perceptions of Population That Believes the Navy, Army, Federal Police, Federal Attorney General's Office, State Police, Judges, Municipal Police, and Transit Police Are Corrupt (2017)

Source: Maureen Meyer and Gina Hinojosa, *Mexico's National Anti-Corruption System: A Historic Opportunity in the Fight against Corruption* (Washington, DC: WOLA, 2018); INEGI, ENVIPE, 2017

However, the institutions continue to be riddled with corruption.[67] There is also a lack of trust between the police forces at different levels, which can hinder intelligence sharing and cooperation.

Measuring Trust in The Police

What are the variables that influence levels of trust in the police? Using the LAPOP 2016/2017 data on Mexico,[68] we conducted a regression analysis to determine what impacts levels of trust in the police (see Table 3.2). Our dependent variable, trust in the national police, ranges from "Not at All" to "A Lot." Another independent variable is age, which ranges from 18 to 88. Using Stata 15.1, we recoded age into six categories. The ideology variables range from one, which represents left, to 10, which is classified as right. The other independent variables include urban, which is divided into urban and rural. We also use the variable skin color, which ranges from 1 through 9, with one being very light to control for potential racism. Finally, the last independent variable that we control for is monthly household income, which ranges from no income to more than $11,050.[69]

The regression results reveal that ideology and monthly household income are statistically significant at the 95-percent confidence level. A one-unit

Table 3.2 Factors Associated With Trust in the National Police

Variable	Coeff (SE)	t-test
Ideology	0.120*	5.73
	(0.021)	
Age	0.032	0.86
	(0.038)	
Sex	0.012	0.11
	(0.106)	
Urban	0.152	1.12
	(0.135)	
Skin Color	−0.034	−0.93
	(0.036)	
Monthly Household Income	−0.028*	−2.68
	(0.011)	
Constant	2.422*	6.88
	(0.352)	
Observations	1,247	
R-Squared	0.041	
Robust Standard Errors in Parentheses		

*** p<0.01, ** p<0.05, * p<0.1

Source: Created by authors with data from the 2016/2017 LAPOP survey

increase in ideology results in a 0.120 change in the dependent variable (trust in the police). This result suggests that someone who is more conservative, on average, will have more trust in the police. The income variables reveal that a one-unit change in monthly household income leads to a −0.028 change in level of trust in the police. Thus, someone who makes more money, on average, has a lower level of trust in the police.

Operationalizing Corruption and State Fragility

The 2016/2017 Mexico survey data conducted by LAPOP[70] reveals that 23.82 percent of the survey responded that a police officer asked for a bribe. This leads one to inquire into the variables that influence whether a police officer asked for a bribe.[71] The dependent variable was whether a police officer has asked for a bribe and was coded as "no" and "yes." The independent variables included sex, urban, skin color, and education. The urban variable was coded into urban and rural,[72] while skin color ranged from one, very light, to nine, very dark. The education variable ranged from no schooling to 18 or more years of school.

The logistic regression shows that sex and education are statistically significant at the 95-percent confidence interval. A one-unit increase in sex

Table 3.3 Factors Associated With Whether a Police Officer Asked for a Bribe in Mexico

Variable	Coeff (SE)	z-test
Sex	−1.117***	−8.6
	(0.130)	
Urban	−0.169	−0.86
	(0.195)	
Skin Color	0.061	1.51
	(0.040)	
Education	0.092***	6.64
	(0.014)	
Constant	−0.520	−1.37
	(0.381)	
Observations	1,552	
Standard Errors in Parentheses		

*** p<0.01, ** p<0.05, * p<0.1

Source: Created by authors with data from the 2016/2017 LAPOP survey

(i.e., male to female) results in a −1.117 change in the log-odds of the dependent variable. This suggests that women, on average, are less likely than men to have an officer ask for a bribe. Furthermore, a one-unit change in education results in a 0.092 shift in the log-odds of the dependent variable. This means that, on average, people who have more education are more likely to have a police officer asked them for a bribe (see Table 3.3). This could be because people who have more education may have higher salaries. This could lead to police officers profiling people based on the car that they drive or the clothes that they wear. Someone who is perceived as driving a "nice" car could be at higher risk of being asked to pay a bribe by officers.

The Mexican survey data also reveals that 11.34 percent of respondents said that a government employee asked for a bribe. This leads one to question what variables impact whether a government employee will ask for a bribe. This logistic regression model controls for age, which was recoded into six categories as well as sex, urban, skin color, and monthly household income.[73]

The logistic regression model[74] indicates that sex is significant at the 95-percent confidence level. Interestingly, skin color, urban, and monthly household income were not statistically significant. A one-unit change in sex (i.e., male to female) leads to a −0.926 shift in the log-odds of the dependent variable. This suggests that females, on average, are less likely to be asked by a government employee for a bribe (see Table 3.4).

Table 3.4 Factors Associated With Whether a Government Employee Asked for a Bribe

Variable	Coeff (SE)	t-test
Sex	−0.926***	−4.79
	(0.193)	
Urban	−0.295	−1.30
	(0.228)	
Skin Color	0.041	0.73
	(0.056)	
Monthly Household Income	0.030*	1.68
	(0.018)	
Constant	−0.777	−1.38
	(0.563)	
Observations	1,382	
Standard Errors in Parentheses		

*** p<0.01, ** p<0.05, * p<0.1

Source: Created by authors with data from the 2016/2017 LAPOP survey

Amnesty to Organized Crime Groups?

Mexico's July 2018 elections led to intense debates among the candidates regarding the best way to combat drug trafficking, organized crime, and the rising levels of violence. As a presidential candidate, Andrés Manuel López Obrador from The National Regeneration Movement (Movimiento Regeneración Nacional, MORENA) argued that Mexico's war on drugs had been a failure. López Obrador has indicated that he will combat the high levels of corruption and impunity in Mexico and is open to alternative strategies to decrease organized crime. In December 2017, he contended that he would be willing to consider granting drug traffickers amnesty to reduce the high levels of violence. He argued: "we will talk about granting amnesty so long as the victims and their families are willing."[75] While there have been negotiations in other countries (e.g., the gang truce in El Salvador or the peace process in Colombia),[76] there are many criminal organizations in Mexico. Brian J. Phillips, a specialist on security-related issues, argues:

> A second issue is that the FARC negotiations involved only one militant group, and the El Salvador gang truce involved only two. In the past 10 years, Mexico has had a rotating cast of national and transnational criminal organizations, combined with a plethora of smaller gangs.[77]

Scholars also question whether the Mexican government could trust these criminal organizations not to partake in violent activities, particularly since violence is the *modus operandi* of these organizations. Phillips contends:

Furthermore, it is unlikely that most or any of the groups could credibly commit to not use violence, or reduce their violence, or whatever the Mexican government might demand. Many Mexican criminal groups operate in cell-like structures and have loosely affiliated factions, so there is usually not a unified leadership that could get all its members to obey a truce.[78]

Therefore, providing amnesty to organized crime groups in Mexico will present many challenges, as there are many organizations. Critics question whether you can trust organized crime groups and whether their promises are credible.[79] There are many individuals involved in drug trafficking organizations, not just the leaders.[80] The negotiations could create high levels of distrust among the public, as some people could feel that the government is promoting impunity and criminal behavior and not implementing the rule of law.

Conclusion

The transition to democracy in 2000 represented a critical juncture in the country's history. Despite the country's democratization, Mexico has continued to be plagued by high levels of corruption and impunity, which has created a ripe environment for criminal activity. Criminal groups desire a state apparatus that is weak and can be corrupted. They seek to avoid prison sentences by bribing corrupt politicians, judges, and police officers.

President Calderón launched a drug war in 2006, deploying the military. The result of the drug war has been that the cartels have not only fought between each other for dominance in the lucrative drug trade but also with the Mexican security forces. The Calderón government ended its term with more than 100,000 deaths. The Peña Nieto administration initially witnessed decreases in violence. However, violence spiked in subsequent years.

Mexico has continued to be plagued by organized crime as the number of groups have fragmented and diversified their criminal activities over time. This criminal landscape has even resulted in some politicians talking about potential amnesty for drug traffickers. There are many criminal groups (some estimates place the number at more than 200), and they will continue to seek to survive in this clandestine business. Unless Mexico changes its approach to combating criminal organizations and drug trafficking and reforms underlying structural issues (e.g., impunity and corruption), criminal groups will thrive and criminal violence will continue.

Notes

1. Ted Galen Carpenter, *The Fire Next Door: Mexico's Drug Violence and the Danger to America* (Washington, DC: CATO, 2012); Jorge Chabat, "Mexico's war on drugs: No margin for maneuver," *The ANNALS of the American Academy of Political and Social Science* 582, no. 1 (2002): pp. 134–148.
2. Gustavo Flores-Macías, "Mexico's 2012 elections: The return of the PRI," *Journal of Democracy* 24, no. 1 (2013): pp. 128–141; Joseph L. Klesner, "Electoral

competition and the new party system in Mexico," *Latin American Politics and Society* 47, no. 2 (2005): pp. 103–142; Andreas Schedler, "The democratic revelation," *Journal of Democracy* 11, no. 4 (2000): pp. 5–19; Marcos Pablo Moloeznik, "The challenges to Mexico in times of political change," *Crime, Law and Social Change* 40, no. 1 (2003): pp. 7–20.

3. "Political Parties in Mexico," *Rice University's Baker Institute for Public Policy*, www.bakerinstitute.org/political-parties-mexico/, accessed June 6, 2018; for more, see Louise Shelley, "Corruption and organized crime in Mexico in the post-PRI transition," *Journal of Contemporary Criminal Justice* 17, no. 3 (2001): pp. 213–231; Luis Astorga, "La cocaína en el corrido," *Revista mexicana de sociología* (2000): pp. 151–173; Luis Astorga, "The limits of anti-drug policy in Mexico," *International Social Science Journal* 53, no. 169 (2001): pp. 427–434.

4. For more, see Chappell Lawson, "Mexico's unfinished transition: Democratization and authoritarian enclaves in Mexico," *Mexican Studies/Estudios Mexicanos* 16, no. 2 (2000): pp. 267–287; Jonathan Fox, "The difficult transition from clientelism to citizenship: Lessons from Mexico," *World Politics* 46, no. 2 (1994): pp. 151–184; José Luis Reyna and Richard S. Weinert, "Authoritarianism in Mexico," *Anthropology News* 18, no. 9 (1977): pp. 23; John A. Booth and Mitchell A. Seligson, "The political culture of authoritarianism in Mexico: A reexamination," *Latin American Research Review* 19, no. 1 (1984): pp. 106–124.

5. Roberto Zepeda Martínez and Jonathan D. Rosen, "Corrupción e inseguridad en México: consecuencias de una democracia imperfecta," *Revista AD UNIVERSA*, Año 4, Vol. 1 (diciembre 2014): pp. 60–85; Jonathan Daniel Rosen and Roberto Zepeda Martínez, "La guerra contra las drogas en Colombia y México: estrategias fracasadas," *Ánfora* 21, no. 38 (2014): pp. 179–200.

6. Christy Thornton and Adam Goodman, "How the Mexican drug trade thrives on free trade," *The Nation*, July 15, 2014, p. 7.

7. Chappell Lawson, "How did we get here? Mexican democracy after the 2006 elections," *PS: Political Science & Politics* 40, no. 1 (2007): 45–48; Rogelio Hernández-Rodríguez, "The renovation of old institutions: State governors and the political transition in Mexico," *Latin American Politics and Society* 45, no. 4 (2003): pp. 97–127; Todd A. Eisenstadt, "Thinking outside the (ballot) box: Informal electoral institutions and Mexico's political opening," *Latin American Politics and Society* 45, no. 1 (2003): pp. 25–54.

8. Luis Gómez Romero, "Governors gone wild: Mexico faces a 'lost generation' of corrupt leaders," *The Conversation*, August 15, 2017, p. 5.

9. "Mexico," *Transparency International: Corruption Perceptions Index*, www.transparency.org/country/MEX, accessed June 6, 2018.

10. James Bargent, "Mexico impunity levels reach 99%: Study," *InSight Crime*, February 4, 2016, www.insightcrime.org/news/brief/mexico-impunity-levels-reach-99-study/, accessed June 6, 2018; for more, Juan D. Lindau, "The drug war's impact on executive power, judicial reform, and federalism in Mexico," *Political Science Quarterly* 126, no. 2 (2011): pp. 177–200; Jonathan Fox, "The difficult transition from clientelism to citizenship: Lessons from Mexico," *World Politics* 46, no. 2 (1994): pp. 151–184; Sara Schatz, "Disarming the legal system: Impunity for the political murder of dissidents in Mexico," *International Criminal Justice Review* 18, no. 3 (2008): pp. 261–291; Stephen D. Morris and Joseph L. Klesner, "Corruption and trust: Theoretical considerations and evidence from Mexico," *Comparative Political Studies* 43, no. 10 (2010): pp. 1258–1285; Stephen D. Morris, "Disaggregating corruption: A comparison of participation and perceptions in Latin America with a focus on Mexico," *Bulletin of Latin American Research* 27, no. 3 (2008): pp. 388–409.

11. Bruce Bagley, *Drug Trafficking and Organized Crime in the Americas: Major Trends in the Twenty-Frist Century* (Washington, DC: Woodrow Wilson Center

International Center for Scholars, 2012); Bruce M. Bagley and Jonathan D. Rosen, eds., *Drug Trafficking, Organized Crime, and Violence in the Americas Today* (Gainesville, FL: University Press of Florida, 2015).

12. Alejandro Moreno, "The 2006 Mexican presidential election: The economy, oil revenues, and ideology," *PS: Political Science & Politics* 40, no. 1 (2007): pp. 15–19; Joseph L. Klesner, "The 2006 Mexican elections: Manifestation of a divided society?" *PS: Political Science & Politics* 40, no. 1 (2007): pp. 27–32; Joy Langston, "The PRI's 2006 electoral debacle," *PS: Political Science & Politics* 40, no. 1 (2007): pp. 21–25.

13. Quoted in James C. McKinley Jr. and Ginger Thompson, "Calderón wins narrow victory in Mexico election," *The New York Times*, July 6, 2006.

14. Jo Tuckman, "Failed Mexican presidential candidate sets up protest camp," *The Guardian*, August 2, 2006, p. 1.

15. Jonathan D. Rosen and Roberto Zepeda, *Organized Crime, Drug Trafficking, and Violence in Mexico: The Transition from Felipe Calderón to Enrique Peña Nieto* (Lanham, MD: Lexington Books, July 2016); Carmen Boullosa and Mike Wallace, *A Narco History: How the United States and Mexico Jointly Created the "Mexican Drug War"* (New York, NY: OR Books, 2015).

16. Quoted in Sara Miller Llana, "With Calderón in, a new war on Mexico's mighty drug cartels," *The Christian Science Monitor*, January 22, 2007.

17. Jorge Castañeda, "Time for an alternative to Mexico's drug war," *CATO Institute*, September 24, 2012, www.cato.org/publications/economic-development-bulletin/time-alternative-mexicos-drug-war, accessed June 6, 2018, p. 3.

18. Lizbeth Diaz, "Mexico troops enter Tijuana in drug gang crackdown," *The Washington Post*, January 3, 2007.

19. Jorge Castañeda, "A U.S. war with Mexican consequences," *CATO Institute*, August 5, 2009, www.cato-unbound.org/2009/08/05/jorge-castaneda/us-war-mexican-consequences, accessed June 7, 2018, p. 5.

20. Ibid., p. 5.

21. Nathaniel Parish Flannery, "'Calderón's war," *Journal of International Affairs* (2013): p. 1; see also: Francisco Resendiz, "Centralismo marcó al sexenio," *El Universal*, December 1, 2012.

22. Quoted in Sara Miller Llana, "With Calderón in, a new war on Mexico's mighty drug cartels."

23. Ted Galen Carpenter, *The Fire Next Door: Mexico's Drug Violence and the Danger to America.*

24. Quoted in Sara Miller Llana, "With Calderón in, a new war on Mexico's mighty drug cartels."

25. Bruce Bagley, *Drug Trafficking and Organized Crime in the Americas: Major Trends in the Twenty-Frist Century.*

26. June S. Beittel, *Mexico: Organized Crime and Drug Trafficking Organizations* (Washington, DC: Congressional Research Service, 2017), p. 24.

27. Patrick Corcoran, "Mexico has 80 drug cartels: Attorney general," *InSight Crime*, December 20, 2012, www.insightcrime.org/news/analysis/mexico-has-80-drug-cartels-attorney-general/, accessed June 28, 2018.

28. June S. Beittel, *Mexico: Organized Crime and Drug Trafficking Organizations*; E. Eduardo Castillo and Elliot Spagat, "Mexico arrests leader of Tijuana Drug Cartel," *Associated Press*, June 24, 2014; for more, see Bruce Bagley, "Carteles de la droga: de Medellín a Sinaloa," *Criterios* 4, no. 1 (2011): pp. 233–247; Shannon O'Neil, "The real war in Mexico: How democracy can defeat the drug cartels," *Foreign Affairs* (2009): pp. 63–77.

29. "Sinaloa Cartel," *InSight Crime*, January 24, 2018, www.insightcrime.org/mexico-organized-crime-news/sinaloa-cartel-profile/, accessed June 6, 2018.

30. Quoted in Mariano Castillo, "Chicago's new public enemy no. 1: 'El Chapo'," *CNN*, February 15, 2013.
31. Quoted in Ibid.
32. "Former DEA agent: Sinaloa Cartel likely to remain strong without 'El Chapo'," *NPR*, January 25, 2017, www.npr.org/2017/01/25/511655811/former-dea-agent-sinaloa-cartel-likely-to-remain-strong-without-el-chapo, accessed June 6, 2018.
33. For more, see Raúl Benítez Manaut, "La crisis de seguridad en México," *Nueva Sociedad* 220 (2009): pp. 173–190; Phil Williams, "El crimen organizado y la violencia en México: una perspectiva comparativa," *ISTOR: Revista de Historia International* 11 (2010): pp. 15–40; Stephanie Brophy, "Mexico: Cartels, corruption and cocaine: A profile of the Gulf cartel," *Global Crime* 9, no. 3 (2008): pp. 248–261.
34. June S. Beittel, *Mexico: Organized Crime and Drug Trafficking Organizations*, p. 18.
35. Ibid.
36. Steven Dudley, "Part II: The modus operandi," *InSight Crime*, September 8, 2011, www.insightcrime.org/investigations/part-2-the-modus-operandi/, accessed June 7, 2018, pp. 3–4.
37. Parker Asmann, "Mexico's Zetas: From criminal powerhouse to fragmented remnants," *InSight Crime*, April 6, 2018, www.insightcrime.org/news/analysis/mexico-zetas-criminal-powerhouse-fragmented-remnants/, accessed June 7, 2018, p. 9.
38. Quoted in Victoria Dittmar, "Is Mexico's CJNG following in the footsteps of the Zetas?" *InSight Crime*, February 19, 2018, www.insightcrime.org/news/analysis/mexicos-cjng-following-footsteps-zetas/, accessed June 7, 2018; Alejandro Hope, "Z-43: Los Zetas después de 'Los Zetas'," *El Universal*, 10 de febrero de 2018.
39. "Jalisco Cartel New Generation (CJNG)," *InSight Crime*, March 30, 2018, www.insightcrime.org/mexico-organized-crime-news/jalisco-cartel-new-generation/, accessed June 7, 2018.
40. "Jalisco Cartel New Generation (CJNG)," *InSight Crime*; for more, see Adam David Morton, "The war on drugs in Mexico: A failed state?" *Third World Quarterly* 33, no. 9 (2012): pp. 1631–1645; Vanda Felbab-Brown, "The rise of militias in Mexico: Citizens' security or further conflict escalation?" *Prism: A Journal of the Center for Complex Operations* 5, no. 4 (2015): p. 172.
41. Victoria Dittmar, "Is Mexico's CJNG following in the footsteps of the Zetas?"
42. Randal C. Archibold, "Mexican helicopter shot down, killing 3 soldiers," *The New York Times*, May 1, 2015, p. 1.
43. Jesús Pérez Caballero, "Mexico's CJNG: Local consolidation, military expansion and vigilante rhetoric," *InSight Crime*, February 8, 2018, www.insightcrime.org/news/analysis/mexico-cjng-local-consolidation-military-expansion-vigilante-rhetoric/, accessed June 6, 2018, p. 2.
44. Michael D. Lyman, *Drugs in Society: Causes, Concepts, and Control* (New York, NY: Routledge, 2016, eighth edition).
45. For more, see June S. Beittel, *Mexico: Organized Crime and Drug Trafficking Organizations*; Eduardo Guerrero-Gutiérrez provided CRS with this information; Raúl Benítez Manaut, "Crimen organizado: fenómeno trasnacional, evolución en México," *Bien Común* 19 (2013): p. 215;
46. June S. Beittel, *Mexico: Organized Crime and Drug Trafficking Organizations*; Eduardo Guerrero-Gutiérrez provided CRS with this information.
47. Jesús Pérez Caballero, "Mexico's CJNG: Local consolidation, military expansion and vigilante rhetoric."
48. Patrick Corcoran, "Mexico President reprises controversial kingpin strategy," *InSight Crime,* June 6, 2017, www.insightcrime.org/news/analysis/mexico-president-reprises-controversial-kingpin-strategy/, accessed June 6, 2018, pp. 4–5.

49. For more, see Jonathan D. Rosen and Roberto Zepeda, *Organized Crime, Drug Trafficking, and Violence in Mexico: The Transition from Felipe Calderón to Enrique Peña Nieto*; Viridiana Ríos, "Why did Mexico become so violent? A self-reinforcing violent equilibrium caused by competition and enforcement," *Trends in Organized Crime* 16, no. 2 (2013): pp. 138–155; Javier Osorio, "The contagion of drug violence: Spatiotemporal dynamics of the Mexican war on drugs," *Journal of Conflict Resolution* 59, no. 8 (2015): pp. 1403–1432; Tomas Kellner and Francesco Pipitone, "Inside México's drug war," *World Policy Journal* 27, no. 1 (2010): pp. 29–37; Richard Snyder and Angélica Durán Martínez, "Drugs, violence, and state-sponsored protection rackets in Mexico and Colombia," *Colombia Internacional* 70 (2009): pp. 61–91.

50. Jonathan D. Rosen and Roberto Zepeda, *Organized Crime, Drug Trafficking, and Violence in Mexico: The Transition from Felipe Calderón to Enrique Peña Nieto*; David Shirk and Joel Wallman, "Understanding Mexico's drug violence," *Journal of Conflict Resolution* 59, no. 8 (2015): 1348–1376.

51. Ted Galen Carpenter, "Mexico's drug violence spikes again," *The National Interest*, May 3, 2017, p. 2.

52. Eli Meixler, "With over 29,000 homicides, 2017 was Mexico's most violent year on record," *Time*, January 22, 2018.

53. Kate Linthicum, "Mexico's bloody drug war is killing more people than ever," *Los Angeles Times*, July 22, 2017.

54. For more, see Carlos Vilalta and Robert Muggah, "Violent disorder in Ciudad Juarez: A spatial analysis of homicide," *Trends in Organized Crime* 17, no. 3 (2014): pp. 161–180; Melissa W. Wright, "Necropolitics, narcopolitics, and femicide: Gendered violence on the Mexico-US border," *Signs: Journal of Women in Culture and Society* 36, no. 3 (2011): pp. 707–731; Alicia R. Schmidt Camacho, "Ciudadana X: Gender violence and the denationalization of women's rights in Ciudad Juarez, Mexico," *CR: The New Centennial Review* 5, no. 1 (2005): pp. 255–292.

55. Luis Fernando Alonso, "Rising violence in Juárez, Mexico may signal return of cartel war," *InSight Crime*, October 31, 2016, www.insightcrime.org/news/brief/rising-violence-in-juarez-mexico-may-signal-return-of-cartel-war/, accessed June 7, 2018, p. 2; Patricia Mayorga, "Octubre rojo en Ciudad Juárez; matan a 10 el viernes y suman 90 asesinatos," *Proceso*, 29 de octubre de 2016.

56. For more on cartel violence, see Robert C. Bonner, "The cartel crackdown: Winning the drug war and rebuilding Mexico in the process," *Foreign Affairs* 91 (2012): p. 12; Paul Rexton Kan, "What we're getting wrong about Mexico," *Parameters* 41, no. 2 (2011): p. 37.

57. Jerjes Aguirre and Hugo Amador Herrera, "Institutional weakness and organized crime in Mexico: The case of Michoacán," *Trends in Organized Crime* 16, no. 2 (2013): pp. 221–238.

58. Mimi Yagoub, "Why a 900% spike in murders in West Mexico state?" *InSight Crime*, May 25, 2016, www.insightcrime.org/news/brief/what-is-behind-900-spike-in-murders-in-west-mexico-state/, accessed June 6, 2018, p. 1.

59. Tristan Clavel, "Organized crime behind spiking homicides in Mexico's most violent municipalities," *InSight Crime*, March 30, 2017, www.insightcrime.org/news/analysis/organized-crime-behind-spiking-homicides-mexico-violent-municipalities/, accessed June 7, 2018.

60. Mimi Yagoub, "Why a 900% spike in murders in West Mexico state?"; Tristan Clavel, "Organized crime behind spiking homicides in Mexico's most violent municipalities."

61. The LAPOP survey team indicates that the following command must be used to set to weight the data: svyset upm [pw=wt], strata(estratopri)

62. The link to the LAPOP data can be found here: http://datasets.americasbarometer.org/database/index.php?freeUser=true

63. Recode q2 (18/28=1) (29/39=2) (40/50=3) (51/61=4) (62/72=5) (73/88=6), gen (age)

64. After running the regression, we test for multicollinearity, model specification, and heteroskedasticity. The variance inflation factor (VIF) results in a mean VIF of 1.06. The rage of the VIF for the variables is between 1.03 and 1.11, demonstrating that there is not multicollinearity as variables with 10 or more require further investigation. In addition, the linktest produces a hatsq that is not statistically significant, which means that the model is properly specified. Finally, the Breusch-Pagan/Cook-Weisberg test for heteroskedasticity leads to a Prob > chi2 of 0.04, which suggest that there is heteroskedasticity in the model. We ran a new regression with the robust standard error command (vce (robust)) in the regression to adjust for heteroskedasticity.

65. Quoted in Sara Miller Llana, "With Calderón in, a new war on Mexico's mighty drug cartels."

66. For more on this topic, see Jonathan D. Rosen and Roberto Zepeda, *Organized Crime, Drug Trafficking, and Violence in Mexico: The Transition from Felipe Calderón to Enrique Peña Nieto*; Diane E. Davis, "Undermining the rule of law: Democratization and the dark side of police reform in Mexico," *Latin American Politics and Society* 48, no. 1 (2006): pp. 55–86.

67. For more, see Daniel M. Sabet, *Police Reform in Mexico: Informal Politics and the Challenge of Institutional Change* (Stanford, CA: Stanford University Press, 2012).

68. The link to the LAPOP data can be found here: http://datasets.americasbarometer.org/database/index.php?freeUser=true

69. After running the regression, we checked the model for multicollinearity, model specification, and heteroskedasticity. The variance inflation factor (VIF) of the model produced a mean VIF of 1.05 and a VIF for all the variables ranging from 1.12 to 1.01. Since the VIF is below 10, the results suggest that the model does not have issues with multicollinearity. The linktest indicates that the model is properly specified. Finally, the results of the Breusch-Pagan/Cook-Weisberg test for heteroskedasticity generate a prob > chi2 of 0.0000, suggesting that there is heteroskedasticity in the model. We ran a new regression with the robust standard error command (vce (robust)) in the regression to correct for heteroskedasticity.

70. LAPOP recommends weighting the data using the following command. svyset upm [pw=wt], strata(estratopri). This command is required prior to running any statistical analysis. The LAPOP team indicates that svy must be used prior to running estimation commands (e.g., svy: reg). For more, see www.vanderbilt.edu/lapop/ab2016/AmericasBarometer_2016-17_Sample_Design.pdf, accessed October 21, 2019.

71. A logit model requires that there is a linear relationship between the odds ratio and the independent variables. I used the Box-Tidwell model to test this. In the original model, monthly household income and age are non-linear in several tests that I ran. I first removed monthly income and then age became non-linear. Thus, I removed both variables and added the education variable. The boxtid command (i.e., Box-Tidwell test) reveals that the model meets the basic assumptions required for a logit model.

72. I ran a logit model because the dependent variable is dichotomous. Moreover, I wanted to determine if the model had issues with multicollinearity as well as the model specification. The model has a mean variance inflation factor (VIF) of 1.03. A VIF of 10 or above requires further investigation. To determine the model specification, I ran the linktest, which produces a linear predicted value squared (hatsq) that is not statistically significant.

73. I originally included age in this model. However, the Box-Tidwell test reveals that age is non-linear. Therefore, this variable violates the assumption that there is a linear relationship between the odds ratio and the independent variables. Thus, I removed the age variable and reran the test.

74. After running the logit model, it is also important to check for multicollinearity and analyze the model specification. The mean VIF is 1.06, which suggests that the model does not have issues with multicollinearity. The linktest is not statistically significant at the 95-percent confidence level, meaning that the model is properly specified.
75. Quoted in David Agren, "Fury as Mexico presidential candidate pitches amnesty for drug cartel kingpins," *The Guardian*, December 4, 2017.
76. Bruce M. Bagley and Jonathan D. Rosen, eds., *Colombia's Political Economy at the Outset of the Twenty-First Century: From Uribe to Santos and Beyond* (Lanham, MD: Lexington Books, 2015); Chris Van der Borgh and Wim Savenije, "Desecuritising and re-securitising gang policies: The Funes government and gangs in El Salvador," *Journal of Latin American Studies* 47, no. 1 (2015): pp. 149–176; José Miguel Cruz and Angélica Durán-Martínez, "Hiding violence to deal with the state: Criminal pacts in El Salvador and Medellín," *Journal of Peace Research* 53, no. 2 (2016): pp. 197–210; Charles M. Katz, Eric C. Hedberg, and Luis Enrique Amaya, "Gang truce for violence prevention, El Salvador," *Bulletin of the World Health Organization* 94, no. 9 (2016): p. 660.
77. Brian J. Phillips, "An amnesty deal for Mexico's drug cartels?" *Political Violence at a Glance*, December 11, 2017, https://politicalviolenceataglance.org/2017/12/11/an-amnesty-deal-for-mexicos-drug-cartels/, accessed June 11, 2018, p. 2.
78. Ibid., p. 3.
79. For more, see Ronna Rísquez, "Could an amnesty in Mexico reduce violence?" *InSight Crime*, December 15, 2017, www.insightcrime.org/news/analysis/mexico-torn-amnesty-narco-leaders-urgent-need-peace/, accessed June 11, 2018.
80. Brian J. Phillips, "An amnesty deal for Mexico's drug cartels?"

Works Cited

Aguirre, Jerjes and Hugo Amador Herrera. "Institutional weakness and organized crime in Mexico: The case of Michoacán," *Trends in Organized Crime* 16, no. 2 (2013): pp. 221–238.

Alonso, Luis Fernando. "Rising violence in Juárez, Mexico may signal return of cartel war," *InSight Crime*, October 31, 2016, www.insightcrime.org/news/brief/rising-violence-in-juarez-mexico-may-signal-return-of-cartel-war/, accessed June 7, 2018.

Archibold, Randal C. "Mexican helicopter shot down, killing 3 soldiers," *The New York Times*, May 1, 2015.

Asmann, Parker. "Mexico's Zetas: From criminal powerhouse to fragmented remnants," *InSight Crime*, April 6, 2018, www.insightcrime.org/news/analysis/mexico-zetas-criminal-powerhouse-fragmented-remnants/, accessed June 7, 2018.

Astorga, Luis. "La cocaína en el corrido," *Revista mexicana de sociología* (2000): pp. 151–173.

Astorga, Luis. "The limits of anti-drug policy in Mexico," *International Social Science Journal* 53, no. 169 (2001): pp. 427–434.

Bagley, Bruce Michael. "Carteles de la droga: de Medellín a Sinaloa," *Criterios* 4, no. 1 (2011): pp. 233–247.

Bagley, Bruce Michael. *Drug Trafficking and Organized Crime in the Americas: Major Trends in the Twenty-Frist Century*. Washington, DC: Woodrow Wilson Center International Center for Scholars, 2012.

Bagley Bruce Michael and Jonathan D. Rosen, eds. *Colombia's Political Economy at the Outset of the Twenty-First Century: From Uribe to Santos and Beyond*. Lanham, MD: Lexington Books, 2015.

Bagley, Bruce Michael and Jonathan D. Rosen, eds. *Drug Trafficking, Organized Crime, and Violence in the Americas Today*. Gainesville, FL: University Press of Florida, 2015.

Bargent, James. "Mexico impunity levels reach 99%: Study," *InSight Crime*, February 4, 2016, www.insightcrime.org/news/brief/mexico-impunity-levels-reach-99-study/, accessed June 6, 2018.

Beittel, June S. *Mexico: Organized Crime and Drug Trafficking Organizations*. Washington, DC: Congressional Research Service, 2017.

Benítez Manaut, Raúl. "La crisis de seguridad en México," *Nueva Sociedad* 220 (2009): pp. 173–190.

Benítez Manaut, Raúl. "Crimen organizado: fenómeno trasnacional, evolución en México," *Bien Común* 19 (2013): p. 215.

Bonner, Robert C. "The cartel crackdown: Winning the drug war and rebuilding Mexico in the process," *Foreign Affairs* 91 (2012): p. 12.

Booth, John A. and Mitchell A. Seligson. "The political culture of authoritarianism in Mexico: A reexamination," *Latin American Research Review* 19, no. 1 (1984): pp. 106–124.

Boullosa, Carmen and Mike Wallace. *A Narco History: How the United States and Mexico Jointly Created the "Mexican Drug War"*. New York, NY: OR Books, 2015.

Brophy, Stephanie. "Mexico: Cartels, corruption and cocaine: A profile of the Gulf cartel," *Global Crime* 9, no. 3 (2008): pp. 248–261.

Carpenter, Ted Galen. *The Fire Next Door: Mexico's Drug Violence and the Danger to America*. Washington, DC: CATO, 2012.

Carpenter, Ted Galen. "Mexico's drug violence spikes again," *The National Interest*, May 3, 2017.

Castañeda, Jorge. "A U.S. war with Mexican consequences," *CATO Institute*, August 5, 2009, www.cato-unbound.org/2009/08/05/jorge-castaneda/us-war-mexican-consequences, accessed June 7, 2018.

Castañeda, Jorge. "Time for an alternative to Mexico's drug war," *CATO Institute*, September 24, 2012, www.cato.org/publications/economic-development-bulletin/time-alternative-mexicos-drug-war, accessed June 6, 2018.

Castillo, E. Eduardo and Elliot Spagat. "Mexico arrests leader of Tijuana Drug Cartel," *Associated Press*, June 24, 2014.

Castillo, Mariano. "Chicago's new public enemy no. 1: 'El Chapo'," *CNN*, February 15, 2013.

Chabat, Jorge. "Mexico's war on drugs: No margin for maneuver," *The ANNALS of the American Academy of Political and Social Science* 582, no. 1 (2002): pp. 134–148.

Clavel, Tristan. "Organized crime behind spiking homicides in Mexico's most violent municipalities," *InSight Crime*, March 30, 2017, www.insightcrime.org/news/analysis/organized-crime-behind-spiking-homicides-mexico-violent-municipalities/, accessed June 7, 2018.

Corcoran, Patrick. "Mexico has 80 drug cartels: Attorney general," *InSight Crime*, December 20, 2012, www.insightcrime.org/news/analysis/mexico-has-80-drug-cartels-attorney-general/, accessed June 28, 2018.

Corcoran, Patrick. "Mexico President reprises controversial kingpin strategy," *InSight Crime*, June 6, 2017, www.insightcrime.org/news/analysis/mexico-president-reprises-controversial-kingpin-strategy/, accessed June 6, 2018.

Cruz, José Miguel and Angélica Durán-Martínez. "Hiding violence to deal with the state: Criminal pacts in El Salvador and Medellin," *Journal of Peace Research* 53, no. 2 (2016): pp. 197–210.

Davis, Diane E. "Undermining the rule of law: Democratization and the dark side of police reform in Mexico," *Latin American Politics and Society* 48, no. 1 (2006): pp. 55–86.

Diaz, Lizbeth. "Mexico troops enter Tijuana in drug gang crackdown," *The Washington Post*, January 3, 2007.

Dittmar, Victoria. "Is Mexico's CJNG following in the footsteps of the Zetas?" *InSight Crime*, February 19, 2018, www.insightcrime.org/news/analysis/mexicos-cjng-following-footsteps-zetas/, accessed June 7, 2018.

Dudley, Steven. "Part II: The modus operandi," *InSight Crime*, September 8, 2011, www.insightcrime.org/investigations/part-2-the-modus-operandi/, accessed June 7, 2018.

Eisenstadt, Todd A. "Thinking outside the (ballot) box: Informal electoral institutions and Mexico's political opening," *Latin American Politics and Society* 45, no. 1 (2003): pp. 25–54.

Felbab-Brown, Vanda. "The rise of militias in Mexico: Citizens' security or further conflict escalation?" *Prism: A Journal of the Center for Complex Operations* 5, no. 4 (2015): p. 172.

Flores-Macías, Gustavo. "Mexico's 2012 elections: The return of the PRI," *Journal of Democracy* 24, no. 1 (2013): pp. 128–141.

"Former DEA agent: Sinaloa Cartel likely to remain strong without 'El Chapo'," *NPR*, January 25, 2017, www.npr.org/2017/01/25/511655811/former-dea-agent-sinaloa-cartel-likely-to-remain-strong-without-el-chapo, accessed June 6, 2018.

Fox, Jonathan. "The difficult transition from clientelism to citizenship: Lessons from Mexico," *World Politics* 46, no. 2 (1994): pp. 151–184.

Gómez Romero, Luis. "Governors gone wild: Mexico faces a 'lost generation' of corrupt leaders," *The Conversation*, August 15, 2017.

Hernández-Rodríguez, Rogelio. "The renovation of old institutions: State governors and the political transition in Mexico," *Latin American Politics and Society* 45, no. 4 (2003): pp. 97–127.

Hope, Alejandro. "Z-43: Los Zetas después de 'Los Zetas'," *El Universal*, 10 de febrero de 2018.

"Jalisco Cartel New Generation (CJNG)," *InSight Crime*, March 30, 2018, www.insightcrime.org/mexico-organized-crime-news/jalisco-cartel-new-generation/, accessed June 7, 2018.

Kan, Paul Rexton. "What we're getting wrong about Mexico," *Parameters* 41, no. 2 (2011): p. 37.

Katz, Charles M., Eric C. Hedberg, and Luis Enrique Amaya. "Gang truce for violence prevention, El Salvador," *Bulletin of the World Health Organization* 94, no. 9 (2016): p. 660.

Kellner, Tomas and Francesco Pipitone. "Inside México's drug war," *World Policy Journal* 27, no. 1 (2010): pp. 29–37.

Klesner, Joseph L. "Electoral competition and the new party system in Mexico," *Latin American Politics and Society* 47, no. 2 (2005): pp. 103–142.

Klesner, Joseph L. "The 2006 Mexican elections: Manifestation of a divided society?" *PS: Political Science & Politics* 40, no. 1 (2007): pp. 27–32.

Langston, Joy. "The PRI's 2006 electoral debacle," *PS: Political Science & Politics* 40, no. 1 (2007): pp. 21–25.

Lawson, Chappell. "Mexico's unfinished transition: Democratization and authoritarian enclaves in Mexico," *Mexican Studies/Estudios Mexicanos* 16, no. 2 (2000): pp. 267–287.

Lawson, Chappell. "How did we get here? Mexican democracy after the 2006 elections," *PS: Political Science & Politics* 40, no. 1 (2007): 45–48.

Lindau, Juan D. "The drug war's impact on executive power, judicial reform, and federalism in Mexico," *Political Science Quarterly* 126, no. 2 (2011): pp. 177–200.

Linthicum, Kate. "Mexico's bloody drug war is killing more people than ever," *Los Angeles Times*, July 22, 2017.

Lyman, Michael D. *Drugs in Society: Causes, Concepts, and Control*. New York, NY: Routledge, 2016, eighth edition.

Mayorga, Patricia. "Octubre rojo en Ciudad Juárez; matan a 10 el viernes y suman 90 asesinatos," *Proceso*, 29 de octubre de 2016.

McKinley Jr., James C. and Ginger Thompson. "Calderón wins narrow victory in Mexico election," *The New York Times*, July 6, 2006.

Meixler, Eli. "With over 29,000 homicides, 2017 was Mexico's most violent year on record," *Time*, January 22, 2018.

"Mexico," *Transparency International: Corruption Perceptions Index*, www. transparency.org/country/MEX, accessed June 6, 2018.

Miller Llana, Sara. "With Calderón in, a new war on Mexico's mighty drug cartels," *The Christian Science Monitor*, January 22, 2007.

Moloeznik, Marcos Pablo. "The challenges to Mexico in times of political change," *Crime, Law and Social Change* 40, no. 1 (2003): pp. 7–20.

Moreno, Alejandro. "The 2006 Mexican presidential election: The economy, oil revenues, and ideology," *PS: Political Science & Politics* 40, no. 1 (2007): pp. 15–19.

Morris, Stephen D. "Disaggregating corruption: A comparison of participation and perceptions in Latin America with a focus on Mexico," *Bulletin of Latin American Research* 27, no. 3 (2008): pp. 388–409.

Morris, Stephen D. and Joseph L. Klesner. "Corruption and trust: Theoretical considerations and evidence from Mexico," *Comparative Political Studies* 43, no. 10 (2010): pp. 1258–1285.

Morton, Adam David. "The war on drugs in Mexico: A failed state?" *Third World Quarterly* 33, no. 9 (2012): pp. 1631–1645.

O'Neil, Shannon. "The real war in Mexico: How democracy can defeat the drug cartels," *Foreign Affairs* (2009): pp. 63–77.

Osorio, Javier. "The contagion of drug violence: Spatiotemporal dynamics of the Mexican war on drugs," *Journal of Conflict Resolution* 59, no. 8 (2015): pp. 1403–1432.

Parish Flannery, Nathaniel. "'Calderón's war," *Journal of International Affairs* (2013): p. 1.

Pérez Caballero, Jesús. "Mexico's CJNG: Local consolidation, military expansion and vigilante rhetoric," *InSight Crime*, February 8, 2018, www.insightcrime.org/news/analysis/mexico-cjng-local-consolidation-military-expansion-vigilante-rhetoric/, accessed June 6, 2018, p. 2.

Phillips, Brian J. "An amnesty deal for Mexico's drug cartels?" *Political Violence at a Glance*, December 11, 2017, https://politicalviolenceataglance.org/2017/12/11/an-amnesty-deal-for-mexicos-drug-cartels/, accessed June 11, 2018, p. 2.

"Political Parties in Mexico," *Rice University's Baker Institute for Public Policy*, www. bakerinstitute.org/political-parties-mexico/, accessed June 6, 2018.

Resendiz, Francisco. "Centralismo marcó al sexenio," *El Universal*, December 1, 2012.

Reyna, José Luis and Richard S. Weinert. "Authoritarianism in Mexico," *Anthropology News* 18, no. 9 (1977): p. 23.

Ríos, Viridiana. "Why did Mexico become so violent? A self-reinforcing violent equilibrium caused by competition and enforcement," *Trends in Organized Crime* 16, no. 2 (2013): pp. 138–155.

Rísquez, Ronna. "Could an amnesty in Mexico reduce violence?" *InSight Crime*, December 15, 2017, www.insightcrime.org/news/analysis/mexico-torn-amnesty-narco-leaders-urgent-need-peace/, accessed June 11, 2018.

Rosen, Jonathan Daniel and Roberto Zepeda Martínez. "La guerra contra las drogas en Colombia y México: estrategias fracasadas," *Ánfora* 21, no. 38 (2014): pp. 179–200.

Rosen, Jonathan Daniel and Roberto Zepeda Martínez. *Organized Crime, Drug Trafficking, and Violence in Mexico: The Transition from Felipe Calderón to Enrique Peña Nieto*. Lanham, MD: Lexington Books, July 2016.

Sabet, Daniel M. *Police Reform in Mexico: Informal Politics and the Challenge of Institutional Change*. Stanford, CA: Stanford University Press, 2012.

Schatz, Sara. "Disarming the legal system: Impunity for the political murder of dissidents in Mexico," *International Criminal Justice Review* 18, no. 3 (2008): pp. 261–291.

Schedler, Andreas. "The democratic revelation," *Journal of Democracy* 11, no. 4 (2000): pp. 5–19.

Schmidt Camacho, Alicia R. "Ciudadana X: Gender violence and the denationalization of women's rights in Ciudad Juarez, Mexico," *CR: The New Centennial Review* 5, no. 1 (2005): pp. 255–292.

Shelley, Louise. "Corruption and organized crime in Mexico in the post-PRI transition," *Journal of Contemporary Criminal Justice* 17, no. 3 (2001): pp. 213–231.

Shirk, David and Joel Wallman. "Understanding Mexico's drug violence," *Journal of Conflict Resolution* 59, no. 8 (2015): pp. 1348–1376.

"Sinaloa cartel," *InSight Crime*, January 24, 2018, www.insightcrime.org/mexico-organized-crime-news/sinaloa-cartel-profile/, accessed June 6, 2018.

Snyder, Richard and Angélica Durán Martínez. "Drugs, violence, and state-sponsored protection rackets in Mexico and Colombia," *Colombia Internacional* 70 (2009): pp. 61–91.

Thornton, Christy and Adam Goodman. "How the Mexican drug trade thrives on free trade," *The Nation*, July 15, 2014.

Tuckman, Jo. "Failed Mexican presidential candidate sets up protest camp," *The Guardian*, August 2, 2006.

Van der Borgh, Chris and Wim Savenije. "De-securitising and re-securitising gang policies: The Funes government and gangs in El Salvador," *Journal of Latin American Studies* 47, no. 1 (2015): pp. 149–176.

Vilalta, Carlos and Robert Muggah. "Violent disorder in Ciudad Juarez: A spatial analysis of homicide," *Trends in Organized Crime* 17, no. 3 (2014): pp. 161–180.

Williams, Phil. "El crimen organizado y la violencia en México: una perspectiva comparativa," *ISTOR: Revista de Historia International* 11 (2010): pp. 15–40.

Wright, Melissa W. "Necropolitics, narcopolitics, and femicide: Gendered violence on the Mexico-US border," *Signs: Journal of Women in Culture and Society* 36, no. 3 (2011): pp. 707–731.

Yagoub, Mimi. "Why a 900% spike in murders in West Mexico state?" *InSight Crime*, May 25, 2016, www.insightcrime.org/news/brief/what-is-behind-900-spike-in-murders-in-west-mexico-state/, accessed June 6, 2018.

Zepeda Martínez, Roberto and Jonathan D. Rosen. "Corrupción e inseguridad en México: consecuencias de una democracia imperfecta," *Revista AD UNIVERSA*, Año 4, Vol. 1 (diciembre 2014): pp. 60–85.

4 El Salvador and Nicaragua
Comparing Regime Type

El Salvador has a long history of violence given the country's civil war, which lasted more than a decade.[1] Yet violence today has surpassed the days of the internal conflict.[2] In 2015, El Salvador became the most violent non-warring country in the world with a homicide rate of 103 per 100,000. August 2015 alone witnessed the murder of more than 900 people. In addition, the country recorded 52 deaths in one day, demonstrating the extreme levels of violence. Nina Lakhani argues, "Last year's death toll is the highest recorded since 1983, at the height of a 12-year civil war that pitted a US-backed military dictatorship against leftwing guerrilla groups."[3] This is quite astounding given the fact that the civil war resulted in 75,000 deaths.[4] This chapter seeks to examine trends in violence and state fragility in El Salvador and how these variables have created ripe conditions for criminal violence. It focuses on the role of gangs as well as the government's strategies and how they have contributed to the high levels of violence impacting El Salvador. The chapter also discusses the comparative case of Nicaragua, which unlike its Northern Triangle neighbors, is not inundated with gang activity and violence. While Nicaragua has been plagued by corruption and state fragility, this chapter contends that Daniel Ortega's government has ruled with an iron fist and has controlled all activity within the country. The practices of the Ortega regime have had disastrous effects for democracy in Nicaragua, but this is one variable that helps explain why gangs, crime, and violence in the country are low.

Salvadoran Street Gangs: MS-13 and 18th Street

Salvadoran street gangs have contributed to the high levels of violence plaguing the country.[5] Mara Salvatrucha, or MS-13, is the most powerful Central American street gang.[6] This organization began in the 1980s in Los Angeles, California, while the rival 18th Street gang formed in the 1960s. Groups of Salvadoran migrants formed MS-13 as the gang provided them with a sense of brotherhood. Gangs provide their members with a sense of identity.[7] In Los Angeles, the Salvadoran MS-13 members had a hard time fitting in. Even the way in which they speak Spanish is different from Mexicans, the predominant group in Los Angeles (e.g., Central Americans use the *vos* conjugation as opposed to *tú*).[8] The first members of MS-13 liked to "hang out" on the streets of California.[9]

However, MS-13 evolved over time.[10] Due to the Illegal Immigration Reform and Immigrant Responsibility Act of 1996,[11] the US government deported gang members back to their countries of origin. These gang members returned to El Salvador without criminal records. Gang members took advantage of the high levels of corruption, impunity, and instability in El Salvador and used these conditions to expand their organizations.[12] According to Sarah Kinosian, a gang expert:

> Gang members deported from Los Angeles took advantage of these conditions, and leveraged their more professional and unified structure to ramp up recruitment, consolidate small local youth gangs into more violent and more organized groups, and expand into the street gangs that control neighborhoods throughout Central America today.[13]

They brought their know-how and gang culture back with them to Guatemala, El Salvador, and Honduras.[14]

Experts debate the number of gang members in El Salvador. According to the UNODC, the country had 8,000 18th Street members and 12,000 MS-13 members in 2012.[15] Officials maintain that there around 29,325 gang members on the Salvadoran streets. In addition to the street gang population, there are slightly less than 10,000 gang members who are in prison or who have been deported.[16] Other estimates place the number of gangs at around 60,000.[17] Yet research indicates that there are around 500,000 people in the country who have connections to gangs.[18] Analysts arrived at the number of gang associations by evaluating the social network of gangs.[19] Thus, the number of gang members in the country differs according to different sources. While it is not possible to calculate the exact number of gang members, estimates show that there are nearly half a million people who have linkages with the gangs, demonstrating the social power of these organizations.

Classifying MS-13: Drug Cartels, Guerrilla Groups, or Street Gangs?

MS-13 and 18th Street are involved in extortion, drug trafficking, and other criminal activities, leading some experts to debate how to classify these groups.[20] In 2012, the United States declared that MS-13 is a transnational criminal organization:

> The U.S. Department of the Treasury today designated the Latin American gang Mara Salvatrucha, known as MS-13, pursuant to Executive Order (E.O.) 13581, which targets significant transnational criminal organizations (TCOs) and their supporters. MS-13 is being targeted for its involvement in serious transnational criminal activities, including drug trafficking,

kidnapping, human smuggling, sex trafficking, murder, assassinations, racketeering, blackmail, extortion, and immigration offenses.[21]

Moreover, some scholars have argued that the organization should be considered an urban guerrilla group.[22]

The Trump administration has used tough rhetoric against MS-13. In December 2017, then Attorney General Jeff Sessions delivered a speech on the initiatives taken by the administration to combat MS-13:

> I have designated MS-13 as a priority for our Organized Crime Drug Enforcement Task Forces. These task forces bring together a broad coalition of federal law enforcement—from DEA, FBI, and ATF to ICE, the Coast Guard, Secret Service, and the IRS. I want to thank Secretary Nielsen and Department of Homeland Security personnel for making an incredible contribution to these task forces.[23]

In addition, President Trump has made speeches and tweeted about the need to combat MS-13. On February 23, 2018, he tweeted:

> MS-13 gang members are being removed by our Great ICE and Border Patrol Agents by the thousands, but these killers come back in from El Salvador, and through Mexico, like water. El Salvador just takes our money, and Mexico must help MORE with this problem. We need The Wall!

Some experts, such as InSight Crime's Steven Dudley, contend that MS-13 is not a drug cartel but, rather, a street gang. He argues that the organization can best be characterized as a group of youth as opposed to a sophisticated network of drug traffickers.[24] Research indicates that in El Salvador the gang makes most of its revenue from extortion. MS-13 is not a major player in the international drug trafficking network. In addition, some experts have noted that the gang is "inept" at drug trafficking.[25]

MS-13 meets the definition of a street gang as they consist of youth who share a common identity and participate in criminal activities. José Miguel Cruz and his colleagues at Florida International University conducted a survey with nearly 1,200 gang members in El Salvador. According to this survey, 19.6 percent of the sample joined the gang at 12 years old or younger, while 39.5 percent joined between the ages of 13 and 15. Moreover, 17.4 percent of the respondents joined their respective gangs between 16 and 17 years old, while 13.1 percent joined between the ages of 18 and 21. Only 10.3 percent of respondents joined at 21 or older.[26]

Tough on Crime Policies

The Salvadoran government sought to combat gangs and gang-related violence.[27] The Francisco Flores government launched iron-fist (*mano dura*) strategies to increase security in El Salvador.[28] The *mano dura* and super *mano dura* policies led to an increase in the number of arrests of suspected gang members. The proliferation of arrests resulted in a massive increase in the prison population. In 2002, El Salvador had a prison population of 10,907. By 2006, the number of prisoners spiked to 14,771. The prison population continued to increase over time. In 2014, El Salvador had a prison population of 28,334. As of 2016, there were 36,824 prisoners in the country. The number of gang members incarcerated makes up a large percentage of the overall prison population. In 2009, for instance, Salvadoran prisons had 7,555 gang members. By 2015, the number of gang members in prison had spiked to 12,983 (see Figure 4.1).

The increasing prison population had unintended consequences. Prison officials had to separate prisoners based on gangs as mixing rival gang members could lead to violence and even riots. The result was that gang members from different cliques throughout the country were united within the prison system. Prisons became schools of crime as gang members networked with their gang colleagues. In addition, the leaders of MS-13 and the 18th Street gang were incarcerated and called the shots from behind the prison walls. Thus, prisons helped gang members better organize, and they have played an integral part in the evolution of the gangs.[29] It is expected that gang members will be arrested, as they are involved in various criminal activities.[30]

The *mano dura* strategies utilized to combat the gangs have resulted in spikes in violence.[31] As has been seen in other countries, hardline strategies to combat organized crime can often lead to fragmentations of criminal groups (e.g., Colombian and Mexican cartels), but it can also lead to more violence.[32] Salvadoran gangs have not only fought for control of territory among themselves, using violence as a tactic to intimidate rivals and civilians.

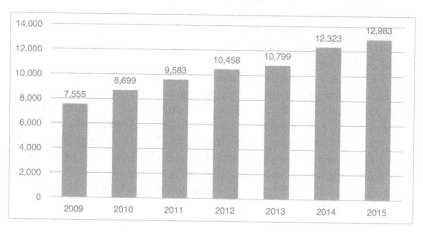

Figure 4.1 Salvadoran Gang Members in Prison

Source: Steven Dudley and Juan José Martínez D'Aubuisson, "El Salvador Prisons and the Battle for the MS13's Soul," *InSight Crime*, February 16, 2017; data from the Universidad Centroamericana (UCA)

The research of Cruz and his colleagues reveals that 35.2 percent of the gang members in the survey had a primary-level education, while 41.6 percent had a middle school education. In addition, 71.3 percent of the respondents in the survey had a monthly family income of less than $250, demonstrating the high levels of poverty that the gang members experience.[33] Cruz's research over the past two decades demonstrates that gangs provide their members with not only material resources but also friends and protection.[34]

In 2014, the Salvadoran Supreme Court labeled gang members as terrorists. Arron Daugherty contends that:

> in the same ruling, the judges rejected multiple lawsuits seeking to declare elements of El Salvador's anti-terrorism laws as unconstitutional. The laws provide for harsher sentencing of MS13 and Barrio 18 members, including 10 to 15 year prison terms for gang leaders convicted under terrorism charges.[35]

This enabled the Salvador Sánchez Cerén administration to demonstrate to the public that the government was serious about the gang threat. Defining gang members as terrorists is a mischaracterization of the organizations. Gang members are youth from marginalized communities who join their respective organizations due to a variety of underlying factors, such as poverty and limited educational opportunities. Gangs provide these individuals with a sense of identity.

What have been the consequences of "tough on crime" policies in El Salvador? The result of these policies has been that violence has increased over time. Salvadoran gangs have fought with the Salvadoran security forces. While the homicide rates have dropped in recent years from over 100 per 100,000 in 2015 to 64 per 100,000 in 2017, the rate is still extremely high (see Figure 4.2). In September 2017, El Salvador recorded 435 homicides alone. Moreover, the data and rising violence levels contradict the victory claims that the current administration has made to demonstrate to the public that El Salvador is becoming safer.[36] This raises questions among human rights activists about the actions of the police, which will be discussed in more detail later.

Despite the efforts of the Sánchez Cerén government, Salvadorans still do not believe that the government has control of the security situation in the country. In a 2017 survey with 1,000 people, 42 percent of the respondents contended that the gangs rule the country, while only 12 percent responded that the government rules. Only six percent of the respondents believed that the president controls the country.[37] According to Vanderbilt's LAPOP, 68.2 percent of Salvadorans believed that security is the most important problem in the country.[38]

Moreover, El Salvador is ranked as one of the most dangerous countries for women (see Figure 4.3).[39] In 2016, more than 500 women were murdered.[40] The National Civil Police (Policia Nacional Civil, PNC) registered 165 cases of sexual aggression and 361 cases of rape from January through August 2015. In

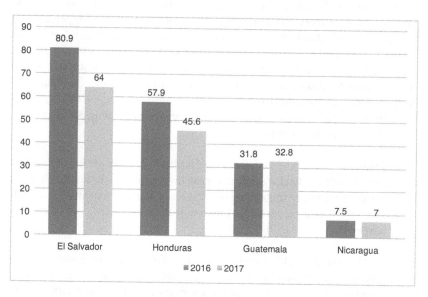

Figure 4.2 Homicide Rate in Central America (per 100,000)

Source: Created by authors with data from Gabriel García/Edwin Segura, "El Salvador es el país con más homicidios de Centroamérica," *La Prensa Gráfica*, January 3, 2018

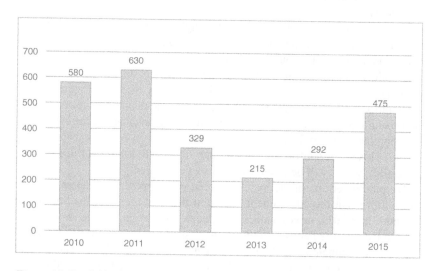

Figure 4.3 Femicides in El Salvador

Source: Created by authors with data from Sarah Kinosian, Angelika Albaladejo, and Lisa Haugaard, El Salvador's Violence: No Easy Way Out (Washington, DC: CIP, 2016); data from the Institute for Legal Medicine (IML)

Note: The 2015 numbers are based on data from January through October 2015

the first eight months of 2015, the Salvadoran police received reports of 1,123 cases of sexual violence.[41]

The culture of *machismo* also helps explains some of the horrific treatment of women in El Salvador.[42] According to Molly O'Toole:

> Magdalena Arce, the president of a network of women's shelters in the foothills of San Salvador, argued that the violence against women comes down to machismo. As academics have argued, the sexism that devalues Salvadoran girls is so ingrained—in El Salvador's politics, culture, even its religion—that many young women "don't even know they have rights," Arce said.[43]

Gangs play a role in perpetuating the violence against women and *machismo* culture.

Gangs have been involved in major human rights abuses against women.[44] Yet there are high levels of impunity for violence against women. Women often fear being harmed if they report a case. Women also often fear that they will not be believed. The impunity rate and levels of corruption present in the judicial system can lead one to question if it is even worth reporting a case.[45] More needs to be done to combat cases of violence against women and strengthen the reporting and prosecuting mechanisms.[46] Otherwise, it is highly likely that the rates of violence against women will continue unabated.

Variables that Determine Gang Presence

What determines where gangs operate? Using the 2016/2017 El Salvador survey[47] from LAPOP at Vanderbilt University, we sought to determine what variables influence the presence of gangs in neighborhoods, our dependent variable. The variable gang presence in neighborhoods was divided into "A Lot," "Some," "Little," and "None." Our independent variables included age, urban, and monthly household income. The age variable was from 18 to 93. However, we recoded it into seven different categories.[48] The urban variable was divided into two categories: urban and rural. Finally, the monthly household income variable ranged from no income to more than $785.[49]

The model reveals that urban and monthly household income are statistically significant. Age is nearly statistically significant at the 95-confidence level. A one-unit increase in urban (i.e., shifting from urban to rural), means a 0.349 change in the dependent variable. In addition, a one-unit change in monthly household income results in a –0.020 shift in the dependent variable. In summary, household income and whether you live in an urban or rural area, on average, have a significant impact on the presence of gangs (see Table 4.1). Gangs take advantage of power vacuums, corruption, and high levels of poverty and operate in zones that lack government presence.

Table 4.1 Factors Associated With Gang Presence in the Neighborhood

Variable	Coeff (SE)	t-test
Age	0.040**	2.14
	(0.018)	
Urban	0.349***	4.16
	(0.084)	
Monthly Household Income	−0.020***	−2.47
	(0.008)	
Constant	2.255***	15.86
	(0.142)	
Observations	1,349	
R-Squared	0.049	
Standard Errors in Parentheses		

*** p<0.01, ** p<0.05, * p<0.1

Source: Created by authors with data from the 2016/2017 LAPOP survey

Police Corruption and Violence

The police, by definition, are supposed to protect and serve and maintain law and order. The Salvadoran police have been involved in numerous scandals and have contributed to state fragility.[50] Working as a police officer in El Salvador is a dangerous job. Reports have emerged that police officers may have been involved in extrajudicial killings. Geoff Thale and Kevin Amaya of the Washington Office on Latin America (WOLA) document the extrajudicial killings:

- March 26, 2015: Eight people were killed on the San Blas coffee farm in La Libertad. According to the investigation by the Salvadoran Human Rights Ombudsman, most victims received more than 10 shots in the body, some on the skull and back. The investigation also concluded that extrajudicial executions did occur and that the crime scene had been tampered with. Later in June of 2016, eight police agents who participated in the alleged confrontation were indicted on aggravated homicide charges relating to the death of Dennis Martinez. On September 2017, a judge in Santa Tecla acquitted the police agents on all charges, citing the prosecution's inability to identify who pulled the trigger that killed Martinez.
- April 30, 2015: Police agents claimed that three people—police officer Deysi Cabrera and married couple Óscar Mejía and Saidra Hernández—died in a "police confrontation" in the town of San Pedro Masahua. The police said that Mejía and his wife were gang members and that Mejía initiated the firefight by shooting and killing Cabrera. However, according to three witnesses, the couple's location made it virtually impossible to shoot Cabrera. Furthermore, the Ombudsman's Office concluded that the couple was killed execution-style, with Hernandez receiving eight shots

in the back and Mejía 29. According to El Faro, when the Mejía Hernández family attempted to denounce the killing of their family members, the prosecutor's office told them that the case had been closed.

- August 15, 2015: The PNC announced that five gang members, two of whom were under the age of 18, died in an armed confrontation in the rural town of Panchimalco. Several witnesses said to the then Human Rights Ombudsman, David Morales, that the alleged gang members were all killed by police and military personnel. One of the witnesses disappeared three days after making these statements and has not been found. Another witness has been detained without cause and has been charged with attempted murder.

- March 28, 2016: After failing to stop at a police checkpoint, police agents shot and killed Ángel Fernando Ábrego. According to the testimony of the IDHUCA, one shot in the chest seemed to occur while Abrego was standing outside of his vehicle and another in the back of the head while he was sitting inside of the vehicle. The only witness, Abrego's uncle, was in the vehicle when the shooting occurred. He was charged with aggravated attempted homicide, even after the police claimed that neither he nor Abrego were armed or had threatened the police officers.

- August 22, 2017: An article published by Revista Factum detailed that a special unit of the National Civilian Police (PNC) allegedly carried out three extrajudicial executions, two sexual assaults against minors, and extortion, among other crimes. Following the publication of the article, four officers identified by the investigation were temporarily detained, but have since returned to duty on the police force. Threats against Factum journalists emerged after the release of the article and recently resulted in the IACHR deciding to grant the publication precautionary measures, ordering the Salvadoran government to investigate the threats.[51]

The extrajudicial killings have tarnished the reputation of police forces, which are already highly distrusted among the population due to their involvement in seemingly countless corruption scandals.

The Salvadoran police must undergo serious reforms as the institution has been riddled with corruption. Experts note that the police forces need to improve the mechanisms designed to ensure accountability. Adriana Beltrán and Carolyn Scorpio, Central American experts, write:

> Beyond investigation, preventing other incidents of police abuse from happening requires a deep commitment to institutional strengthening and reform, and to improving community relations, as well as a commitment to establishing effective accountability mechanisms to ensure that police officers are performing their difficult jobs in compliance with the law and with respect for human rights.[52]

The police forces can also improve their relations with the community. A major challenge in policing—not just in El Salvador—is that community members do not trust the police. In addition, witnesses to crimes fear providing the police with information because they could be threatened or killed by the perpetrators. Thus, the high level of distrust in the government creates major obstacles.[53]

Determining Trust in the National Civil Police

Given the various incidents of corruption, it would be useful to measure the determinants of police trust in El Salvador. Using the 2016/2017 El Salvador survey from LAPOP at Vanderbilt University, we decided to run a regression controlling for age, sex, monthly household income, ideology, and urban versus rural.[54] The dependent variable, trust in the National Civil Police, was coded from one to seven, with one being "Not at All" and seven being "A Lot." The age variable was from eighteen to ninety three, but we recoded it into seven different categories. The sex variable was divided into male and female, while the monthly household income variable ranged from no income to more than $785. The ideology variable ranged from left, coded as 1, to right, coded as 10. Finally, the urban variable is urban to rural.[55]

The regression model reveals that urban, age, ideology, and monthly household income are all statistically significant at the 95-percent confidence interval. A one-unit change in urban (i.e., urban to rural) leads to a 0.518 change in the dependent variable. This implies that people living in rural areas, on average, have more trust in the National Civil Police. A one-unit change in age leads to a 0.172 change in trust in the National Civil Police. This suggests that trust in the institution increases the older one is (see Table 4.2).

Table 4.2 Factors Associated With Trust in National Civil Police

Variable	Coeff (SE)	t-test
Age	0.172*	5.36
	(0.032)	
Sex	0.064	0.65
	(0.099)	
Monthly Household Income	−0.025*	−2.35
	(0.011)	
Ideology	0.064*	3.23
	(0.020)	
Urban	0.518*	4.03
	(0.129)	
Constant	2.961*	10.63
	(0.279)	
Observations	1,218	
R-Squared	0.061	
Standard Errors in Parentheses		

*** $p<0.01$, ** $p<0.05$, * $p<0.1$

Source: Created by authors with data from the 2016/2017 LAPOP survey

Operationalizing Corruption and State Fragility

What variables determine whether a police officer has asked for a bribe in El Salvador, which is a measure of corruption and state fragility? Using LAPOP's 2016 data on El Salvador, the regression equation controls for age, sex, urban, skin color, and monthly household income. The dependent variable, a police officer asking for a bribe, is a dichotomous variable: no and yes. The age variable is from 18 to 93, but it has been recoded it into seven categories.[56] The sex variable is coded male and female, while urban is coded urban and rural.[57] The skin color variable is coded 1, for very light, through 9, for very dark. Finally, monthly household income[58] is coded from no income to more than $785.[59]

The logistic regression model indicates that sex, skin color, and monthly household income are statistically significant at the 95-percent confidence level (see Table 4.3). A one-unit change in sex (i.e., male to female) results in a −1.304 shift in the log-odds of the dependent variable. This means that females, on average, are less likely to pay bribes than men are and is something that could be explored further in future studies. The model also indicates that a one-unit change in skin color leads to a −0.282 shift in the log-odds of whether a police officer has asked for a bribe. Finally, a one-unit shift in monthly household income results in a 0.113 change in the log-odds of the dependent variable. This means that people who earn more money, on average, are more likely to have been asked by an officer to pay a bribe. As demonstrated, men, on average, are targeted more than women are. This creates the possibility that officers target men and individuals who appear to have more money based, perhaps, on the car that they drive, the neighborhood listed on their license, or the clothes they wear.

Table 4.3 Factors Associated With Whether a Police Officer Asked for a Bribe in El Salvador

Variables	Coeff (SE)	t-test
Sex	−1.304***	−4.31
	(0.302)	
Urban	−0.528	−1.57
	(0.336)	
Skin Color	−0.282**	−2.21
	(0.127)	
Monthly Household Income	0.113***	4.16
	(0.027)	
Constant	−0.696	−0.88
	(0.789)	
Observations	1,366	
Standard Errors in Parentheses		

*** $p<0.01$, ** $p<0.05$, * $p<0.1$

Source: Created by authors with data from the 2016/2017 LAPOP survey

The survey also asks participants if a government employee asked for a bribe. Only 2.26 percent said yes, while 97.74 percent said no. The no category had 1,516 respondents, while the yes category only had 35. The survey data also asked if one had been asked to pay a bribe to the courts. The results reveal that 7.53 percent of the respondents said yes. However, this question only had 93 total respondents: 86 said yes and seven said no. Given the small sample of people who responded yes, conducting a logistic regression model would have severe limitations.

Institutional Corruption

El Salvador faces many challenges with corruption at all levels of government. El Salvador scored a 33 in 2017 on the CPI, with zero being the most corrupt and 100 being the least corrupt. The country's score has worsened over time: it received a score of 36 in 2016 and 39 in 2015 (see Figure 4.4).

El Salvador has had serious challenges because of the high levels of corruption among government officials.[60] Reports have emerged about the relationship between the gangs and Salvadoran political parties. Cruz contends:

> In August, prosecutors there showed that El Salvador's two main political parties had colluded with MS-13 and other gangs, paying them more than US$300,000 for help winning the country's 2014 presidential election. Party officials allegedly utilized MS-13 to mobilize some voters and suppress others. Still, the attorney general's office has not indicted party leaders.[61]

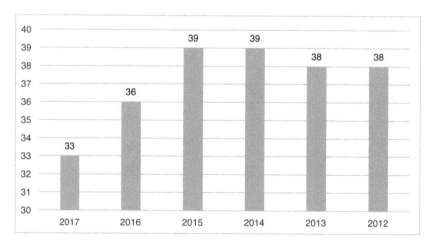

Figure 4.4 Corruption Perceptions Index Score

Source: "Corruption Perceptions Index 2017," *Transparency International*, February 21, 2018

The high levels of impunity have enabled such activities to occur unabated. In February 2018, for example, El Salvador made some minor progress with the conviction of José Elías Hernández, the former mayor of Apopa, for his relationship with the 18th Street gang. Hernández granted various benefits to members of 18th Street while in office as well as during his reelection (e.g., access to vehicles as well as money transfers). Because of such transgressions, the court sentenced him to 12 years in Salvadoran prison.[62]

Corruption has been a major problem at the presidential level. Mauricio Funes, the president from 2009 to 2014, fled to Nicaragua in 2016. In June 2018, the government ordered the arrest of Funes and 30 of his colleagues for stealing $351 million from the government. The attorney general contended: "In the government of Mauricio Funes there were serious and outrageous cases of corruption in which they extracted $351 million from public accounts."[63] Tony Saca, the president from 2004 to 2009, was arrested in 2016 from money laundering as well as embezzlement and illicit association.[64] Saca stole more than $300 million from the government. In 2018, a judge indicated that the former president will go to trial and could face 25 years in prison if he is convicted of his alleged crimes. He is currently incarcerated.[65] Finally, Francisco Flores, the president from 1999 to 2004, allegedly diverted $15 million from the government.[66] However, he died while awaiting trial.

Given the high levels of corruption among politicians, it is not surprising that the 2016/2017 survey conducted by LAPOP found that 31.81 percent of the survey responded "Not at All" when asked if they had trust in political parties. Only 3.39 percent said that they had "A Lot" of trust in political parties. A regression model can help determine what variables impact trust in political parties. Using the 2016/2017 LAPOP data on El Salvador, we built a model using trust in political parties as the dependent variable. The trust variable ranged from one, "Not at All," to seven, "A Lot." We also controlled for age, which was from 18 to 93. We recoded the age variable into seven categories. The other variables were urban and monthly household income. Finally, we controlled for ideology where left was 1 and right was 10.[67]

The results reveal that age, sex, urban, household monthly income, and ideology are statistically significant at the 95-percent confidence level (see Table 4.4). The results suggest that a one-unit increase in age leads to a 0.133 change in the dependent variable. In addition, a one-unit change in sex (i.e., male to female) leads to a 0.195 change in the dependent variable. Furthermore, a one-unit change in urban (i.e., urban to rural) results in a 0.502 change in trust in political parties. One-unit change in monthly household income and ideology leads to changes in the dependent variable of –0.027 and 0.069, respectively.

Table 4.4 Factors Associated With Trust in Political Parties

Variable	Coeff (SE)	t-test
Age	0.133*	4.05
	(0.033)	
Sex	0.195*	1.98
	(0.099)	
Urban	0.502*	4.42
	(0.113)	
Monthly Household Income	−0.027*	−2.53
	(0.011)	
Ideology	0.069*	3.52
	(0.020)	
Constant	1.479*	4.92
	(0.301)	
Observations	1,214	
R-Squared	0.068	
Robust Standard Errors in Parentheses		

*** p<0.01, ** p<0.05, * p<0.1

Source: Created by authors with data from the 2016/2017 LAPOP survey

Nicaragua

Nicaragua has a long history of conflict dating back to the Cold War.[68] However, the country, until recently, has been one of the safest in the region in terms of violence. In 2017, for example, Nicaragua had a homicide rate of seven per 100,000 (see Figure 4.5).[69] Why is Nicaragua so much less violent than its Northern Triangle neighbors? Moreover, why does this country not have gang members like El Salvador, Honduras, and Guatemala?[70]

The reason is that the Nicaraguan government has maintained very strict control over neighborhoods and communities throughout the country. Daniel Ortega, the leader of the Sandinista National Liberation Front (Frente Sandinista de Liberación Nacional, FSLN) has been the president since 2007. Ortega ran for reelection in 2016, and he selected his wife, Rosario Murillo, to be his vice president. Orlando J. Pérez, an expert on Central American security, contends:

> Whether a "self-coup" or not (as claimed by the opposition), the unprecedented consolidation of power by President Ortega and his wife, Rosario Murillo (previously his spokesperson and now his vice-presidential running mate) has been made possible by a hapless opposition, a growing economy and a ruthless dedication to methodically controlling every branch of government.[71]

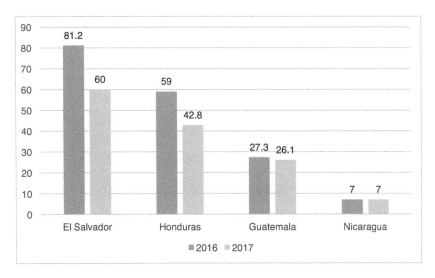

Figure 4.5 Homicide Rate per 100,000 (2016 and 2017)

Source: Created by authors with data from Tristan Clavel, "InSight Crime's 2017 Homicide Round-Up," *InSight Crime*, January 19, 2018; David Gagne, "InSight Crime's 2016 Homicide Round-up," *InSight Crime*, January 16, 2017

To no one's surprise, the husband-and-wife team won the elections. The Ortega government has been shrouded in corruption and lack of transparency. Nicaragua scored a 26 on the 2017 CPI, with zero being highly corrupt and 100 being not very corrupt.[72]

While in power, the FSLN has maintained tight control over the political system.[73] According to the Freedom House Index, the country scored a five out of seven in terms of political rights, with one being the freest and seven being the least free. Regarding civil liberties, the country scored a four out of seven.[74] The Nicaraguan government has also had strict oversight of communities through established neighborhood watch organizations, which have enabled the Ortega government to gain intelligence and control the events that transpire in Nicaragua.[75] The police today are a product of the revolution. According to Argentina Martínez, the director of Save the Children in Nicaragua, the Sandinista revolution had an impact on the policing and security apparatus. She argues, "It also altered consciousness. That consciousness and the reforms to the police remain one of the most important and lasting legacies of the revolution, something we're very proud of."[76] In summary, the police maintain tight control and a close relationship with the communities (see Figures 4.6–4.8).[77]

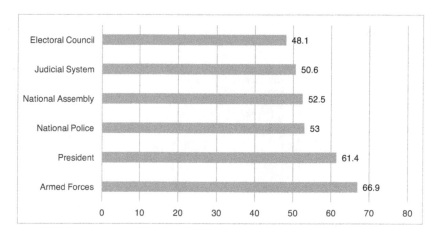

Figure 4.6 Confidence in Nicaraguan Institutions, by Percentage (2016)

Source: Created by authors with data from José Miguel Cruz, Eduardo Marenco, Mariana Rodrí-guez, *Cultura política de la democracia en Nicaragua y en las Américas, 2016/17: Un estudio comparado sobre democracia y gobernabilidad* (Nashville, TN: LAPOP, 2018)

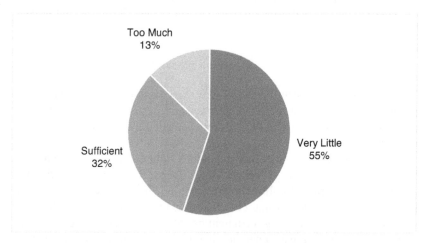

Figure 4.7 Freedom of Expression for Political Opinions (2016)

Source: Created by authors with data from José Miguel Cruz, Eduardo Marenco, Mariana Rodrí-guez, *Cultura política de la democracia en Nicaragua y en las Américas, 2016/17: Un estudio comparado sobre democracia y gobernabilidad* (Nashville, TN: LAPOP, 2018)

In April 2018, the Nicaraguan government announced reforms to the social security system, which sparked outrage among the populace being asked to accept less money. According to Evan Ellis:

the change, formally published on April 17th, deeply offended Nicaraguan sensibilities. Given the almost universal perception of widespread corruption within the Sandinista government..., Nicaraguans who had fought in

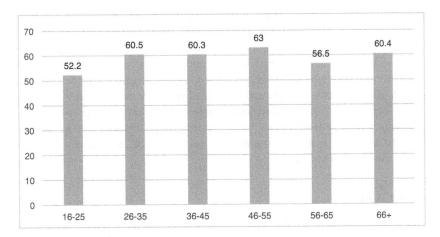

Figure 4.8 Perceptions That There is Little Protection for Human Rights in the Country, According to Age

Source: Created by authors with data from José Miguel Cruz, Eduardo Marenco, Mariana Rodríguez, *Cultura política de la democracia en Nicaragua y en las Américas, 2016/17: Un estudio comparado sobre democracia y gobernabilidad* (Nashville, TN: LAPOP, 2018)

and suffered during the revolution, and who had paid taxes and paid into the pension system all of their lives, were now being asked to accept less to compensate for monies that the government had presumably stolen or mismanaged.[78]

Protest ensued as the population responded to the authoritarian rule of the Ortega government.

Ortega has participated in dialogues, but his critics are skeptical that there will be changes as he holds on to power and control of the political and security apparatus. According to the spokesman for the Civic Alliance for Justice and Democracy, Juan Sebastián Chamorro, "Ortega's response to return to dialogue on Friday shows that these civic measures are giving results." He added, "But we haven't seen any willingness from the government to respond to our democratization agenda."[79] The violent protests have resulted in the death of more than 100 people since April. This has led some individuals to question whether it is possible to have a dialogue with an authoritarian government that has used repression to kill innocent people. Gonzalo Carrión of the Nicaraguan Center for Human Rights asked, "How can you dialogue with your assassins?" He continued: "This was the biggest rally yet. It was a homage to mothers who lost their sons at rallies in April and May, and they wound up adding 15 more mothers to that list."[80] The level of violence against protesters has led to many organizations calling for Ortega to leave office. Many international organizations have denounced the violence conducted by the Ortega administration.[81]

The future of Nicaragua remains uncertain, as citizens have grown tired of President Ortega's control of the entire system and oppressive tactics.

In summary, Nicaragua, unlike its Northern Triangle neighbors, has maintained a tight grip on gangs and criminal activities. The Ortega government has controlled the entire country through undemocratic practices. Thus, there are various lessons about strategies for combating organized crime and the relationship between the state and organized crime. Nicaragua shows that its undemocratic practices coupled with community policing have prevented the flourishing of organized crime. As of January 2020, the future of Nicaragua remains uncertain as the government tightens its control and Ortega will likely run in the election in 2021.

Conclusion

El Salvador has suffered from high levels of violence. Gangs have contributed to the increasing levels of violence as they fight among each other to control territory. The *mano dura* approach implemented by the government also has contributed to the high levels of gang violence. Gang members have fought with the police and armed forces, resulting in El Salvador surpassing Honduras as the most violent country in the world.

The iron-fist strategies have also resulted in spikes in the prison population. Youths often feel that it is a crime to be young and from a poor neighborhood in El Salvador, as they are targeted by the police.[82] The increasing prison populations have created major challenges for the prison system. Prisons have played an integral part in the gang life, serving as schools of crime where gang members can network with different clique leaders. The prison system is extremely overcrowded and does not effectively rehabilitate gang members. Given the fact that El Salvador does not have the death penalty, most gang members will be released back into society.

Moreover, El Salvador faces major challenges with its institutions, which can be best characterized as extremely fragile. The country is plagued by corruption as demonstrated by the countless scandals involving politicians and government authorities. Previous presidents have stolen hundreds of millions of dollars from the government. Major reforms are required to strengthen institutions to combat corruption and impunity.

The case of Nicaragua presents an interesting anomaly. The country's Northern Triangle neighbors have been ravaged by gangs and high levels of violence. On the other hand, Nicaragua, until the recent 2018 protests, had not been plagued by violence and did not have a major issue with gangs. The Ortega government has iron-fist control of the entire country. President Ortega and his wife control all levels of government and micromanage the country. While the country can be characterized as non-democratic given the limitations of free press and freedom of speech, the country has controlled its borders and limited delinquent activity occurring within its territory.

Notes

1. Philippe Bourgois, "The power of violence in war and peace: Post-Cold War lessons from El Salvador," *Ethnography* 2, no. 1 (2001): pp. 5–34; Caroline Hartzell and Matthew Hoddie, "Institutionalizing peace: Power sharing and post-civil war conflict management," *American Journal of Political Science* 47, no. 2 (2003): pp. 318–332; Robin Maria DeLugan, "Peace, culture, and governance in post-civil war El Salvador (1992–2000)," *Journal of Human Rights* 4, no. 2 (2005): 233–249.

2. For more, see *BBC*, "El Salvador violence up to civil war-era level," *BBC*, September 2, 2015; Lainie Reisman, "Breaking the vicious cycle: Responding to Central American youth gang violence," *SAIS Review of International Affairs* 26, no. 2 (2006): pp. 147–152; Roque Planas, "How El Salvador became the world's most violent peacetime country," *The Huffington Post*, January 16, 2017.

3. Nina Lakhani, "Violent deaths in El Salvador spiked 70% in 2015, figures reveal," *The Guardian*, January 4, 2016, p. 2.

4. For more on the civil war, see Elisabeth Jean Wood, *Insurgent Collective Action and Civil War in El Salvador* (New York, NY: Cambridge University Press, 2003).

5. For more, see Elana Zilberg, "Fools banished from the kingdom: Remapping geographies of gang violence between the Americas (Los Angeles and San Salvador)," *American Quarterly* 56, no. 3 (2004): pp. 759–779; Donna DeCesare, "The children of war street gangs in El Salvador," *NACLA Report on the Americas* 32, no. 1 (1998): pp. 21–29.

6. Sonja Wolf, "Mara Salvatrucha: The most dangerous street gang in the Americas?" *Latin American Politics and Society* 54, no. 1 (2012): pp. 65–99; Andrew M. Grascia, "Gang violence: Mara Salvatrucha-Forever Salvador," *Journal of Gang Research* 11, no. 2 (2004): pp. 29–36; Sonja Wolf, "Maras transnacionales: Origins and transformations of Central American street gangs," *Latin American Research Review* 45, no. 1 (2010): pp. 256–265.

7. For more, see David C. Pyrooz, Gary Sweeten, and Alex R. Piquero, "Continuity and change in gang membership and gang embeddedness," *Journal of Research in Crime and Delinquency* 50, no. 2 (2013): pp. 239–271; Scott H. Decker, Chris Melde, and David C. Pyrooz, "What do we know about gangs and gang members and where do we go from here?" *Justice Quarterly* 30, no. 3 (2013): pp. 369–402; Robert Garot, "'Where you from!' Gang identity as performance," *Journal of Contemporary Ethnography* 36, no. 1 (2007): pp. 50–84.

8. T. W. Ward, *Gangsters Without Borders: An Ethnography of a Salvadoran Street Gang* (New York, NY: Oxford University Press, 2013); Samuel Logan, *This Is for the Mara Salvatrucha: Inside the MS-13, America's Most Violent Gang* (New York, NY: Hyperion, 2009).

9. José Miguel Cruz, "Central American gangs like MS-13 were born out of failed anti-crime policies," *The Conversation*, March 9, 2017, https://theconversation.com/central-american-gangs-like-ms-13-were-born-out-of-failed-anti-crime-policies-76554, accessed June 12, 2018, p. 2; José Miguel Cruz, "The root causes of the Central American crisis," *Current History* 114, no. 769 (2015): p. 43.

10. José Miguel Cruz, "Central American maras: From youth street gangs to transnational protection rackets," *Global Crime* 11, no. 4 (2010): 379–398.

11. Sonia Chen, "The Illegal Immigration Reform and Immigrant Responsibility Act of 1996: Another congressional hurdle for the courts," *Indiana Journal of Global Legal Studies* (2000): pp. 169–195; Austin T. Fragomen, "The illegal immigration reform and immigrant responsibility act of 1996: An overview," *The International Migration Review* 31, no. 2 (1997): 438–460.

12. José Miguel Cruz, "Central American maras: From youth street gangs to transnational protection rackets."

13. Sarah Kinosian, "Seven facts about MS-13 and how to combat the gang," *Washington Office on Latin America*, June 18, 2017, www.wola.org/analysis/ms-13-not-immigration-problem/, accessed June 13, 2018, p. 1.
14. José Miguel Cruz, "Central American maras: From youth street gangs to transnational protection rackets."
15. Clare Ribando Seelke, *Gangs in Central America* (Washington, DC: Congressional Research Service, 2016); United Nations Office on Drugs and Crime (UNODC), *Transnational Organized Crime in Central America and the Caribbean: A Threat Assessment* (Vienna: UNODC, 2012).
16. James Bargent, "Nearly half a million Salvadorans connected to street gangs: Study," *InSight Crime*, May 28, 2013, www.insightcrime.org/news/brief/nearly-half-a-million-salvadorans-connected-to-street-gangs-study/, accessed June 14, 2018, p. 2.
17. Óscar Martínez, Efren Lemus, Carlos Martínez, and Deborah Sontag, "Killers on a shoestring: Inside the gangs of El Salvador," *The New York Times*, November 20, 2016.
18. Molly O'Toole, "El Salvador's gangs are targeting young girls," *The Atlantic*, March 4, 2018; James Bargent, "Nearly half a million Salvadorans connected to street gangs: Study."
19. James Bargent, "Nearly half a million Salvadorans connected to street gangs: Study," p. 2.
20. For more, see John P. Sullivan, "Maras morphing: Revisiting third generation gangs," *Global Crime* 7, no. 3–4 (2006): pp. 487–504.
21. *US Department of Treasury*, "Treasury sanctions Latin American criminal organization," *US Department of Treasury*, October 11, 2012, www.treasury.gov/press-center/press-releases/Pages/tg1733.aspx, accessed March 9, 2020, p. 1.
22. For more, see John P. Sullivan, "Maras morphing: Revisiting third generation gangs;" Dennis Rodgers and Robert Muggah, "Gangs as non-state armed groups: The Central American case," *Contemporary Security Policy* 30, no. 2 (2009): pp. 301–317; Oliver Jütersonke, Robert Muggah, and Dennis Rodgers, "Gangs, urban violence, and security interventions in Central America," *Security Dialogue* 40, no. 4–5 (2009): pp. 373–397.
23. Department of Justice, "Attorney General sessions delivers remarks on the administration's efforts to combat MS-13 and carry out its immigration priorities," *Department of Justice*, December 12, 2017, www.justice.gov/opa/speech/attorney-general-sessions-delivers-remarks-administrations-efforts-combat-ms-13-and-carry, accessed March 9, 2020.
24. Steven S. Dudley, "MS-13 is a street gang, not a drug cartel—and the difference matters," *The Conversation*, March 20, 2018, https://theconversation.com/ms-13-is-a-street-gang-not-a-drug-cartel-and-the-difference-matters-92702, accessed June 12, 2018, p. 2.
25. Ibid., p. 3.
26. José Miguel Cruz, Jonathan D. Rosen, Luis Enrique Amaya, and Yulia Vorobyeva, *The New Face of Street Gangs: The Gang Phenomenon in El Salvador* (Miami, FL: FIU, 2017).
27. For more, see Jonathan D. Rosen and Hanna Samir Kassab, *Drugs, Gangs, and Violence* (New York, NY: Palgrave Macmillan, 2018).
28. Mo Hume, "Mano dura: El Salvador responds to gangs," *Development in Practice* 17, no. 6 (2007): pp. 739–751; Alisha C. Holland, "Right on crime? Conservative Party politics and Mano Dura policies in El Salvador, *Latin American Research Review* 48, no. 1 (2013): pp. 44–67.
29. Sarah Kinosian and Angelika Albaladejo," El Salvador's security strategy in 2016: Change or more Mano Dura?" *Latin American Working Group*, http://lawg.org/action-center/lawg-blog/69-general/1599-el-salvadors-security-strategy-in-2016-change-or-more-mano-dura-, accessed March 9, 2020, p. 2; José Miguel Cruz, "Central American maras: From youth street gangs to transnational protection rackets."

30. Jonathan D. Rosen and Marten W. Brienen, eds., *Prisons in the Americas in the Twenty-First Century: A Human Dumping Ground* (Lanham, MD: Lexington Books, 2015).

31. Jonathan D. Rosen, "Estrategias contra-pandillas en América Central: prisión y mano dura no funcionan," *democraciaAbierta*, December 21, 2017, www.opendemocracy.net/democraciaabierta/jonathan-d-rosen/estrategias-contra-pandillas-en-am-rica-central-laprisi-n-y-la-ma, accessed June 13, 2018.

32. Bruce M. Bagley and Jonathan D. Rosen, eds., *Drug Trafficking, Organized Crime, and Violence in the Americas Today* (Gainesville, FL: University Press of Florida, 2015).

33. José Miguel Cruz, Jonathan D. Rosen, Luis Enrique Amaya, and Yulia Vorobyeva, *The New Face of Street Gangs: The Gang Phenomenon in El Salvador*.

34. José Miguel Cruz and Nelson Portillo Peña, *Solidaridad y violencia en las pandillas del gran San Salvador: más allá de la vida loca* (San Salador: UCA editores, 1998); José Miguel Cruz, Jonathan D. Rosen, Luis Enrique Amaya, and Yulia Vorobyeva, *The New Face of Street Gangs: The Gang Phenomenon in El Salvador*; for more on the issue of youth deliquency, see René Olate, Christopher Salas-Wright, and Michael G. Vaughn, "Predictors of violence and delinquency among high risk youth and youth gang members in San Salvador, El Salvador," *International Social Work* 55, no. 3 (2012): pp. 383–401.

35. Arron Daugherty, "El Salvador Supreme Court labels street gangs as terrorist groups," *InSight Crime*, August 26, 2015, www.insightcrime.org/news/brief/el-salvador-supreme-court-labels-street-gangs-as-terrorist-groups/, accessed June 13, 2018, p. 2.

36. Héctor Silva Ávalos, "El Salvador violence rising despite 'extraordinary' anti-gang measures," *InSight Crime*, October 3, 2017, www.insightcrime.org/news/analysis/violence-el-salvador-rise-despite-extraordinary-anti-gang-measures/, accessed June 13, 2018, p. 4.

37. Parker Asmann, "El Salvador citizens say gangs, not government 'rule' the country," *InSight Crime*, November 8, 2017, November 8, 2017, www.insightcrime.org/news/brief/el-salvador-citizens-say-gangs-not-government-rules-country/, accessed June 13, 2018; Redacción DEM, "El 42 % cree que las pandillas mandan más que el Gobierno," *El Mundo*, 8 de noviembre de 2017.

38. Ricardo Córdova Macías, Mariana Rodríguez y Elizabeth J. Zechmeister, *Cultura política de la democracia en El Salvador y en las Américas, 2016/17: Un estudio comparado sobre democracia y gobernabilidad* (Nashville, TN: LAPOP, 2017).

39. Mo Hume, "'It's as if you don't know, because you don't do anything about it': Gender and violence in El Salvador," *Environment and Urbanization* 16, no. 2 (2004): pp. 63–72; Catalina Lobo-Guerrero, "In El Salvador, 'girls are a problem'," *The New York Times*, September 2, 2017.

40. Catalina Lobo-Guerrero, "In El Salvador, 'girls are a problem'"; Laura Aguierre, "300 feminicidios al año 'no son nada' en el país más violento del continente," *Univision*, 7 de marzo de 2017.

41. Angelika Albaladejo, "How violence affects women in El Salvador," *Latin America Working Group*, February 22, 2016, www.lawg.org/action-center/lawg-blog/69-general/1590-how-violence-affects-women-in-el-salvador, accessed June 14, 2018; original data from PNC.

42. For more on violence against women, see Cynthia L. Bejarano, "Las super madres de Latino America: Transforming motherhood by challenging violence in Mexico, Argentina, and El Salvador," *Frontiers: A Journal of Women Studies* 23, no. 1 (2002): pp. 126–150; Mo Hume, "The myths of violence: Gender, conflict, and community in El Salvador," *Latin American Perspectives* 35, no. 5 (2008): pp. 59–76.

43. Molly O'Toole, "El Salvador's gangs are targeting young girls," p. 4; Bron B. Ingoldsby, "The Latin American family: Familism vs. machismo," *Journal of*

Comparative Family Studies (1991): pp. 57–62; Evelyn P. Stevens, "Machismo and marianismo," *Society* 10, no. 6 (1973): pp. 57–63.

44. Quoted in Angelika Albaladejo, "How violence affects women in El Salvador."
45. Ibid., p. 6.
46. For more, see Orlando J. Pérez, "Democratic legitimacy and public insecurity: Crime and democracy in El Salvador and Guatemala," *Political Science Quarterly* 118, no. 4 (2003): pp. 627–644; Charles T. Call, "Democratisation, war and state-building: Constructing the rule of law in El Salvador," *Journal of Latin American Studies* 35, no. 4 (2003): pp. 827–862; Marina Prieto-Carrón, Marilyn Thomson, and Mandy Macdonald, "No more killings! Women respond to femicides in Central America," *Gender & Development* 15, no. 1 (2007): pp. 25–40.
47. The LAPOP team indicates that the following command must be used to weight the data: svyset upm [pw=wt], strata(estratopri)
48. Recode q2 (18/28=1) (29/39=2) (40/50=3) (51/61=4)(62/72=5) (73/83=6) (84/93=7), gen (age)
49. We sought to control for multicollinearity, model specification, and heteroskedasticity after running our regression model. The model has a variance inflation factor (Vif) range from 1.01 to 1.20. Moreover, the mean VIF is 1.13, suggesting that there is no multicollinearity in the model. The linktest produces a hatsq that is not statistically significant, which indicates that the model is properly specified. The Breusch-Pagan/Cook-Weisberg test for heteroskedasticity produces a Prob > chi2 of 0.21. Thus, the model does not have issues with heteroskedasticity.
50. For more on this issue of police, see Jose Miguel Cruz, "Police misconduct and political legitimacy in Central America," *Journal of Latin American Studies* 47, no. 2 (2015): pp. 251–283; William Stanley, "Building new police forces in El Salvador and Guatemala: Learning and counter-learning," *International Peacekeeping* 6, no. 4 (1999): pp. 113–134; John Bailey and Lucía Dammert, *Public Security and Police Reform in the Americas* (Pittsburgh, PA: University of Pittsburgh Press, 2006).
51. Quoted directly from Geoff Thale and Kevin Amaya, "Amid rising violence, El Salvador fails to address reports of extrajudicial killings," *WOLA*, November 3, 2017, www.wola.org/analysis/amid-rising-violence-el-salvador-fails-address-reports-extrajudicial-killings/, accessed June 21, 2018, p. 4; see also Óscar Martínez y Roberto Valencia, "PDDH concluye que Policía y militares cometieron ejecuciones extralegales," *El Faro*, 25 de abril de 2016; *El Faro*, "Policía mató a joven ebrio que huyó de retén policial en San Salvador," *El Diario*, 30 de marzo de 2016; Bryan Avelar y Juan Martínez d'Aubuisson, "En la intimidad del escuadrón d la muerte de la policía," *Revista Factum*, 22 de agosto de 2017; Revista Factum, "CIDH ordena investigar amenazas contra periodistas de Revista Factum," *Revista Factum*, 3 de noviembre de 2017.
52. Adriana Beltrán and Carolyn Scorpio, "El Salvador: Turning a blind eye to police abuse and extrajudicial executions?" *Washington Office on Latin America*, August 16, 2016, www.wola.org/analysis/el-salvador-turning-blind-eye-police-abuse-extrajudicial-executions/, accessed June 13, 2018, p. 3.
53. José Miguel Cruz, "In Central America, gangs like MS-13 are bad—but corrupt politicians may be worse," *The Conversation*, October 23, 2017, https://theconversation.com/in-central-america-gangs-like-ms-13-are-bad-but-corrupt-politicians-may-be-worse-86113, accessed June 13, 2018, p. 3.
54. The dataset can be found at: http://datasets.americasbarometer.org/database/index.php?freeUser=true
55. After running the regression, we sought to control for multicollinearity, model specification, and heteroskedasticity. The model has a variance inflation factor (Vif) range from 1.23 to 1.01. The mean VIF is 1.10, revealing that the regression does not have issues with multicollinearity. The linktest indicates that the model

is properly specified. Next, the Breusch-Pagan/Cook-Weisberg test for heteroskedasticity results in a Prob > chi2 of 0.204, revealing that the model does not have heteroskedasticity.

56. The recode is as follows: recode q2 (18/28=1) (29/39=2) (40/50=3) (51/61=4) (62/72=5) (73/83=6) (84/93=7), gen (age)

57. I ran the Box-Tidwell test to determine linearity. However, the age variable has a non-linear relationship. Therefore, I removed this variable from the model and re-ran the test.

58. After running the regression, it is important to determine model specification and if there are any issues with multicollinearity. The linktest determines if the model is properly specified. Running the linktest produces a hatsq that is not statistically significant at the 95-percent confidence level. Thus, the model does not have specification issues. The mean VIF is 1.13. Thus, the model does not have issues with multicollinearity.

59. The monthly household income is divided into 17 categories from no income, less than $50, $50–80, $81–95, and so forth.

60. Mitchell A. Seligson, "The impact of corruption on regime legitimacy: A comparative study of four Latin American countries," *The Journal of Politics* 64, no. 2 (2002): pp. 408–433; Orlando J. Pérez, "Democratic legitimacy and public insecurity: Crime and democracy in El Salvador and Guatemala."

61. José Miguel Cruz, "In Central America, gangs like MS-13 are bad—but corrupt politicians may be worse," p. 2; Óscar Martínez, Carlos Martínez y Efren Lemus, "Relato de un fraude electoral, narrado por un pandillero," *El Faro*, 11 de agosto de 2017; José Miguel Cruz, "Violence, citizen insecurity, and elite maneuvering in El Salvador," *Public security and police reform in the Americas* (2006): pp. 148–168.

62. Angelika Albaladejo, "El Salvador convicts first mayor for ties to gangs," *InSight Crime*, February 2, 2018, www.insightcrime.org/news/analysis/elsalvador-convicts-mayor-ties-gangs/, accessed June 13, 2018, p. 2.

63. Quoted in Marcos Aleman, "El Salvador prosecutors order arrest of ex-president Funes," *AP News*, June 9, 2018.

64. Parker Asmann, "Former El Salvador President to stand trial for money laundering," *InSight Crime,* May 17, 2018, www.insightcrime.org/news/brief/former-el-salvador-president-trial-money-laundering/, accessed June 13, 2018.

65. Reuters Staff, "El Salvador court to try former president for money laundering," *Reuters*, May 16, 2018.

66. Sam Roberts, "Francisco Flores, tainted Ex-President of El Salvador, dies at 56," *The New York Times*, February 2, 2016, p. 1.

67. Using Stata 15.1, we tested the regression for multicollinearity, model specification, and heteroskedasticity. The variance inflation factor (VIF) produces a mean VIF or 1.10. The VIF for the numbers ranged from 1.01 to 1.23, demonstrating that the model does not have issues with multicollinearity. The linktest indicates that the model does not have issues with specification, Furthermore, the Breusch-Pagan/Cook-Weisberg test for heteroskedasticity produced a Prob > chi2 of 0.00, suggesting that there is heteroskedasticity in the model. We ran the regression command using vce(robust) to correct the model.

68. Thomas W. Walker, *Nicaragua: Living in the Shadow of the Eagle* (Boulder, CO: Westview Press, 2003).

69. Tristan Clavel, "InSight Crime's 2017 homicide round-up," *InSight Crime*, January 19, 2018, www.insightcrime.org/news/analysis/2017-homicide-round-up/, accessed June 19, 2018.

70. For more, see José Miguel Cruz, "Criminal violence and democratization in Central America: The survival of the violent state," *Latin American Politics and Society* 53, no. 4 (2011): pp. 1–33.

71. Orlando J. Pérez, "The slow 'auto-golpe' in Nicaragua," *Global Americans*, August 24, 2016, https://theglobalamericans.org/2016/08/slow-auto-golpe-nicaragua/, accessed June 19, 2018, p. 1.

72. Corruption Perceptions Index 2017, *Transparency International*, February 21, 2018, www.transparency.org/news/feature/corruption_perceptions_index_2017#table, accessed June 19, 2018.

73. For more on political participation and politics, see José Miguel Cruz, Jonathan D. Rosen, Yulia Vorobyeva y Daniela Campos, *Participación política en Nicaragua: Concepciones, comportamientos y actitudes políticas de la* ciudadanía (Miami, FL: Florida International University, 2017); Salvador Martí i Puig, "The adaptation of the FSLN: Daniel Ortega's leadership and democracy in Nicaragua," *Latin American Politics and Society* 52, no. 4 (2010): pp. 79–107; Leslie E. Anderson and Lawrence C. Dodd, "Nicaragua: Progress amid regress?" *Journal of Democracy* 20, no. 3 (2009): pp. 153–167.

74. "Nicaragua Profile," *Freedom House*, https://freedomhouse.org/report/freedom-world/2017/Nicaragua, accessed June 19, 2018.

75. Tracy Wilkinson, "Few Nicaraguans among Central America's exodus to U.S.," *Los Angeles Times*, August 30, 2014, p. 3.

76. Roberto Lovato, "Why is Nicaragua's homicide rate so far below that of its Central American neighbors?" *The Nation*, February 2, 2018, pp. 8–9.

77. For more, see J. Thomas Ratchford III, "Policing in partnership: Nicaraguan policies with implications for US Police forces," *Emory International Law Review* 32 (2017): p. 173;

78. R. Evan Ellis, "Nicaragua's struggle for dignity and survival," *Global Americans*, May 27, 2018, https://theglobalamericans.org/2018/05/nicaraguas-struggle-for-dignity-and-survival/, pp. 3–4.

79. Quoted in Alfonso Flores Bermúdez and Elisabeth Malkin, "Nicaragua protests take a new turn: Empty streets," *The New York Times*, June 14, 2018.

80. Quoted in Frances Robles, "Nicaragua protests grow increasingly violent, 100 killed since April," *The New York Times*, May 31, 2018.

81. Quoted in "Nicaragua: Authorities unleashed a lethal strategy of repression against protesters," *Amnesty International*, May 29, 2018, www.amnesty.org/en/latest/news/2018/05/nicaragua-authorities-unleashed-a-lethal-strategy-of-repression-against-protesters/, accessed June 19, 2018.

82. Jonathan D. Rosen and José Miguel Cruz, "Overcoming stigma and discrimination: Challenges for reinsertion of gang members in developing countries," *International Journal of Offender Therapy and Comparative Criminology* 62, no. 15 (2018): pp. 4758–4775.

Works Cited

Acemoglu, Daron, Simon Johnson, and James A. Robinson. "The colonial origins of comparative development: An empirical investigation," *American Economic Review* 91, no. 5 (2001): pp. 1369–1401.

Adelman, Jeremy. *Colonial Legacies: The Problem of Persistence in Latin American History*. New York, NY: Routledge, 1999.

Adriana Beltrán and Carolyn Scorpio. "El Salvador: Turning a blind eye to police abuse and extrajudicial executions?" *Washington Office on Latin America*, August 16, 2016, www.wola.org/analysis/el-salvador-turning-blind-eye-police-abuse-extrajudicial-executions/, accessed June 13, 2018.

Aguierre, Laura. "300 feminicidios al año 'no son nada' en el país más violento del continente," *Univision*, 7 de marzo de 2017.

Albaladejo, Angelika. "How violence affects women in El Salvador," *Latin America Working Group*, February 22, 2016, www.lawg.org/action-center/lawg-blog/69-general/1590-how-violence-affects-women-in-el-salvador, accessed June 14, 2018.

Albaladejo, Angelika. "El Salvador convicts first mayor for ties to gangs," *InSight Crime*, February 2, 2018, www.insightcrime.org/news/analysis/elsalvador-convicts-mayor-ties-gangs/, accessed June 13, 2018.

Aleman, Marcos. "El Salvador prosecutors order arrest of ex-president Funes," *AP News*, June 9, 2018.

Anderson, Leslie E. and Lawrence C. Dodd. "Nicaragua: Progress amid regress?" *Journal of Democracy* 20, no. 3 (2009): pp. 153–167.

Asmann, Parker. "El Salvador citizens say gangs, not government 'rule' the country," *InSight Crime*, November 8, 2017, www.insightcrime.org/news/brief/el-salvador-citizens-say-gangs-not-gove rnment-rules-country/, accessed June 13, 2018.

Asmann, Parker. "Former El Salvador President to stand trial for money laundering," *InSight Crime*, May 17, 2018, www.insightcrime.org/news/brief/former-el-salvador-president-trial-money-laundering/, accessed June 13, 2018.

Astorga, Luis. "La cocaína en el corrido," *Revista mexicana de sociología* (2000): pp. 151–173.

Astorga, Luis. "The limits of anti-drug policy in Mexico," *International Social Science Journal* 53, no. 169 (2001): pp. 427–434.

Avelar, Bryan y Juan Martínez d'Aubuisson. "En la intimidad del escuadrón d la muerte de la policía," *Revista Factum*, 22 de agosto de 2017.

Bagley, Bruce Michael. "Colombia and the war on drugs," *Foreign Affairs* 67, no. 1 (1988): pp. 70–92.

Bagley, Bruce Michael. "The new hundred years war? US national security and the war on drugs in Latin America," *Journal of Interamerican Studies and World Affairs* 30, no. 1 (1988): pp. 161–182.

Bagley, Bruce Michael. "US foreign policy and the war on drugs: Analysis of a policy failure," *Journal of Interamerican Studies and World Affairs* 30, no. 2–3 (1988): pp. 189–212.

Bagley, Bruce Michael. *Drug Trafficking and Organized Crime in the Americas*. Washington, DC: Woodrow Wilson Center, 2012.

Bagley, Bruce Michael and Jonathan D. Rosen, eds. *Drug Trafficking, Organized Crime, and Violence in the Americas Today*. Gainesville, FL: University Press of Florida, 2015.

Bailey, John and Lucía Dammert. *Public Security and Police Reform in the Americas*. Pittsburgh, PA: University of Pittsburgh Press, 2006.

Beittel, June S. *Colombia: Background, U.S. Relations, and Congressional Interest*. Washington, DC: Congressional Research Service, 2012.

Beittel, June S. *Mexico: Organized Crime and Drug Trafficking Organizations*. Washington, DC: Congressional Research Service, 2017.

Bejarano, Cynthia L. "Las super madres de Latino America: Transforming motherhood by challenging violence in Mexico, Argentina, and El Salvador," *Frontiers: A Journal of Women Studies* 23, no. 1 (2002): pp. 126–150.

Bernabe, Father. *History of the Inca Empire: An Account of the Indian's Customs and their Origin, Together with a Treatise on Inca Legend*. Austin, TX: University of Texas Press, 1979.

Booth, John A. and Mitchell A. Seligson. "The political culture of authoritarianism in Mexico: A reexamination," *Latin American Research Review* 19, no. 1 (1984): pp. 106–124.

Boudon, Lawrence. "Guerrillas and the state: The role of the state in the Colombian peace process," *Journal of Latin American Studies* 28, no. 2 (1996): pp. 279–297.

Bourgois, Philippe. "The power of violence in war and peace: Post-Cold War lessons from El Salvador," *Ethnography* 2, no. 1 (2001): pp. 5–34.

Brenneman, Robert. *Homies and Hermanos: God and Gangs in Central America.* New York, NY: Oxford University Press, 2012.

Call, Charles T. "Democratisation, war and state-building: Constructing the rule of law in El Salvador," *Journal of Latin American Studies* 35, no. 4 (2003): pp. 827–862.

Chernick, Marc W. "Negotiated settlement to armed conflict: Lessons from the Colombian peace process," *Journal of Interamerican Studies and World Affairs* 30, no. 4 (1988): pp. 53–88.

Clavel, Tristan. "InSight Crime's 2017 homicide round-up," *InSight Crime*, January 19, 2018, www.insightcrime.org/news/analysis/2017-homicide-round-up/, accessed June 19, 2018.

Córdova Macías, Ricardo, Mariana Rodríguez, y Elizabeth J. Zechmeister. *Cultura política de la democracia en El Salvador y en las Américas, 2016/17: Un estudio comparado sobre democraciay gobernabilidad.* Nashville, TN: LAPOP, 2017.

Corruption Perceptions Index 2017. *Transparency International*, February 21, 2018, www.transparency.org/news/feature/corruption_perceptions_index_2017#table, accessed June 19, 2018.

Crandall, Russell. *Driven by Drugs: US Policy Toward Colombia.* Boulder, CO: Lynne Rienner, 2008, second edition.

Cruz, José Miguel. "Violence, citizen insecurity, and elite maneuvering in El Salvador," *Public Security and Police Reform in the Americas* (2006): pp. 148–168.

Cruz, José Miguel. "Central American maras: From youth street gangs to transnational protection rackets," *Global Crime* 11, no. 4 (2010): pp. 379–398.

Cruz, José Miguel. "Criminal violence and democratization in Central America: The survival of the violent state," *Latin American Politics and Society* 53, no. 4 (2011): pp. 1–33.

Cruz, Jose Miguel. "Police misconduct and political legitimacy in Central America," *Journal of Latin American Studies* 47, no. 2 (2015): pp. 251–283.

Cruz, José Miguel. "In Central America, gangs like MS-13 are bad—but corrupt politicians may be worse," *The Conversation*, October 23, 2017, https://theconversation.com/in-central-america-gangs-like-ms-13-are-bad-but-corrupt-politicians-may-be-worse-86113, accessed June 13, 2018.

Cruz, José Miguel and Nelson Portillo Peña. *Solidaridad y violencia en las pandillas del gran San Salvador: más allá de la vida loca.* San Salador: UCA Editores, 1998.

Cruz, José Miguel, Jonathan D. Rosen, Luis Enrique Amaya, and Yulia Vorobyeva. *The New Face of Street Gangs: The Gang Phenomenon in El Salvador.* Miami, FL: FIU, 2017.

Cruz, José Miguel, Jonathan D. Rosen, Yulia Vorobyeva, y Daniela Campos. *Participación política en Nicaragua: Concepciones, comportamientos y actitudes políticas de la ciudadanía.* Miami, FL: Florida International University, 2017.

Daugherty, Arron. "El Salvador Supreme Court labels street gangs as terrorist groups," *InSight Crime*, August 26, 2015, www.insightcrime.org/news/brief/el-salvador-supreme-court-labels-street-gangs-as-terrorist-groups/, accessed June 13, 2018.

Davis, Diane E. "Undermining the rule of law: Democratization and the dark side of police reform in Mexico," *Latin American Politics and Society* 48, no. 1 (2006): pp. 55–86.

DeCesare, Donna. "The children of war street gangs in El Salvador," *NACLA Report on the Americas* 32, no. 1 (1998): pp. 21–29.

Decker, Scott H. and Margaret Townsend Chapman. *Drug Smugglers on Drug Smuggling: Lessons from the Inside*. Philadelphia, PA: Temple University Press, 2008.

Department of Justice. "Attorney General sessions delivers remarks on the administration's efforts to combat MS-13 and carry out its immigration priorities," *Department of Justice*, December 12, 2017, www.justice.gov/opa/speech/attorney-general-sessions-delivers-remarks-administrations-efforts-combat-ms-13-and-carry, accessed March 9, 2020.

Dion, Michelle L. and Catherine Russler. "Eradication efforts, the state, displacement and poverty: Explaining coca cultivation in Colombia during Plan Colombia," *Journal of Latin American Studies* 40, no. 3 (2008): pp. 399–421.

Dudley, Steven S. "MS-13 is a street gang, not a drug cartel—and the difference matters," *The Conversation*, March 20, 2018, https://theconversation.com/ms-13-is-a-street-gang-not-a-drug-cartel-and-the-difference-matters-92702, accessed June 12, 2018.

El Faro. "Policía mató a joven ebrio que huyó de retén policial en San Salvador," *El Diario*, 30 de marzo de 2016.

Evan Ellis, R. "Nicaragua's struggle for dignity and survival," *Global Americans*, May 27, 2018, https://theglobalamericans.org/2018/05/nicaraguas-struggle-for-dignity-and-survival/.

Filippone, Robert. "The Medellin Cartel: Why we can't win the drug war," *Studies in Conflict & Terrorism* 17, no. 4 (1994): pp. 323–344.

Flores Bermúdez, Alfonso and Elisabeth Malkin. "Nicaragua protests take a new turn: Empty streets," *The New York Times*, June 14, 2018.

Flores-Macías, Gustavo. "Mexico's 2012 elections: The return of the PRI," *Journal of Democracy* 24, no. 1 (2013): pp. 128–141.

Fox, Jonathan. "The difficult transition from clientelism to citizenship: Lessons from Mexico," *World Politics* 46, no. 2 (1994): pp. 151–184.

Garot, Robert. "'Where you from!' Gang identity as performance," *Journal of Contemporary Ethnography* 36, no. 1 (2007): pp. 50–84.

Gold, Jessica, Kimberly Frost-Pineda, and Mark S. Gold. "A brief history of cocaine," *JAMA* 295, no. 22 (2006): pp. 2665–2666.

Gootenberg, Paul. *Cocaine: Global Histories*. New York, NY: Routledge, 1999.

Grascia, Andrew M. "Gang violence: Mara Salvatrucha-Forever salvador," *Journal of Gang Research* 11, no. 2 (2004): pp. 29–36.

Hartzell, Caroline and Matthew Hoddie. "Institutionalizing peace: Power sharing and post-civil war conflict management," *American Journal of Political Science* 47, no. 2 (2003): pp. 318–332.

Hernández-Rodríguez, Rogelio. "The renovation of old institutions: State governors and the political transition in Mexico," *Latin American Politics and Society* 45, no. 4 (2003): pp. 97–127.

Hinojosa, Victor J. *Domestic Politics and International Narcotics Control: U.S. Relations with Mexico and Colombia, 1989–2000*. New York, NY: Routledge, 2007.

Holland, Alisha C. "Right on crime? Conservative Party politics and Mano Dura policies in El Salvador," *Latin American Research Review* 48, no. 1 (2013): pp. 44–67.

Holmes, Jennifer S., Kevin M. Curtin, and Sheila Amin Gutiérrez de Piñeres. *Guns, Drugs, and Development in Colombia*. Austin, TX: University of Texas Press, 2008.

Hume, Mo. "'It's as if you don't know, because you don't do anything about it': Gender and violence in El Salvador," *Environment and Urbanization* 16, no. 2 (2004): pp. 63–72.

Hume, Mo. "Mano dura: El Salvador responds to gangs," *Development in Practice* 17, no. 6 (2007): pp. 739–751.

Hume, Mo. "The myths of violence: Gender, conflict, and community in El Salvador," *Latin American Perspectives* 35, no. 5 (2008): pp. 59–76.

Jonathan D. Rosen and José Miguel Cruz. "Overcoming stigma and discrimination: Challenges for reinsertion of gang members in developing countries," *International Journal of Offender Therapy and Comparative Criminology* 62, no. 15 (2018): pp. 4758–4775.

Jütersonke, Oliver Robert Muggah, and Dennis Rodgers. "Gangs, urban violence, and security interventions in Central America," *Security Dialogue* 40, no. 4–5 (2009): pp. 373–397.

Kassab, Hanna Samir. *Weak States in International Relations Theory: The Cases of Armenia, St. Kitts and Nevis, Lebanon and Cambodia*. New York, NY: Palgrave, 2015.

Kassab, Hanna Samir and Jonathan D. Rosen. *Corruption, Institutions, and Fragile States*. New York, NY: Palgrave Macmillan, 2018.

Kassab, Hanna Samir and Jonathan D. Rosen, eds. *Violence in the Americas*. Lanham, MD: Lexington Books, 2018.

Kinosian, Sarah and Angelika Albaladejo. "El Salvador's security strategy in 2016: Change or more Mano Dura?" *Latin American Working Group*, http://lawg.org/action-center/lawg-blog/69-general/1599-el-salvadors-security-strategy-in-2016-change-or-more-mano-dura, accessed March 9, 2020.

Kleiman, Mark A. R., Jonathan P. Caulkins, and Angela Hawken. *Drugs and Drug Policy: What Everyone Needs to Know*. New York, NY: Oxford University Press, 2011.

Klesner, Joseph L. "Electoral competition and the new party system in Mexico," *Latin American Politics and Society* 47, no. 2 (2005): pp. 103–142.

Kruijt, Dirk. *Armed Actors: Organised Violence and State Failure in Latin America*. London, UK: Zed Books, 2004.

Langston, Joy. "The PRI's 2006 electoral debacle," *PS: Political Science & Politics* 40, no. 1 (2007): pp. 21–25.

Lawson, Chappell. "Mexico's unfinished transition: Democratization and authoritarian enclaves in Mexico," *Mexican Studies/Estudios Mexicanos* 16, no. 2 (2000): pp. 267–287.

Lee, Rensselaer W. "Colombia's cocaine syndicates," *Crime, Law and Social Change* 16, no. 1 (1991): pp. 3–39.

Lessing, Benjamin. *Making Peace in Drug Wars: Crackdowns and Cartels in Latin America*. New York, NY: Cambridge University Press, 2018.

Lindau, Juan D. "The drug war's impact on executive power, judicial reform, and federalism in Mexico," *Political Science Quarterly* 126, no. 2 (2011): pp. 177–200.

Lobo-Guerrero, Catalina. "In El Salvador, 'girls are a problem'," *The New York Times*, September 2, 2017.

Logan, Samuel. *This is for the Mara Salvatrucha: Inside the MS-13, America's Most Violent Gang*. New York, NY: Hyperion, 2009.

Lovato, Roberto. "Why is Nicaragua's homicide rate so far below that of its Central American neighbors?" *The Nation*, February 2, 2018.

Marcy, William L. *Politics of Cocaine: How U.S. Foreign Policy Has Created a Thriving Drug Industry in Central and South America.* Chicago: Chicago Review Press, 2010.

Martínez, Óscar, Carlos Martínez, y Efren Lemus. "Relato de un fraude electoral, narrado por un pandillero," *El Faro*, 11 de agosto de 2017.

Martínez, Óscar y Roberto Valencia. "PDDH concluye que Policía y militares cometieron ejecuciones extralegales," *El Faro*, 25 de abril de 2016.

McGirr, Lisa. *The War on Alcohol: Prohibition and the Rise of the American State.* New York, NY: W.W. Norton & Company, Inc., 2015.

Moloeznik, Marcos Pablo. "The challenges to Mexico in times of political change," *Crime, Law and Social Change* 40, no. 1 (2003): pp. 7–20.

Morris, Stephen D. "Disaggregating corruption: A comparison of participation and perceptions in Latin America with a focus on Mexico," *Bulletin of Latin American Research* 27, no. 3 (2008): pp. 388–409.

"Nicaragua: Authorities unleashed a lethal strategy of repression against protesters," *Amnesty International*, May 29, 2018, www.amnesty.org/en/latest/news/2018/05/nicaragua-authorities-unleashed-a-lethal-strategy-of-repression-against-protesters/, accessed June 19, 2018.

"Nicaragua profile," *Freedom House*, https://freedomhouse.org/report/freedomworld/2017/Nicaragua, accessed June 19, 2018.

Olate, René, Christopher Salas-Wright, and Michael G. Vaughn. "Predictors of violence and delinquency among high risk youth and youth gang members in San Salvador, El Salvador," *International Social Work* 55, no. 3 (2012): pp. 383–401.

O'Toole, Molly. "El Salvador's gangs are targeting young girls," p. 4; Bron B. Ingoldsby. "The Latin American family: Familism vs. machismo," *Journal of Comparative Family Studies* (1991): pp. 57–62.

Pacheco, Fernando Celaya. "Narcofearance: How has narcoterrorism settled in Mexico?" *Studies in Conflict & Terrorism* 32, no. 12 (2009): pp. 1021–1048.

Pansters, Wil G. "Drug trafficking, the informal order, and caciques. Reflections on the crime-governance nexus in Mexico," *Global Crime* 19, no. 3–4 (2018): pp. 315–338.

Pérez, Orlando J. "Democratic legitimacy and public insecurity: Crime and democracy in El Salvador and Guatemala," *Political Science Quarterly* 118, no. 4 (2003): pp. 627–644.

Pérez, Orlando J. "The slow 'auto-golpe' in Nicaragua," *Global Americans*, August 24, 2016, https://theglobalamericans.org/2016/08/slow-auto-golpe-nicaragua/, accessed June 19, 2018.

Prieto-Carrón, Marina, Marilyn Thomson, and Mandy Macdonald. "No more killings! Women respond to femicides in Central America," *Gender & Development* 15, no. 1 (2007): pp. 25–40.

Puig, Salvador Martí i. "The adaptation of the FSLN: Daniel Ortega's leadership and democracy in Nicaragua," *Latin American Politics and Society* 52, no. 4 (2010): pp. 79–107.

Pyrooz, David C., Gary Sweeten, and Alex R. Piquero. "Continuity and change in gang membership and gang embeddedness," *Journal of Research in Crime and Delinquency* 50, no. 2 (2013): pp. 239–271.

Quijano, Anibal. "Coloniality of power and Eurocentrism in Latin America," *International Sociology* 15, no. 2 (2000): pp. 215–232.

Ramírez, Jorge Giraldo and Juan Pablo Mesa. "Reintegración sin desmovilización: el caso de las milicias populares de Medellín," *Colombia Internacional* 77 (2013): pp. 217–239.

Ratchford III, J. Thomas. "Policing in partnership: Nicaraguan policies with implications for US Police forces," *Emory International Law Review* 32 (2017): p. 173.

Redacción DEM. "El 42 % cree que las pandillas mandan más que el Gobierno," *El Mundo*, 8 de noviembre de 2017.

Reisman, Lainie. "Breaking the vicious cycle: Responding to Central American youth gang violence," *SAIS Review of International Affairs* 26, no. 2 (2006): pp. 147–152.

Relly, Jeannine E. "Journalism in times of violence: Social media use by US and Mexican journalists working in northern Mexico," *Digital Journalism* 2, no. 4 (2014): pp. 507–523.

Reuters Staff. "El Salvador court to try former president for money laundering," *Reuters*, May 16, 2018.

Revista Factum. "CIDH ordena investigar amenazas contra periodistas de Revista Factum," *Revista Factum*, 3 de noviembre de 2017.

Roberts, Sam. "Francisco Flores, tainted Ex-President of El Salvador, dies at 56," *The New York Times*, February 2, 2016.

Robles, Frances. "Nicaragua protests grow increasingly violent, 100 killed since April," *The New York Times*, May 31, 2018.

Rodgers, Dennis and Robert Muggah. "Gangs as non-state armed groups: The Central American case," *Contemporary Security Policy* 30, no. 2 (2009): pp. 301–317.

Rosen, Jonathan D. "Estrategias contra-pandillas en América Central: prisión y mano dura no funcionan," *democraciaAbierta*, December 21, 2017, www.opendemocracy.net/democraciaabierta/jonathan-d-rosen/estrategias-contra-pandillas-en-am-rica-central-laprisi-n-y-la-ma, accessed June 13, 2018.

Rosen, Jonathan D. and Bruce M. Bagley. "Is Plan Colombia a model? An analysis of counternarcotics strategies in Colombia," *Global Security Review* 1 (2017): pp. 8–14.

Rosen, Jonathan D., Bruce M. Bagley, and Jorge Chabat, eds. *The Criminalization of States: The Relationship Between States and Organized Crime*. Lanham, MD: Lexington Books, 2019.

Rosen, Jonathan D. and Marten W. Brienen, eds. *Prisons in the Americas in the Twenty-First Century: A Human Dumping Ground*. Lanham, MD: Lexington Books, 2015.

Rosen, Jonathan D. and Hanna Samir Kassab, eds. *Fragile States in the Americas*. Lanham, MD: Lexington Books, 2016.

Rosen, Jonathan D. and Hanna Samir Kassab. *Drugs, Gangs, and Violence*. New York, NY: Palgrave Macmillan, 2018.

Rosen, Jonathan D. and Roberto Zepeda. *Organized Crime, Drug Trafficking, and Violence in Mexico: The Transition from Felipe Calderón to Enrique Peña Nieto*. Lanham, MD: Lexington Books, 2016.

Seligson, Mitchell A. "The impact of corruption on regime legitimacy: A comparative study of four Latin American countries," *The Journal of Politics* 64, no. 2 (2002): pp. 408–433.

Shelley, Louise. "Corruption and organized crime in Mexico in the post-PRI transition," *Journal of Contemporary Criminal Justice* 17, no. 3 (2001): pp. 213–231.

Shirk, David A. *Mexico's New Politics: The Pan and Democratic Change*. Boulder, CO: Lynne Rienner Publishers, 2005.

Shirk, David A. "Drug violence in Mexico: Data and analysis from 2001–2009," *Trends in Organized Crime* 13, no. 2–3 (2010): pp. 167–174.

Silva Ávalos, Héctor. "El Salvador violence rising despite 'extraordinary' anti-gang measures," *InSight Crime*, October 3, 2017, www.insightcrime.org/news/analysis/violence-el-salvador-rise-despite-extraordinary-anti-gang-measures/, accessed June 13, 2018.

Snyder, Richard and Angélica Durán Martínez. "Drugs, violence, and state-sponsored protection rackets in Mexico and Colombia," *Colombia Internacional* 70 (2009): pp. 61–91.

Stanley, William. "Building new police forces in El Salvador and Guatemala: Learning and counter-learning," *International Peacekeeping* 6, no. 4 (1999): pp. 113–134.

Stevens, Evelyn P. "Machismo and marianismo," *Society* 10, no. 6 (1973): pp. 57–63.

Sullivan, John P. "Maras morphing: Revisiting third generation gangs," *Global Crime* 7, no. 3–4 (2006): pp. 487–504.

Tate, Winifred. "Repeating past mistakes: Aiding counterinsurgency in Colombia," *NACLA Report on the Americas* 34, no. 2 (2000): pp. 16–19.

Thale, Geoff and Kevin Amaya. "Amid rising violence, El Salvador fails to address reports of extrajudicial killings," *WOLA*, November 3, 2017, www.wola.org/analysis/amid-rising-violence-el-salvador-fails-address-reports-extrajudicial-killings/, accessed June 21, 2018.

Thornton, Mark. *The Economics of Prohibition*. Salt Lake City, UT: University of Utah Press, 1991.

US Department of Treasury. "Treasury sanctions Latin American criminal organization," *US Department of Treasury*, October 11, 2012, www.treasury.gov/press-center/press-releases/Pages/tg1733.aspx, accessed March 9, 2020.

Van der Borgh, Chris and Wim Savenije. "De-securitising and re-securitising gang policies: The Funes government and gangs in El Salvador," *Journal of Latin American Studies* 47, no. 1 (2015): pp. 149–176.

Walker, Thomas W. *Nicaragua: Living in the Shadow of the Eagle*. Boulder, CO: Westview Press, 2003.

Ward, T.W. *Gangsters Without Borders: An Ethnography of a Salvadoran Street Gang*. New York, NY: Oxford University Press, 2013.

Watt, Peter and Roberto Zepeda. *Drug War Mexico: Politics, Neoliberalism and Violence in the New Narcoeconomy*. London, UK: Zed Books, 2012.

Weyland, Kurt Gerhard. "The politics of corruption in Latin America," *Journal of Democracy* 9, no. 2 (1998): pp. 108–121.

Wilkinson, Tracy. "Few Nicaraguans among Central America's exodus to U.S.," *Los Angeles Times*, August 30, 2014.

Wolf, Sonja. "Maras transnacionales: Origins and transformations of Central American street gangs," *Latin American Research Review* 45, no. 1 (2010): pp. 256–265.

Wolf, Sonja. "Mara Salvatrucha: The most dangerous street gang in the Americas?" *Latin American Politics and Society* 54, no. 1 (2012): pp. 65–99.

Wolf, Sonja. *Mano Dura: The Politics of Gang Control in El Salvador*. Austin, TX: University of Texas Press, 2017.

Wood, Elisabeth Jean. *Insurgent Collective Action and Civil War in El Salvador*. New York, NY: Cambridge University Press, 2003.

Youngers, Coletta and Eileen Rosin, eds. *Drugs and Democracy in Latin America: The Impact of US Policy*. Boulder, CO: Lynne Rienner Publishers, 2005.

5 External Actors and Power Vacuums

Many Latin American countries suffer from chronic underdevelopment and corruption. These elements, when taken together, create the perfect illicit business environment, which will attract organized criminal groups. Russian and Chinese mafia groups have enriched themselves in the trafficking of people and narcotics. People from China seek escape through Latin America en route to more developed countries like the United States and Canada for $70,000 a person according to some estimates.[1] Similarly, one group called the Triads is gaining ground from Mexico down to Argentina. This chapter traces the history of Chinese and Russian organized crime in Latin America. First, we will look at specific cases of narcotics trafficking. Second, we will focus on push and pull factors driving the human trafficking market. Applying the theoretical framework, the fragility of Latin America makes the location an ideal illicit business environment as well as providing a perfect transshipment point. In other words, this environment facilitates the meeting point of supply locations (people from China) and demand (the port of arrival).[2]

The first section will study the development of the Triads and their business model as they develop, expand, and protect their illicit supply chain. Special attention to the deep level of complex cooperation between the Triads and other domestic gang groups will be given. The Triads are aware of the costs of penetration into Latin America. Rather than directly challenging local groups, they cooperate with existing groups. In this manner, the Triads have become a serious force in Latin America since the early 1990s, leading one expert to conclude that they are "the most powerful and important ethnic group in transnational Chinese organized crime."[3]

The chapter also discusses the Russian mafia in Latin America. The Russian mob enriches itself in Latin America due to the wealth potential located there. Like any business, supply fills demand. Products flow into areas that demand certain commodities, and then there is payment for those products or services rendered. Since the fall of the Soviet Union, the Russian mafia has expanded into Latin America for those reasons. First, beginning in Russia, we see how corruption breeds further corruption, fueling not just a cycle of violence, but chronic and persistent underdevelopment, political and economic instability, and whole generations lost to war. Second, economic inequality is another consequence. As we shall see in the following section, corruption may flow finance to those in the right place at the right time. In the Soviet Union, bureaucrats, due to their management experience, could purchase state owned enterprises during the period of liberalization we know as Glasnost and Perestroika. These enterprises were allowed to produce great profits, and with all the work to build the company already complete, the new owner just had to make it run efficiently for a monetary reward.

Triads in Latin America and Local Cooperation

Like the Italian and Russian mafias, the Chinese mafia, most notably the Tongs[4] and the Triads, boast a proud, yet secretive, history.[5] The Triads were founded sometime between 1662 and 1722 by 120 rebel monks recruited by Ming Emperor Kangzi. Together, they sought to overthrow the conquering Qing dynasty and restore the Ming Dynasty.[6] The attempt ultimately failed, leading to violent reprisals by the occupying force that killed all but five monks. The surviving monks set up a secret society with the purpose of pushing the Qing out of their country. The five went to different parts of the state to mobilize the wider society.[7] Before departing, the monks developed a set of signs and symbols for recognizing each other. With the overthrow of the Qing Dynasty in 1911 by the Republic of China, the Triad's objective had finally been achieved. It is thought that this moment was pivotal to the movement into criminality. Legend has it that the name "Triad" came from a Western interpretation of the society's original name, the Tiandihui (the Heaven and Earth Society).[8] Tiandihui, the area around Three Rivers, is viewed as the founding place of the group.[9]

Chinese scholars are skeptical of this origin story, claiming that the Triads had very little to do with the aim of throwing out the Qing dynasty. They instead argue that the Triads offered people protection during the social and economic dislocation in the southern areas of the Fujian province.[10] From here, they expanded into other areas of China, most notably Hong Kong and the rest of mainland China.[11] From there, they spread into Southeast Asia, smuggling heroin into the United States.[12] To be successful, the Triads developed connections with local groups such as the Sinaloa cartel and Los Zetas in Mexico to reduce the risk of narcotics trafficking. A US Senate report in 1986 stated:

> The ones who are responsible for the importation and the financing are basically the business people—generally, importers and exporters and financiers. . . . They make the arrangements for the heroin to go directly from Southeast Asia to the gang, where the gang is then responsible for distribution.[13]

For example, the first heroin shipment in 1983 transported less than 10 kilograms of heroin from Bangkok, Thailand, to Malaysia, to Singapore, and to its final port in Toronto, Canada.[14] In another case, three kilograms of heroin moved from Thailand to Japan to New York City in the United States. From there, the heroin was sold to African-American gangs who then sold it on the street across the East Coast.[15] Hence, from these and many more examples, the Triads can be understood as middlemen, not wanting to remake the wheel or encroach on other gangs. Instead, they preferred to work with already established gangs and individuals who were well experienced and organized in a particular field of illicit business.

Today, it seems the Triads are pushing forward with a similar strategy of working with local groups to reduce the risk of getting caught. Like Southeast Asia, Latin America seems to be an ideal location. Latin American cartels, whether in Colombia, Peru, Argentina, Bolivia, or Mexico, already have the know-how and appropriate skillset to supply narcotics. This fact provides a unique opportunity for the Triads in the import and export business.

In Mexico, the Triads are cooperating with the Sinaloa cartel in the manufacture and sale of methamphetamine.[16] At the core of this cooperation is the idea of mutual comparative advantage: the Chinese provide the raw materials manufactured legally in China (due to loosened controls), and the Mexican mafia does the manufacturing. Robert Bunker, a security expert, describes how this relationship spills into other illicit areas:

> These cartels benefit via linkages with Chinese organized crime by obtaining access to bulk precursor chemicals whose regulation has been severely tightened in Mexico and the United States. . . . The Chinese and HK triads get cash providing the bulk of precursor materials . . . small arms and ammunition.[17]

Bunker also notes that the network has even begun a human trafficking branch, funneling people from China as well as other Asian countries into the United States.

Returning to the discussion of cooperation in the development and sale of synthetic drugs, in 2014, one major narcotics trafficker, Joaquín "El Chapo" Guzmán Loera of the Sinaloa cartel, put together the alliance between his group and two other Triads. One group, known as the 14K Triad, is 25,000 members strong, while the other, the Sun Yee On, boasts over 50,000 members.[18] Once the Triads transport the synthetic drug ingredients to ports in Guatemala and El Salvador, the Sinaloa cartel drives the product to the factory located in secret areas throughout Mexico. Once the drugs are made, they are then delivered to markets in the United States, Canada, Europe, Africa, and locations in Latin America like Argentina, Guatemala, El Salvador, and Mexico.[19]

In addition to supplying methamphetamine ingredients to the Sinaloa cartel, the Triads maintain close relationships with traffickers in major demand locations in American cities. Similarly, the Sinaloa cartel maintains locations in Africa and Russia.[20] Thus, they have a global presence. Indeed, it seems as if the Triads have cornered the market in the sale of precursor chemicals so much so that they control a major profit source. In one instance, the Mexican government seized 32 tons of chemicals linked to methamphetamine production.[21] In 2014, the Mexican government seized 900 tons of chemicals in a six-month period.[22] Similar shipments may be worth up to $10 billion, a highly profitable enterprise.

The Triads also work with Los Zetas and the Knights Templar, two rivals of the Sinaloa cartel. Such freedom to operate regardless of affiliation is significant as it allows the Triads the opportunity to maximize profit in the region regardless of inter-cartel conflict.[23] Working with rival groups allows the Triads the opportunity to break into Central American republics, most notably Honduras, Guatemala, and El Salvador.[24] Connections between gangs freely operating in those states allow the Triads even more space in which to maneuver.[25] Furthermore, there is potential to work with the FARC.[26] Connections do not end there, as we begin to see methamphetamine move to West and North Africa.[27] Associations with Al Qaeda in North Africa are suspected.[28] A Lebanese narcotics trafficker working in Latin America, Chrekry Harb, donates 12 percent of his income to the terrorist group Hezbollah.[29] Some reports have emerged that Los Zetas began cooperating with Hezbollah in the trafficking of illicit goods as early as 2011.[30] Evidence also suggests that the Triads are exporting other drugs, like cocaine, to Asia.[31]

Like many terrorist and criminal groups, the tri-border area is a hotbed of illegal activity.[32] This is where Argentina, Paraguay, and Brazil meet, and it is heavily porous and insecure—textbook state fragility.[33] Some experts contend that the Triads, along with Iranian, Hezbollah, and Hamas networks and other cartels operate free of law enforcement in this region.[34] Here, criminal groups and terrorist organizations have been working together to achieve their goals alongside the Triads and Hezbollah.[35] Although many have argued that this relationship may be exaggerated, and that there are bigger threats to be concerned about, other experts maintain that these groups exist in the region.[36]

The production of fentanyl is another concern similar to the production of methamphetamine in that chemical compounds are shipped to Mexico for processing.[37] These chemical compounds are shipped legally because they differ on a molecular level when compared to fentanyl. However, they can be transformed and then smuggled into the United States.[38] Chinese mafia connections to Mexican cartels are the driving force of the exportation of fentanyl into the United States. The Chinese government has done little to actually curb the supply of these compound chemicals, deferring to the demand of the United States as being at the core of the problem.[39] Yu Haibin of the China National Narcotics Control Commission relays this attitude: "The biggest difficulty China faces in opioid control is that such drugs are in enormous demand in the U.S."[40] In the United States, a 2018 report showed that of the 42,249 opioid-related overdose deaths in 2016, fentanyl was used in 19,413 (45.9 percent of total deaths).[41]

Central American states have also faced increased criminal activity due to their location as a midway point between major supply locations in Mexico and demand in the United States.[42] Honduras and El Salvador continue to face serious strain. Honduras is the number one cocaine transshipment route into the United States from Mexico.[43] The forested areas in that country provide excellent cover, with corrupt practices assuring concealment. There, the drugs are sent on go-fast boats into Guatemalan areas with little to no law enforcement.[44] According to US officials, entire villages are dependent on cocaine trafficking:

> When the traffickers are unloading a go-fast boat in (the Atlantic coast province of) Gracias a Dios, you can sometimes see 70 to 100 people of all ages out there helping unload it. . . . The traffickers look for support among local populations.[45]

El Salvador faces a similar predicament.[46]

The Triads also maintain a serious presence in South America. In his article "Chinese Organized Crime in Latin America," R. Evan Ellis documents the many cities and sites of major Triads activity, from Venezuela and the islands of Trinidad and Tobago in the north to the city of Mendoza in Argentina.[47] The Triads run several operations wherever there are sizable Chinese minority populations. This is because, as Evan Ellis notes, non-members of the Triads are less likely to turn informant against the organized criminal group. This could be for several reasons, which range from nationalistic pride to active participation.[48] Fear may be another reason for not cooperating with Argentinian law enforcement. Extortion of Chinese-Argentinian businesses has plagued the city for 10 years. There have also been instances of kidnapping and murder.[49] The Chinese businesses there may also be engaged in illegal activity, which explains their reluctance to work with law enforcement. A federal police officer, Camilla S. Cabello, describes the situation:

> Chinese people just work with cash and never use credit cards. We do not have any idea of how they import their products. . . . We do not understand anything to what they say. Besides, the Chinese do not want the help of the Argentine police.[50]

These businesses may be hosting illegal immigrants, as Argentina does not have any reliable statistics keeping track of immigration.[51]

Of less importance in terms of national security and human health is the trafficking of contraband goods such as software and clothing.[52] Since the 1990s, a city named Ciudad del Este has served as the center for a number of schemes such as "counterfeit goods, smuggling, cheap electronics and clothing, drug-trafficking, prostitution, the trade of minors and the small arms trade."[53] This location is ideal as the Triads are sprinkled in with other Chinese minorities living there legally and illegally.[54]

The mindset of the Triads is ultimately mercenary; they have no allegiances other than to the accumulation of wealth.[55] Pursuing narcotics trafficking in today's globalized world comes with its successes and its failures. However, attitudes toward failure, namely, being caught by law enforcement, increase the drive of criminal groups. For instance, in an interview, one Triads member named Johnny Kon helps us understand the motivation of the group:

I think it is important for you to know that although we lost half our heroin shipments to law enforcement or stealing that did not discourage us from continuing in the business. It only pushed us to smuggle more drugs to make up the losses.[56]

Kon was one the most notorious heroin smugglers, successfully importing a half ton of product in three years, from 1984 to when he was caught in 1987.

Yet countering the Triads has proved remarkably difficult due to their profiting off of the fragility of the region. According to a study done by the US-China Economic and Security Review Commission, the Triads as well as other organized criminal networks across Latin America utilize Latin American state fragility to enrich themselves.[57] Since China allows the sale of precursor chemicals, the Triads have the freedom to move their product from point A to point B.[58] The report pinpoints several areas that the Triads depend on to maximize profitability, all stemming from state fragility and indirect Chinese cooptation:

- Mislabeling: Mislabeling shipments of precursor chemicals is one way Chinese drug traffickers avoid detection by US and foreign authorities.
- Modifying Chemicals: Precursors can also be chemically modified, making them technically legal and permissible to export. These modified chemicals contain compounds similar to banned precursors and are designed to mimic their use, but are not included on the UN or US lists of banned chemicals.
- Shipping Pre-Precursor Chemicals: As precursor chemicals have become more difficult to ship undetected, Chinese drug traffickers have begun transporting pre-precursors, or the chemicals used to create precursors. By shipping noncontrolled pre-precursor chemicals—including APAAN (alpha-phenylacetoacetonitrile), benzaldehyde, and nitroethane, among others—traffickers are able to avoid detection.
- Insufficient Partner Country Counternarcotic Capabilities: Many Central American countries still lack the institutional and regulatory capabilities to identify and seize illegal precursor chemical shipments. Chinese drug traffickers take advantage of these weaknesses in global counternarcotic operations, sending precursor chemicals to countries where the chances of detection and seizure are lower.
- Illegal Activity: Because they are illicit, drug shipments facilitated by criminal organizations limit the effectiveness of the PICS and the PEN system, customs and port authority inspections, and other regulations governing precursor flows.[59]

What can be done to face these challenges? Increased cooperation between Mexico, China, and the United States would be a logical approach. Chinese customs agents and other security forces must combat trafficking, and the government must close loopholes and clamp down on exporters. The United States must also begin to deal with demand. Jorge Chabat recommends institutional reform across all involved states: "As part of international cooperation, institutions should be strengthened in all countries at the international level in the fight against synthetic drugs."[60] These reforms should be based on a mutual understanding that all states have something to lose from the status quo. This makes negotiation and change a necessity going forward. However, as legitimate exchange between China and Latin America continues, we may expect continued illicit trafficking.[61] It is altogether possible that closer ties will bring more opportunities for Triads as well as for Latin American cartels and gangs.

Human Trafficking in Latin America

According to a 2002 report, Guatemala was marked as "a significant transit country for alien smuggling, both from neighboring Central American countries and Ecuador and from China, Taiwan, and South Asia."[62] Human trafficking has been a serious problem for the region for many decades. In 2014, a report by the International Labour Organization (ILO) estimates that there are 21 million persons trafficked each year, making it a $150 billion per year business.[63] If China is indeed becoming more developed and wealthier, what could possibly explain these numbers? This section will look at Chinese state fragility in terms of underdevelopment and the push factors that drive the human trafficking market. As noted in the previous section, the Triads are a major force creating and maintaining this illicit market of people. They create the infrastructure necessary for people to be brought into Latin America, working with Latin American criminal groups to assure entry into developed states.[64]

Push-Pull Factors that Drive the Human Trafficking Market

What are the push-pull forces that encourage people to leave their state and enter another illegally? How exactly does the infrastructure facilitate this work? The political and economic lack of robust economic growth coupled with a static and unequal political system is a main contributor. While China is indeed an economic powerhouse and a rising military power, its economic system lacks a creative-deterrence mechanism due to its one-party system. A fundamental lack of innovation could be a possible driver of poor job security for unskilled labor. The closer China and the states of Latin America become, the more people will be trafficked into the region.[65]

According to a February 2016 Migration Policy Institute report, job insecurity in China is the cause for the increase.[66] The report argues that wealthier, skilled Chinese looking for opportunity abroad usually find it easier to migrate. Poorer, unskilled workers have a more difficult time given changes in regulations and legal expenses. The report states that new regulations are now in place to discourage legal migration altogether.[67] The report also finds that these government reforms have even more negative effects that increase social and economic inequality in China.[68] This means unskilled laborers are under pressure to find alternative means of switching their visas or affording new ones. All the while, they are increasingly becoming worse off. This has a wide range of effects on illegal immigration, forcing people to take drastic measures to find a better life. Slowing economic growth in the Chinese economy combined with a high population means higher than usual levels of unemployment. Thus, individuals who attempt to find employment in other countries are vulnerable to being trafficked.[69] With more people anxious for work, the demand for being trafficked into other states increased. In June 2016, a San Diego Border Patrol report recorded a 1,281 percent increase in the number of Chinese caught crossing illegally in the previous eight months.[70] In total, it is estimated that 268,000 Chinese are living illegally in the United States.[71] This is of course small when compared to other illegal immigrants. As of June 2018, Mexican numbers were estimated at 6,177,000 individuals, with the next largest being Guatemalans at 723,000.[72] Other countries in Latin America have also experienced high levels of Chinese human trafficking. Since 2010, Argentina has seen an increase in convictions in human trafficking, averaging about two per month.[73] Paraguay, Brazil, Bolivia, and the Dominican Republic record similar figures. These individuals are seeking a better life but often fall victim to sexual exploitation and slavery.

Latin American states experiencing an influx of Chinese human trafficking often serve as a transit point. For instance, Brazil serves as a transshipment point for individuals seeking a foothold in the region.[74] As Brazil is an easily corruptible state, immigration officials make approximately $12,000 for trafficked persons to bypass customs and security.[75] Some of these individuals are then sold into slavery, doing hard labor in areas like cattle ranching, mining, logging, agriculture, or manufacturing.[76] A terrible instance of slave labor involved a large number of Chinese workers coming to Brazil on the promise of a $570 monthly salary with free room and board. Upon arrival, worker passports were taken away. They were then forced to work under slave-like conditions.[77] Peru and Argentina also facilitate the trafficking of illegal Chinese citizens for slave labor.[78] Like Brazil, people are brought in through bribery.

Argentina's case of human trafficking and these accounts of the Chinese mafia illuminate dynamic transnationalism. As mentioned earlier, the Triads have a foothold wherever there is a sizable Chinese minority. On November 30, 2016, Argentina clamped down on a major Chinese smuggling ring, capturing major organizing members. Police forces also arrested the head of Argentina's national migration commission, Leonardo Javier Rende, on bribery charges.[79] These arrests created a vacuum in the criminal group, leading to clashes.[80] While this may seem like progress, further examination shows the issue to be more complicated. People are funneled into Argentina through other Latin American states like Bolivia and Brazil. Since there is a sizable Chinese minority in Argentina, many migrants prefer to go there to settle.[81] State fragility in developing states in Latin America provides organized criminal groups with the business environment necessary to make enormous profits. However, we cannot simply conclude by placing blame on the weakness of political institutions in Latin America. Since migrants are coming from China, and Chinese organized crime networks are the major beneficiaries, then it must be concluded that the Chinese state itself is fragile.

Criminal Networks and State Fragility

This chapter highlights the need for institutional change and reform in both Latin America and China. Both states have serious problems to deal with, specifically their political structures that hinder economic growth and development. Corruption and an established organized criminal element promote further crime.[82] Human trafficking is a source of income for the Triads because there is a demand to leave the state of China. The problem itself is the Chinese political system. China does not have strong inclusive democratic institutions. It wields a heavy hand against its citizens, countenances corrupt practices, and maintains a stagnant and altogether inflexible economic system and an untenable foreign policy of expansion (specifically its controversial island building activity in the South China Sea). The political system retards the economic system, which may be the reason for the success of the Triads and the need for unskilled persons to leave the state. Linked to China's political weaknesses are other factors that are ultimately weakening the regime's hold: corruption, poor economic and environmental regulation, extreme poverty, a rising middle class, dependence on coal, unclean air, and so forth greatly hinder Chinese development and undermine their sovereignty.[83] The Triads take advantage of the weakness of the political, economic, and social system, giving rise to its wealth and power globally. Thus, as argued, China's corrupt political system and its lack of democratic political institutions contribute to the success of the Triads and their infiltration into Latin America.

Due to the vacuum created by Latin American state fragility (a product of underdevelopment and corruption), non-state organized criminal actors are filling the void. The opportunity presented by state weakness is astounding when considering wealth potential. Johnny Kon, the most infamous Triads heroin trafficker in the 1980s, took advantage of the fragility of Latin American states to store his wealth and property in Panama, Paraguay, and Bolivia.[84] This is true in New York City and San Francisco as well. Today, however, Latin America is an ideal place to launder money. In 2007, Panama City, Panama, experienced a property boom like no other due to the influx of drug profit.[85] One anonymous US government official describes the process: "It has become more difficult to transfer money through banks, so we have seen a lot more people carrying cash into Panama through Panama City airport."[86] Furthermore, increasing legitimate economic ties with China is also making it easier to launder money.[87] One such case is the Brazilian gang First Capital Command, which uses Chinese banks and Brazilian front companies to buy weapons and launder money. Increasing economic ties will only make this process easier.

While organized criminal groups do seek out weak and fragile states in an effort to expand their economic influence, there is also an increase in Triads activity in developed states of North America and Europe as well as in Australia, directing sales to overseas demand locations.[88] The following is a listing of areas of Triads activity in these regions:

- Chinese organized crime has established a significant foothold in Australian cities, and Australian authorities consider it a serious law enforcement problem.
- Chinese trafficking groups still use routes that were established through Eastern Europe in the corrupt late-Communist era.
- "Snakehead" groups, which move illegal Chinese migrants to Western Europe and North America using networks of specialized accomplices in local communities, are an active and persistent feature of Chinese crime in many countries.
- In recent years, Chinese criminal activity in Japan has increased noticeably, often in cooperation with indigenous groups.
- Canada has become an important site for Chinese narcotics trafficking and financial crimes.
- In the United States, Chinese groups established their initial footholds on the West Coast and in New York City; from there, they have spread to other large metropolitan areas, and their activities have diversified.
- Chinese criminal activity in Russia has been concentrated in Moscow and the Russian Far East, where numerous forms of trafficking have proliferated.
- Several countries of Southeast Asia are the sites of narcotics and human trafficking, money laundering, and counterfeiting of electronic products.[89]

The next section will show that similar trends exist in Russia. Russian economic weakness and the success of its organized criminal networks are fundamentally connected. A culture of corruption seems to be institutionalized. Since Latin America shares a similar world problem, we see penetration into areas that benefit all parties. This seemingly peaceful pursuit of wealth among these actors is ultimately to their benefit at the expense of citizens choosing more legitimate enterprises.

The Russian Mafia: A Global Enterprise

The Russian mafia has sought to operate in states plagued by corruption. It, along with other mafia groups from Italy and Albania, operates in Mexico.[90] These groups take advantage of the poorly regulated casino industry there.[91] They are involved with various illicit activities (e.g., drugs, prostitution, and gambling).[92] There is a relationship between corrupt states and organized crime groups. The success of the Russian mob has everything to do with the three factors explored in this book's theoretical framework, which happen to be present in Latin America: rampant poverty, stark corruption, and thus, ultimately, fragile state institutions. Like the Triads, the Russian mafia seeks out areas of common cooperation and pursues them peaceably with cartels that already exist in Latin America. Deals have been struck between major Colombian networks including rebel and terrorist groups operating freely in provinces outside state control. The FARC and ELN are major players here as they sell cocaine to the Russian mafia in exchange for weapons. According to reports, the exchange rate was negotiated to one gun per kilogram of cocaine.[93] Each party benefitted from the exchange in terms of their needs: the rebel groups need arms and, the Russian mafia group in question needed cocaine to expand business back home.

Apart from Colombia, the Russian mafia can be found in several other Latin American areas, from Ecuador and Peru to Honduras down to southern cone nations. State fragility within these nations allows mafia members to hide from authorities seeking to extradite them, sometimes in plain sight. In 2012, authorities finally arrested Russian criminal Grigory Basalygin for drug trafficking.[94] The state is useful to criminal groups for many reasons. One reason that could easily be overlooked is that it has little to no criminal control and little to no border control.[95] This fact, coupled with the waiving of all visa requirements to enter the state, made Ecuador a haven for organized crime and even terrorist activity. In 2008, Osama bin Laden's own nephew was found hiding in Quito.[96] As a result, Ecuador is an interesting fragile state from which organized criminals operate diplomatic efforts. However, over two decades, criminal networks have slowly penetrated the state. Due to Ecuador's permeable borders, human trafficking organized by the Russian (as well as the Chinese) mafia has grown steadily.[97]

In this case, Ecuador has served as a meeting ground for the various cartels from different parts of the globe.[98] This is all part of a wider trend of cartels to cooperate rather than compete. Some groups choose to be smaller to bolster concealment of operation and minimize the chance of being penetrated by an informant.[99] This is known as the Predatory Micro-Network. It is defined as "a set of individuals who work together in a specific territory to exploit others (persons, groups or sector) for personal and organizational profit, taking advantage of the black-market and informality, and taxing legal and criminals activities therein."[100] While the domestic area becomes a major victim of cartel and gang violence and predation, it also means that these groups will have to cooperate with one another for access to other areas and markets. Such a dramatic move has only increased the viability of the Russian mafia and its access to overseas markets.

The use of Predatory Micro-Networks to ensure concealment still requires the use of weaponry for defense against other groups. In that regard, the Russian mafia is a major player. In Honduras, gun violence remains among the highest in the region.[101] The violence there has proved to be quite a boon to suppliers as violence breeds insecurity and demand for guns.[102] This violence assisted by the Russian mafia spills over into neighboring states, worsening the already dire situation.[103]

Increasing violence in the region still does not negate the fact that serious coordination efforts between all factions are being carried out. A recent report describes relations between Russian and Latin American criminal groups.[104] In this report, Russian, Central American, and Mexican criminal networks collaborated in several drug smuggling projects. There were no reports of gang wars or conflicts; the cooperation between these two groups was mature and advanced.[105] The dramatic presence of the Russian mafia since the fall of the Soviet Union has brought them untold wealth. From the Russian perspective, the Russian mafia has worsened the economic and political climate in Russia despite the election of Vladimir Putin.

The more powerful the Russian mafia, the more of a challenge it is to state power. This fact has forced Russian law enforcement to step up efforts in Latin America, increasing their presence there.[106] However, rather than cooperating with established institutions led by the United States, Russia has sought to go it alone and utilize a heavy-handed approach toward crime.[107] Interestingly, Russia in the past criticized American heavy-handed approaches toward crime in Latin America. Regardless, such a policy has led to American suspicion that Russia is itself moving in on the traditional American sphere of influence in Latin America. During a time where lines are being drawn in Europe over the Russian annexation of Crimea, Americans are indeed quite suspicious of any kind of Russian involvement, especially when many suspect that the Russian mafia and the Russian state are actually working together toward similar goals.[108] One instance of this was in February 2018, when a half ton of cocaine was discovered at the Russian embassy in Argentina.[109] A 14-month investigation illuminated the depth of corruption in Russia, as Russian assets were being used to conceal and transport narcotics in Europe.[110] This episode would lead anyone to conclude that corruption causes state fragility, which in turn breeds illicit markets.

Conclusion

In China, a large population of low-skilled labor combined with a slowing Chinese economy has increased the demand for alternatives. The Triads are one of the major criminal groups preying upon unskilled individuals seeking wealth and opportunity outside of the state that forgot them. This is a relatively new phenomenon, beginning in 1993 with the alliance between the Chinese mafia and Latin American gangs.[111] Hence, the learning curve has already been established and the alliance still holds due to the profitability of the illegal enterprise. Further, as described in the previous section, the intelligent relationships developed by the Triads with local groups in Latin America are at the core of success. They have been shipping narcotics, arms, and, most importantly, precursor chemicals necessary for the cooking of methamphetamine Experts note:

- Chinese crime organizations outside China and Taiwan are varied in size and flexible in structure, retaining some traditional triad and tong structures, but adapting readily to conditions in host countries.

- Chinese crime organizations are found in most world population centers having substantial ethnic Chinese populations.
- In most cases, the starting point of Chinese crime is extortion and protection practiced against indigenous Chinese populations; subsequently, expansion into other crimes and into the general population often occurs.
- Chinese groups adjust pragmatically to conditions in a country; for example, law enforcement in France has forced a movement away from narcotics trafficking toward trafficking in humans.
- Several large criminal groups have established footholds in more than one country; numerous smaller groups are independent or allied with the large groups in a particular country.
- In some countries, Chinese groups have formed pragmatic, temporary alliances with other ethnic criminal groups.[112]

Altogether, much more must be done to stem the flow of illicit goods, and the road may be through China. Their lack of regulation over precursor chemicals as well as their development strategy may be inherent sources of vulnerability for Latin America and the world. If the Triads continue to benefit from the way things are, it is altogether possible to expect them to challenge the Chinese state in the years to come if attempts to regulate precursor chemicals fail.

Organized crime groups from China and Russia will take advantage of power vacuums that are present in Latin America. The Russian mafia and Chinese organized crime groups are opportunists and are looking to expand their markets. Countries that have high levels of corruption and weak institutions serve as an ideal place for organized crime groups, including external actors. Latin American countries must strengthen institutions in an effort to decrease the power vacuums that are present, which enables external criminal actors to thrive.

Notes

1. R. Evan Ellis, "Chinese organized crime in Latin America," *Prism: A Journal of the Center for Complex Operations* 4, no. 1 (2012): p. 67.
2. Economic Commission for Latin America and the Caribbean (ECLAC), *Latin America and the Caribbean in the World Economy: 2008–2009* (New York, NY: ECLAC, 2009).
3. Willard Myers, "The emerging threat of transnational organized crime from the East," *Crime, Law and Social Change* 24 (1994): 195; cited in Ko-Lin Chin, Sheldon Zhang, and Robert J. Kelly, "Transnational Chinese organized crime activities: Patterns and emerging trends," *Transnational Organized Crime* 4, no. 3–4 (2002): p. 128.
4. Norman W. Philcox, *An Introduction to Organized Crime* (Springfield: Charles C. Thomas Publisher, 1978), p. 18.
5. Michelle Chen, "A cultural crossroads at the 'bloody angle': The Chinatown Tongs and the development of New York City's Chinese American community," *Journal of Urban History* 40, no. 2 (2014): p. 360.
6. Yiu-kong Chu, *The Triads as Business* (London: Taylor and Francis, 2002), p. 11.

7. Ibid.

8. Ibid., p. 12.

9. Ibid., p. 13.

10. Ibid., p. 12.

11. For an in-depth look at the history and development of the Triads, please see: Glenn E. Curtis, Seth L. Elan, Rexford A. Hudson, and Nina A. Kollars, "Transnational activities of Chinese crime organizations," *Trends in Organized Crime* 7, no. 3 (2002): pp. 19–57.

12. Ibid., p. 112.

13. Quoted in Ko Lin Chin, *Chinese Subculture and Criminality: Non-traditional Crime Groups in America* (New York, NY: Greenwood Press, 1990), p. 152.

14. Yiu-kong Chu, *The Triads as Business* (London: Taylor and Francis, 2002), p. 113.

15. Ibid.

16. Bryan Harris, "Hong Kong triads supply meth ingredients to Mexican drug cartels," *South China Morning Post*, January 12, 2014.

17. Ibid.

18. Julieta Pelcastrem, "'El Chapo' conspires with Chinese mafias to produce synthetic drugs in Latin America," *Diálogo Americas*, February 19, 2014.

19. Ibid.

20. Peter Shadbolt, "Philippines raid reveals Mexican drug cartel presence in Asia," *CNN*, February 25, 2014.

21. Geoffrey Ramsey, "Mexico seizes 32 tons of Chinese precursor chemicals," *InSight Crime*, May 8, 2012, www.insightcrime.org/news-briefs/mexico-seizes-32-tons-of-chinese-precursor-chemicals, accessed June 25, 2018; see also R. Evan Ellis, "Chinese organized crime in Latin America."

22. Bryan Harris, "Hong Kong triads supply meth ingredients to Mexican drug cartels," *South China Morning Post*, January 12, 2014.

23. Peter Kouretsos, "Dragon on the border: Mexican and Chinese transnational criminal networks and implications for the United States," *Small Wars Journal*, http://smallwarsjournal.com/jrnl/art/dragon-on-the-border-mexican-and-chinese-transnational-criminal-networks-and-implications-f, accessed June 2, 2018.

24. Lindsay Stewart and Jennifer Griffin, "America's third war: US secretly trains Guatemalan Forces," *FOXNEWS*, December 14, 2010.

25. Manu Brabo, "Gang wars in El Salvador, bloodiest year," *Al Jazeera*, September 16, 2015.

26. Hannah Stone, "FARC-Mexican cartel middlemen captured in Colombia," *Colombia Reports*, August 31, 2010, colombiareports.com/colombia-news/news/11604-farc-mexican-cartel-middlemen-captured-in-colombia.html, accessed June 25, 2018.

27. Alex Pena, "DEA: Mexican drug cartels reach further across Africa," *VOA*, June 15, 2012.

28. Phillip Sherwell, "Cocaine, kidnapping and the Al Qaeda cash squeeze," *Sunday Telegraph*, March 6, 2010; Aida Alami, "Morocco battles Al Qaeda in the Islamic Maghreb," *Global Post*, November 2, 2010.

29. Stephen Dudley, "Terrorism and crime in the Americas—'It's business'," *InSight Crime*, April 9, 2014, www.insightcrime.org/news-analysis/terrorism-and-crime-in-the-americas-its-business, accessed June 25, 2018.

30. Jason Ryan, "Lebanese drug lord charged in US: Links to Zetas and Hezbollah," *ABC News*, December 13, 2011.

31. "Arestan a 5 mexicanos en Hong Kong por tráfico de droga," *Milenio*, September 19, 2011.

32. Gregory Weeks, *US and Latin American Relations* (New York, NY: Pearson, 2008), p. 251.

33. Edwin Mora, "Napolitano: Terrorist enter US from Mexico 'From time to time'," *Cnsnews.com*, July 30, 2012.
34. For more on this issue, see Guido Nejamkis, "Iran set up terrorist networks in Latin America: Argentine prosecutor," *Reuters*, May 29, 2013; Ana R. Sverdlick, "Terrorists and organized crime entrepreneurs in the 'triple frontier' among Argentina, Brazil, and Paraguay," *Trends in Organized Crime* 9, no. 2 (2005): pp. 84–93; Matthew Levitt, "Iranian and Hezbollah operations in South America: Then and now," *Prism: A Journal of the Center for Complex Operations* 5, no. 4 (2015): p. 118.
35. "Paraguay: 'Strong ties' seen between Hong Kong Mafia, tri-border based Hizballah," *ABC Color*, November 22, 2002.
36. Geoffrey Ramsey, "Hezbollah in Latin America: An over-hyped threat?" *CS Monitor*, January 13, 2012.
37. Esmé E. Deprez, Li Hui and Ken Wills, "Deadly Chinese Fentanyl is creating a new era of drug kingpins," *Bloomberg*, May 22, 2018.
38. Sean O'Connor, "Fentanyl: China's deadly export to the United States," *US-China Economic and Security Review Commission* (2017), p. 6.
39. Dan Levin, "In China, illegal drugs are sold online in an unbridled market," *The New York Times*, June 21, 2015.
40. Esmé E. Deprez, Li Hui and Ken Wills "Deadly Chinese Fentanyl is creating a new era of drug kingpins."
41. "Nearly half of opioid-related overdose deaths involve fentanyl," *National Institute of Drug Abuse*, May 1, 2018.
42. See: United Nations Office on Drugs and Crime (UNODC), *Transnational Organized Crime in Central America and the Caribbean: A Threat Assessment* (New York, NY: UNODC, 2012).
43. Mark Stevenson, "Honduras becomes main transit route for cocaine trafficking," *Huffington Post*, December 30, 2011.
44. Ibid.
45. Ibid.
46. Jason Beaubien, "El Salvador fears ties between cartels, street gangs," *National Public Radio*, June 1, 2011.
47. R. Evan Ellis, "Chinese organized crime in Latin America," p. 65.
48. Ibid., p. 67.
49. Kamilia Lahrichi, "Chinese criminal gangs hit Argentina," *Huffington Post*, October 5, 2016.
50. Quoted in ibid.
51. Ibid.
52. R. Evan Ellis, "Chinese organized crime in Latin America," p. 65.
53. Khatchik der Ghougassian, "Developing a sub-regional approach to combat weapons proliferation," *Connecting Weapons with Violence* (ISS Monograph no. 25, May 1998).
54. LaVerle B. Berry, Glenn E. Curtis, Seth L. Elan, Rexford A. Hudson and Nina A. Kollars, *Transnational Activities of Chinese Crime Organizations* (Washington, DC: Library of Congress, 2003), p. 2.
55. Diane Stormont, "Hong Kong's secret triad societies spread their wings," *Reuters Report*, November 6, 1994.
56. Quoted in Yiu-kong Chu, *The Triads as Business*, p. 114.
57. Sean O'Connor, *Meth Precursor Chemicals from China: Implications for the United States* (Washington, DC: US-China Economic and Security Review Commission, 2016), p. 12.
58. Joshua Philipp, "China is fueling a drug war against the US," *Epoch Times*, December 18, 2015.

59. Sean O'Connor, *Meth Precursor Chemicals from China: Implications for the United States* (Washington, DC: U.S.-China Economic and Security Review Commission, 2016), p. 3; see also Joshua Philipp, "China is fueling a drug war against the US," *Epoch Times*, December 18, 2015, pp. 12–13.

60. Jorge Chabat quoted in Julieta Pelcastre, "'El Chapo' conspires with Chinese mafias to produce synthetic drugs in Latin America," *Diálogo Americas*, February 19, 2014.

61. United Nations Economic Commission on Latin America and the Caribbean (ECLAC), *Chinese Foreign Direct Investment in Latin America and the Caribbean: China-Latin America Cross-Council Taskforce* (Abu Dhabi: ECLAC, 2013).

62. US Department of State, *Guatemala: Country Reports on Human Rights Practices* (Washington, DC: US Department of State, 2002), p. 44.

63. "Human trafficking by the numbers," *Human Rights First*, www.humanrights-first.org/resource/human-trafficking-numbers, accessed June 25, 2018; "Forced labour, modern slavery and human trafficking," International Labour Organization, www.ilo.org/global/topics/forced-labour/lang-en/index.htm, accessed June 25, 2018.

64. "Illegal Chinese immigrants are flocking to San Diego, smuggled over the border with Mexico," *South China Morning Post*, June 8, 2016.

65. Sheldon X. Zhang and Chin Ko-lin, *The Social Organization of Chinese Human Smuggling: A Cross National Study* (San Diego, CA: San Diego State University, 2006).

66. Biao Xiang, *Emigration Trends and Policies in China* (Washington DC: Migration Policy Institute, 2016), p. 1.

67. Ibid.

68. Ibid.

69. Antje Dieterich, "Human trafficking of Chinese citizens is big business in Argentina," *InSight Crime*, September 20, 2016, www.insightcrime.org/news-briefs/human-trafficking-big-business-china-argentina, accessed June 25, 2018, p. 2.

70. Rachel Brown, "Chinese human smuggling and the U.S. border security debate," *Council on Foreign Relations*, July 18, 2016; "Illegal Chinese immigrants are flocking to San Diego, smuggled over the border with Mexico," *South China Morning Post*, June 8, 2016.

71. "Profile of the unauthorized population: United States," *Migration Policy Center*, www.migrationpolicy.org/data/unauthorized-immigrant-population/state/US, accessed June 3, 2018.

72. Ibid.

73. Miriam Wells, "Report shows dynamics of human trafficking in Argentina," *InSight Crime*, June 24, 2013, www.insightcrime.org/news-briefs/report-breaks-down-dynamics-of-human-trafficking-in-argentina, accessed June 25, 2018; Gonzalo Prado, "Cada dos meses se dicta una sentencia por trata de personas," *La Nación*, 24 de junio de 2013.

74. James Bargent, "Corruption fuels China-Brazil human trafficking," *InSight Crime*, August 5, 2015, www.insightcrime.org/news-briefs/corruption-fuels-china-brazil-human-trafficking, accessed June 25, 2018.

75. Ibid.

76. James Bargent, "Sweatshop raid raises concerns over Peru to Brazil human trafficking," *InSight Crime*, March 13, 2014, www.insightcrime.org/news/brief/sweatshop-raid-raises-concern-over-peru-to-brazil-human-trafficking/, accessed June 25, 2018.

77. James Bargent, "Corruption fuels China-Brazil human trafficking."

78. James Bargent, "Sweatshop raid raises concerns over Peru to Brazil human trafficking."

79. David Gagne, "Investigation of Argentina's largest Chinese Mafia leads to new arrests," *InSight Crime*, December 2, 2016, www.insightcrime.org/news/brief/investigation-of-argentina-largest-chinese-mafia-leads-to-new-arrests/, accessed June 25, 2018.

80. Alistair Thompson and David Gagne, "Power vacuum leads to fighting among Chinese Mafias in Argentina," *InSight Crime*, February 28, 2017, www.insightcrime.org/news/brief/power-vacuum-leads-to-fighting-among-chinese-mafias-in-argentina/, accessed June 25, 2018.

81. Antje Dieterich, "Human trafficking of Chinese citizens is big business in Argentina," p. 2.

82. See Jeffrey Scott McIllwain, "Organized crime: A social network approach," *Crime, Law and Social Change* 32, no. 4 (1999): pp. 301–323.

83. Hanna Samir Kassab, *Prioritization Theory and Defensive Foreign Policy Systemic Vulnerabilities in International Politics* (New York, NY: Palgrave, 2017), p. 90.

84. Ronald Koziol "Chinese invading Mafia turf," *Chicago Tribune*, May 3, 1988.

85. Andrew Beatty, "Construction boom in Panama is built on drug money," *Reuters*, December 30, 2007.

86. Ibid.

87. Kyra Gurney, "Brazil's PCC, mimicking the country, shifts towards China," *InSight Crime*, January 19, 2015, www.insightcrime.org/news/brief/brazil-pcc-gang-launder-money-in-china-united-states/, accessed June 25, 2018.

88. Yui-Kong Chu, *The Triads as a Business*, p. 1.

89. LaVerle B. Berry, Glenn E. Curtis, Seth L. Elan, Rexford A. Hudson, and Nina A. Kollars, *Transnational Activities of Chinese Crime Organizations* (Washington, DC: Library of Congress, 2003), p. 2.

90. Phil Williams, "El crimen organizado y la violencia en México: una perspectiva comparativa," *ISTOR: Revista de Historia International* 11 (2010): pp. 15–40.

91. Douglas Farah, "Money laundering and bulk cash smuggling: Challenges for the Merida initiative," in *Shared Responbility: U.S.-Mexico Policy Options for Confronting Organized Crime*, eds. Eric L. Olson, David A. Shirk, and Andrew Selee (Washington, DC: Woodrow Wilson International Center for Scholars, Mexico Institute, October 2010), pp. 141–166.

92. James O. Finckenauer, "The Russian 'mafia'," *Society* 41, no. 5 (2004): pp. 62.

93. Charles Parkinson, "US-Colombia operation uncovers FARC, ELN links to Russian Mafia," *InSight Crime*, February 17, 2014, www.insightcrime.org/news/brief/us-colombia-operation-uncovers-farc-eln-links-to-russian-mafia/, accessed March 10, 2020.

94. Edward Fox, "Ecuador captures suspected Russian Drug trafficker," *InSight Crime*, August 8, 2012, www.insightcrime.org/news/brief/ecuador-captures-suspected-russian-drug-trafficker/, accessed June 24, 2018.

95. Geoffrey Ramsey, "UN: Ecuador threatened by Mafia-style homicides," *InSight Crime*, June 17, 2011, www.insightcrime.org/news/analysis/un-ecuador-threatened-by-mafia-style-homicides/, accessed June 25, 2018.

96. Elyssa Pachico, "Bin Laden's cousin arrested in Ecuador?" *InSight Crime*, May 5, 2011, www.insightcrime.org/news/analysis/bin-ladens-cousin-arrested-in-ecuador/, accessed June 25, 2018.

97. Geoffrey Ramsey, "UN: Ecuador threatened by Mafia-style homicides."

98. Ibid.

99. Juan Carlos Garzon Vergara, "Fragmentation and the changing face of LatAm organized crime," *InSight Crime*, November 21, 2015, www.insightcrime.org/news/analysis/what-the-fragmentation-of-organized-crime-means-for-latin-america/, accessed June 25, 2018.

100. Ibid.

101. For more, see "Mafia of the poor: Gang violence and extortion in Central America," *International Crisis Group*, April 6, 2017, www.crisisgroup.org/latin-america-caribbean/central-america/62-mafia-poor-gang-violence-and-extortion-central-america, accessed June 25, 2018; Deborah T. Levenson, *Adiós Niño: The Gangs of Guatemala City and the Politics of Death* (Durham, NC: Duke University Press, 2013); Steven Dudley, "Homicides in Guatemala: Analyzing the data," *InSight Crime*, April 20, 2017, www.insightcrime.org/investigations/homicides-in-guatemala-analyzing-the-data/, accessed June 24, 2018; Anastasia Moloney, "Hundreds flee gang warfare in Honduras' murder city," *Reuters*, May 15, 2017.
102. Edward Fox, "Honduras, Russia to sign pact to strengthen drug fight," *InSight Crime*, September 7, 2012, www.insightcrime.org/news/brief/honduras-russia-to-sign-pact-to-strengthen-drug-fight/, accessed June 25, 2018.
103. Michael Lohmuller and Steven Dudley, "Appraising violence in Honduras: How much is 'gang-related'?" *InSight Crime*, May 18, 2016, www.insightcrime.org/news/analysis/appraising-violence-in-honduras-how-much-is-gang-related/, accessed June 25, 2018.
104. Aïssata Maïga and Walter Kegö, "New frontiers: Russian-speaking organized crime in Latin America," *Institute for Security & Development*, Policy Brief no. 133 (2013): p. 1.
105. Ibid., p. 1.
106. James Bargent, "Russia looks to increase influence in Latin America drug war," *InSight Crime*, March 20, 2013, www.insightcrime.org/news/brief/russia-influence-latin-america-drug-war/, accessed June 25, 2018.
107. R. Evan Ellis, *The New Russian Engagement with Latin America: Strategic Position, Commerce and Dreams of the Past* (Carlisle, PA: US Army War College, 2015), p. 10.
108. Mark Galeotti, "Putin welcomes the return of the Russian Mafia," *Newsweek*, July 18, 2016.
109. Angelika Albaladejo, "Cocaine ring in Russia's Argentina embassy dismantled," *InSight Crime*, February 23, 2018, www.insightcrime.org/news/brief/cocaine-ring-russia-embassy-argentina-dismantled/, accessed June 24, 2018.
110. Ibid.
111. Sebastian Rotella and Lee Romney, "Smugglers use Mexico as a gateway for Chinese immigration," *LA Times*, June 3, 1993.
112. Direct quote from LaVerle B. Berry, Glenn E. Curtis, Seth L. Elan, Rexford A. Hudson, and Nina A. Kollars, *Transnational Activities of Chinese Crime Organizations*, p. 1.

Works Cited

Alami, Aida. "Morocco battles Al Qaeda in the Islamic Maghreb," *Global Post*, November 2, 2010.

Albaladejo, Angelika. "Cocaine ring in Russia's Argentina embassy dismantled," *InSight Crime*, February 23, 2018, www.insightcrime.org/news/brief/cocaine-ring-russi a-embassy-argentina-dismantled/, accessed June 24, 2018.

"Arestan a 5 mexicanos en Hong Kong por tráfico de droga," *Milenio*, September 19, 2011.

Bargent, James. "Russia looks to increase influence in Latin America drug war," *InSight Crime*, March 20, 2013, www.insightcrime.org/news/brief/russia-influence-latin-america-drug-war/, accessed June 25, 2018.

Bargent, James. "Sweatshop raid raises concerns over Peru to Brazil human trafficking," *InSight Crime*, March 13, 2014, www.insightcrime.org/news/brief/sweatshop-raid-raises-concern-over-peru-to-brazil-human-trafficking/, accessed June 25, 2018.

Bargent, James. "Corruption fuels China-Brazil human trafficking," *InSight Crime*, August 5, 2015, www.insightcrime.org/news-briefs/corruption-fuels-china-brazil-human-trafficking, accessed June 25, 2018.

Beatty, Andrew. "Construction boom in Panama is built on drug money," *Reuters*, December 30, 2007.

Beaubien, Jason. "El Salvador fears ties between cartels, street gangs," *National Public Radio*, June 1, 2011.

Berry, LaVerle B., Glenn E. Curtis, Seth L. Elan, Rexford A. Hudson, and Nina A. Kollars. *Transnational Activities of Chinese Crime Organizations*. Washington, DC: Library of Congress, 2003.

Brabo, Manu. "Gang wars in El Salvador, bloodiest year," *Al Jazeera*, September 16, 2015.

Brown, Rachel. "Chinese human smuggling and the U.S. border security debate," *Council on Foreign Relations*, July 18, 2016.

Chen, Michelle. "A cultural crossroads at the 'bloody angle': The Chinatown Tongs and the development of New York City's Chinese American community," *Journal of Urban History* 40, no. 2 (2014): p. 360.

Chin, Ko Lin. *Chinese Subculture and Criminality: Non-traditional Crime Groups in America*. New York, NY: Greenwood Press, 1990.

Chin, Ko-Lin, Sheldon Zhang, and Robert J. Kelly. "Transnational Chinese organized crime activities: Patterns and emerging trends," *Transnational Organized Crime* 4, nos. 3–4 (2002): p. 128.

Chu, Yiu-kong. *The Triads as Business*. London, UK: Taylor and Francis, 2002.

Curtis, Glenn E., Seth L. Elan, Rexford A. Hudson, and Nina A. Kollars. "Transnational activities of Chinese crime organizations," *Trends in Organized Crime* 7, no. 3 (2002): pp. 19–57.

Deprez, Esmé E., Li Hui, and Ken Wills. "Deadly Chinese Fentanyl is creating a new era of drug kingpins," *Bloomberg*, May 22, 2018.

der Ghougassian, Khatchik. "Developing a sub-regional approach to combat weapons proliferation," *Connecting Weapons with Violence*. ISS monograph no. 25, May 1998.

Dieterich, Antje. "Human trafficking of Chinese citizens is big business in Argentina," *InSight Crime*, September 20, 2016, www.insightcrime.org/news-briefs/human-trafficking-big-business-china-argentina, accessed June 25, 2018.

Dudley, Stephen. "Terrorism and crime in the Americas—'It's business'," *InSight Crime*, April 9, 2014, www.insightcrime.org/news-analysis/terrorism-and-crime-in-the-americas-its-business, accessed June 25, 2018.

Dudley, Steven. "Homicides in Guatemala: Analyzing the data," *InSight Crime*, April 20, 2017, www.insightcrime.org/investigations/homicides-in-guatemala-analyzing-the-data/, accessed June 24, 2018.

Economic Commission for Latin America and the Caribbean (ECLAC). *Latin America and the Caribbean in the World Economy: 2008–2009*. New York, NY: ECLAC, 2009.

Evan Ellis, R. "Chinese organized crime in Latin America," *Prism: A Journal of the Center for Complex Operations* 4, no. 1 (2012): p. 67.

Evan Ellis, R. *The New Russian Engagement with Latin America: Strategic Position, Commerce and Dreams of the Past*. Carlisle, PA: US Army War College, 2015, p. 10.

Farah, Douglas. "Money laundering and bulk cash smuggling: Challenges for the Merida initiative," in *Shared Responbility: U.S.-Mexico Policy Options for Confronting Organized Crime*, eds. Eric L. Olson, David A. Shirk, and Andrew Selee. Washington, DC: Woodrow Wilson International Center for Scholars, Mexico Institute, October 2010, pp. 141–166.

Finckenauer, James O. "The Russian 'mafia'," *Society* 41, no. 5 (2004): p. 62.

Fox, Edward. "Ecuador captures suspected Russian drug trafficker," *InSight Crime*, August 8, 2012, www.insightcrime.org/news/brief/ecuador-captures-suspected-russian-drug-trafficker/, accessed June 24, 2018.

Fox, Edward. "Honduras, Russia to sign pact to strengthen drug fight," *InSight Crime*, September 7, 2012, www.insightcrime.org/news/brief/honduras-russia-to-sign-pact-to-strengthen-drug-fight/, accessed June 25, 2018.

Gagne, David. "Investigation of Argentina's largest Chinese Mafia leads to new arrests," *InSight Crime*, December 2, 2016, www.insightcrime.org/news/brief/investigation-of-argentina-largest-chinese-mafia-leads-to-new-arrests/, accessed June 25, 2018.

Galeotti, Mark. "Putin welcomes the return of the Russian Mafia," *Newsweek*, July 18, 2016.

Garzon Vergara, Juan Carlos. "Fragmentation and the changing face of LatAm organized crime," *InSight Crime*, November 21, 2015, www.insightcrime.org/news/analysis/what-the-fragmentation-of-organized-crime-means-for-latin-america/, accessed June 25, 2018.

Gurney, Kyra. "Brazil's PCC, mimicking the country, shifts towards China," *InSight Crime*, January 19, 2015, www.insightcrime.org/news/brief/brazil-pcc-gang-launder-money-in-china-united-states/, accessed June 25, 2018.

Harris, Bryan. "Hong Kong triads supply meth ingredients to Mexican drug cartels," *South China Morning Post*, January 12, 2014.

"Human trafficking by the numbers," *Human Rights First*, www.humanrightsfirst.org/resource/human-trafficking-numbers, accessed June 25, 2018; "Forced labour, modern slavery and human trafficking," International Labour Organization, www.ilo.org/global/topics/forced-labour/lang-en/index.htm, accessed June 25, 2018.

"Illegal Chinese immigrants are flocking to San Diego, smuggled over the border with Mexico," *South China Morning Post*, June 8, 2016.

Kassab, Hanna Samir. *Prioritization Theory and Defensive Foreign Policy Systemic Vulnerabilities in International Politics*. New York, NY: Palgrave, 2017.

Kouretsos, Peter. "Dragon on the border: Mexican and Chinese transnational criminal networks and implications for the United States," *Small Wars Journal*, http://smallwarsjournal.com/jrnl/art/dragon-on-the-border-mexican-and-chinese-transnational-criminal-networks-and-implications-f, accessed June 2, 2018.

Lahrichi, Kamilia. "Chinese criminal gangs hit Argentina," *Huffington Post*, October 5, 2016.

Levenson, Deborah T. *Adiós Niño: The Gangs of Guatemala City and the Politics of Death*. Durham, NC: Duke University Press, 2013.

Levin, Dan. "In China, illegal drugs are sold online in an unbridled market," *The New York Times*, June 21, 2015.

Levitt, Matthew. "Iranian and Hezbollah operations in South America: Then and now," *Prism: A Journal of the Center for Complex Operations* 5, no. 4 (2015): p. 118.

Lohmuller, Michael and Steven Dudley. "Appraising violence in Honduras: How much is 'gang-related'?" *InSight Crime*, May 18, 2016, www.insightcrime.org/news/analysis/appraising-violence-in-honduras-how-much-is-gang-related/, accessed June 25, 2018.

"Mafia of the poor: Gang violence and extortion in Central America," *International Crisis Group*, April 6, 2017, www.crisisgroup.org/latin-america-caribbean/central-america/62-mafia-poor-gang-violence-and-extortion-central-america, accessed June 25, 2018.

Maïga, Aïssata and Walter Kegö. "New frontiers: Russian-speaking organized crime in Latin America," *Institute for Security & Development*, Policy Brief No. 133 (2013): p. 1.

McIllwain, Jeffrey Scott. "Organized crime: A social network approach," *Crime, Law and Social Change* 32, no. 4 (1999): pp. 301–323.

Moloney, Anastasia. "Hundreds flee gang warfare in Honduras' murder city," *Reuters*, May 15, 2017.

Mora, Edwin. "Napolitano: Terrorist enter US from Mexico 'From time to time'," *Cnsnews.com*, July 30, 2012.

Myers, Willard. "The emerging threat of transnational organized crime from the East," *Crime, Law and Social Change* 24 (1994): 195.

"Nearly half of opioid-related overdose deaths involve fentanyl," *National Institute of Drug Abuse*, May 1, 2018.

Nejamkis, Guido. "Iran set up terrorist networks in Latin America: Argentine prosecutor," *Reuters*, May 29, 2013.

O'Connor, Sean. *Meth Precursor Chemicals from China: Implications for the United States*. Washington, DC: US-China Economic and Security Review Commission, 2016.

O'Connor, Sean. "Fentanyl: China's deadly export to the United States," *US-China Economic and Security Review Commission* (2017): p. 6.

Pachico, Elyssa. "Bin Laden's cousin arrested in Ecuador?" *InSight Crime*, May 5, 2011, www.insightcrime.org/news/analysis/bin-ladens-cousin-arrested-in-ecuador/, accessed June 25, 2018.

"Paraguay: 'Strong ties' seen between Hong Kong Mafia, tri-border based Hizballah," *ABC Color*, November 22, 2002.

Pelcastrem, Julieta. "'El Chapo' conspires with Chinese mafias to produce synthetic drugs in Latin America," *Diálogo Americas*, February 19, 2014.

Pena, Alex. "DEA: Mexican drug cartels reach further across Africa," *VOA*, June 15, 2012.

Philcox, Norman W. *An Introduction to Organized Crime*. Springfield: Charles C. Thomas Publisher, 1978.

Philipp, Joshua. "China is fueling a drug war against the US," *Epoch Times*, December 18, 2015.

Prado, Gonzalo. "Cada dos meses se dicta una sentencia por trata de personas," *La Nación*, 24 de junio de 2013.

"Profile of the unauthorized population: United States." *Migration Policy Center*, www.migrationpolicy.org/data/unauthorized-immigrant-population/state/US, accessed June 3, 2018.

Ramsey, Geoffrey. "UN: Ecuador threatened by Mafia-Style homicides," *InSight Crime*, June 17, 2011, www.insightcrime.org/news/analysis/un-ecuador-threatened-by-mafia-style-homicides/, accessed June 25, 2018.

Ramsey, Geoffrey. "Hezbollah in Latin America: An over-hyped threat?" *CS Monitor*, January 13, 2012.

Ramsey, Geoffrey. "Mexico seizes 32 tons of Chinese precursor chemicals," *Insight Crime*, May 8, 2012, www.insightcrime.org/news-briefs/mexico-seizes-32-tons-of-chinese-precursor-chemicals, accessed June 25, 2018.

Ronald, Koziol. "Chinese invading Mafia turf," *Chicago Tribune*, May 3, 1988.

Rotella, Sebastian and Lee Romney. "Smugglers use Mexico as a gateway for Chinese immigration," *LA Times*, June 3, 1993.

Ryan, Jason. "Lebanese drug lord charged in US: Links to Zetas and Hezbollah," *ABC News*, December 13, 2011.

Shadbolt, Peter. "Philippines raid reveals Mexican drug cartel presence in Asia," *CNN*, February 25, 2014.

Sherwell, Phillip. "Cocaine, kidnapping and the Al Qaeda Cash squeeze," *Sunday Telegraph*, March 6, 2010.

Stevenson, Mark. "Honduras becomes main transit route for cocaine trafficking," *Huffington Post*, December 30, 2011.

Stewart, Lindsay and Jennifer Griffin. "America's third war: US secretly trains Guatemalan Forces," *FOXNEWS*, December 14, 2010.

Stone, Hannah. "FARC-Mexican cartel middlemen captured in Colombia," *Colombia Reports*, August 31, 2010, colombiareports.com/colombia-news/news/11604-farc-mexican-cartel-middlemen-captured-in-colombia.html, accessed June 25, 2018.

Stormont, Diane. "Hong Kong's secret triad societies spread their wings," *Reuters Report*, November 6, 1994.

Sverdlick. Ana R. "Terrorists and organized crime entrepreneurs in the 'triple frontier' among Argentina, Brazil, and Paraguay," *Trends in Organized Crime* 9, no. 2 (2005): pp. 84–93.

Thompson, Alistair and David Gagne. "Power vacuum leads to fighting among Chinese Mafias in Argentina," *InSight Crime*, February 28, 2017, www.insightcrime.org/news/brief/power-vacuum-leads-to-fighting-among-chinese-mafias-in-argentina/, accessed June 25, 2018.

United Nations Economic Commission on Latin America and the Caribbean (ECLAC). *Chinese Foreign Direct Investment in Latin America and the Caribbean: China-Latin America Cross-council Taskforce.* Abu Dhabi: ECLAC, 2013.

United Nations Office on Drugs and Crime (UNODC). *Transnational Organized Crime in Central America and the Caribbean: A Threat Assessment.* New York, NY: UNODC, 2012.

US Department of State. *Guatemala: Country Reports on Human Rights Practices.* Washington, DC: US Department of State, 2002.

Weeks, Gregory. *US and Latin American Relations.* New York, NY: Pearson, 2008.

Wells, Miriam. "Report shows dynamics of human trafficking in argentina," *InSight Crime*, June 24, 2013, www.insightcrime.org/news-briefs/report-breaks-down-dynamics-of-human-trafficking-in-argentina, accessed June 25, 2018.

Williams, Phil. "El crimen organizado y la violencia en México: una perspectiva comparativa," *ISTOR: Revista de Historia International* 11 (2010): pp. 15–40.

Xiang, Biao. *Emigration Trends and Policies in China.* Washington, DC: Migration Policy Institute, 2016.

Zhang, Sheldon X. and Chin Ko-lin. *The Social Organization of Chinese Human Smuggling: A Cross National Study.* San Diego, CA: San Diego State University, 2006.

6   Conclusion

Fragile states are the fundamental reason for the success of organized criminal networks.[1] Weak and fragile states lack the institutional capability necessary to encourage and protect legitimate enterprise.[2] Rather, they are easily corruptible and lack access to resources.[3] Underdevelopment is the result of institutional incapacity in this respect. Further, underdevelopment, combined with corrupt political institutions and the growth of illicit markets, encourage organized crime groups to pursue illegal livelihoods.[4] Such matters worsen already critical situations, creating quintessential fragile states that in turn threaten the rest of the world.[5] This is due to the spillover of violence into neighboring states as well as those located on the other side of the world.[6] Cocaine and heroin imported from Colombia or heroin from Afghanistan, already violent communities, could lead to increases in violent criminal behavior in the United States and Europe.[7] All states in the system are made worse off due to the presence of fragile states and the persistence of underdevelopment in those states.[8]

The key to improvement is to increase the resilience factor within these states. Resilience is the ability of any state to deal with threats within their own borders.[9] Effective states with strong capacity and institutions enjoy higher levels of resilience when compared to fragile states. Fragile states cannot adequately neutralize these issues due to the penetration of criminal actors within governing institutions. This, then, is the great conundrum of fragile states in the twenty-first century. The idea of non-growth, the mechanism that destroys the ability of fragile states to become better off over time, is rooted in rampant corruption and, thus, state incapacity.[10] Non-growth is a factor that can spread. For instance, since drug supply markets usually target more developed states that demand illegal substances, non-growth may spread to poorer segments of societies within demand countries like the United States.[11] This is all to move product to the final consumer; people are still needed on the ground to sell drugs. Corruption may also spread as governing officials across the various levels of the supply chain need to be bribed. Hence, governing structures of any illicit market in supply and demand locations are ultimately at risk.[12]

When analyzing the risk generated by weak and fragile states to the globe, it is important to begin at the micro level. State institutions should be a neutral ground for individuals and groups to pursue interests independent of wealth and power. This borrows from the Douglass North definition: "institutions include any form of constraint that human beings devise to shape human interaction."[13]

If institutions are strong in that they defend property rights, protect those seeking justice and punish wrongdoers, then such behavior and practices will be reproduced in citizens. Alternatively, corrupt institutions breed corrupt behavior. Without proper punishment to deter those breaking the law, people will have no regard for the law. Indeed, if it becomes profitable to violate the law such as through narcotics trafficking, then such behavior is not only encouraged but rewarded.[14] On the other hand, strong institutions are designed to deter criminality by punishing those who break the law. In states with strong institutions, leaders are not held above the law or given freedom to operate, but are held to the same standard as other citizens, both rich and poor.

Reforming Institutions

Countries in Latin America face severe institutional challenges. As demonstrated in the case studies throughout this book, many countries in Latin America are inundated by high levels of corruption.[15] However, reforms are required in multiple institutions. In other words, for instance, a country should not reform the police, yet neglect to reform the judicial system.[16] This requires political will and deep-seated reforms. In other words, a corrupt politician may talk about the need to combat corruption, but this person benefits from the current system and does not have many incentives to change it.

As demonstrated throughout this book, the police are one of the major institutions in need of reforms in many countries throughout the Americas given the high levels of corruption and low levels of trust in the institution (Figure 6.1). The

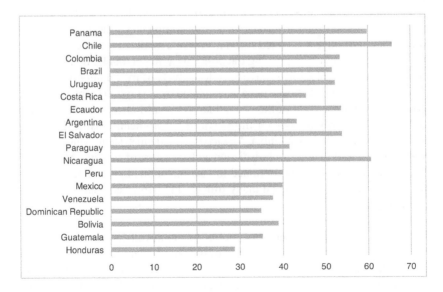

Figure 6.1 Trust in Police Force (0–100)

Source: Created by authors with data from Mimi Yagoub, "From Chile to Mexico: Best and Worst of LatAm Police," *InSight Crime*, March 20, 2017; data from LAPOP 2012 data

police in Colombia are under the Department of Defense. Many experts believe that the police should not be housed within the defense department and should be a separate entity.[17] They argue that there should be a distinct separation between the police and military. In the United States, for example, the Posse Comitatus Act of 1878 does not allow the military to be involved in internal security operations and patrol the streets.[18] President Calderón deployed the military to partake in internal security operations because of his high levels of distrust in the Mexican police forces, which are riddled with corruption. Not only are the Mexican police poorly paid, but there is a high level of unprofessionalism in the institution. In addition, this is a dangerous job, and organized crime groups can use fear and exploit the low salaries of the police to bribe them. This is the age-old problem of *plata o plomo*.[19] In other words, drug trafficking organizations can bribe police officers, who can either accept the cash, or suffer the consequences—hence the lead part of the equation.

There has also been the emergence of hybrid militarized police forces. While the homicide rate decreased in Honduras, for instance, there have been major concerns of human rights abuses. Soldiers have been accused of participating in 30 illegal detentions as well as 20 cases of torture and nine homicides, if not more, in just a two-year period, raising serious concerns about human rights abuses.[20] Thus, while Honduras has seen a decrease in the homicide rate, the question has become what has been the price as the police forces are still plagued by corruption. Mike LaSusa maintains, "While Honduras has seen a substantial drop in its murder rate in recent years, the militarized security strategy pursued by the government has largely failed to tackle longstanding issues like corruption and lack of capacity in police and judicial institutions."[21]

In addition to the need to combat corruption, another lesson of this book is that context matters. The Álvaro Uribe administration made various reforms to the Colombian police and touted such reforms as a model for other countries in the region. Despite Uribe praising the police as a model, public opinion polls demonstrate that Colombians have very low levels of trust among the police forces.[22] In addition, the police have been tainted by corruption scandals. Óscar Naranjo, the former chief of the Colombian National Police, went to Mexico to become a security adviser for the Mexican government.[23] While there can be lessons learned from Colombia, Mexico has a federal system, which creates various challenges in terms of jurisdiction and the nature of policing. Moreover, the Colombian police have continued to face major challenges. For example, the Colombian police removed many officers in 2016 to combat corruption. Mimi Yagoub writes:

> In just 80 days, the Colombian police has removed 1,427 officials from its 180,000 strong ranks. The head of the police, General Jorge Hernando Nieto, said in a press conference that 373 police officers had been dismissed as a result of corruption cases ranging from drug distribution to bribery, while others were removed due to incompetence.[24]

In sum, critics have questioned whether the Colombian police are a model for Mexico not only given the vast differences between the countries, but also as a result of the many challenges still faced by the institution.

Along with reforming the police, many countries in Latin America face many challenges with the judicial system. The instinct often is to pass a new law. Yet scholars note that many of these laws already exist and, therefore, the problem is not the lack of laws. Instead, the laws must be enforced.[25] Countries like Mexico have undergone major judicial reforms. In 2008, Mexico began judicial reforms, including oral trials, to make the system more efficient. Critics of the reform have argued that many of the changes have not been implemented. The implementation of the reforms also requires the retraining of lawyers, judges, and support staff. Patrick Corcoran contends:

> Many analyses point to the failure to adequately train personnel to work within the new system. While foreign exchanges have gone a long way to bring lawyers and judges up to speed, many Mexican law schools have yet to fully adjust their curriculum to the new system, and it has not been possible to train all the current practitioners.[26]

There have been many academic studies on judicial reform that address the challenges of such tasks.[27] Recommendations often focus on the need to be able to evaluate the implementation of programs to ensure effectiveness. In *Judicial Reform in Latin America: An Assessment*, the authors provide many useful recommendations:

- Promote the exchange of relevant experiences and information across the region to permit benchmarking among judicial systems as a means of encouraging change. International organizations can play an important role in this effort.
- Give preference to reforms initiated in areas that are most sensitive and urgent and that are capable of being reproduced. This conforms with the strategy carried out in most countries of first emphasizing reforms in criminal procedure, which is a priority concern of citizens. Also, give special weight to reforms that can demonstrate success over relatively short timeframes, in order to enlist political support for change.
- Enlist the participation in the reform process of sectors having a stake in specific improvements in justice. In the case of criminal justice, for example, human rights organizations and organizations representing victims of crime should be involved. In the case of civil law reform, consumers and the business community should be represented. This helps ensure that the reform agenda remains intact and that the process is not coopted by the legal community or by the judiciary itself.
- Set concrete goals that can be measured in quantifiable ways, promoting evaluation as a fundamental practice and ensuring that participants in the reform process adhere to the goals and objectives established. Funding

provided for judicial reform should likewise be disbursed in line with the accomplishment of the established goals.

- Task credible, independent entities—domestic or international—with responsibility for the periodic evaluation of the reform process and the public dissemination of their findings.
- Ensure the careful technical planning of reforms, with particular emphasis on producing short-term successes. This implies prioritizing areas where relatively rapid progress can be achieved.[28]

Moreover, prisons play an integral part in the criminal justice system and the implementation of the rule of law. In functioning systems, people who violate the law must be prosecuted for crimes, and individuals who have been convicted are sent to prison. As examined in some of the cases throughout this book, prisons do not effectively rehabilitate prisoners. There should be more emphasis on rehabilitation and education to avoid prisons becoming a revolving door. In reality, prisons often serve as schools of crime. The Salvadoran case shows how prisons have played an important part in the gang structure. Prison officials separated gangs within the prison system to avoid the tensions that could arise by mixing members from different gangs. However, gangs from different cliques around the country organized and networked within the prison system.[29]

Decreasing the Demand for Drugs

The drug war has focused on reducing the supply of drugs. It is estimated that the United States has spent more than $1 trillion since Richard Nixon declared the drug war in 1971.[30] Drug trafficking exists because there is a demand for such products. Traffickers are opportunists and will continue to evolve over time to meet market demand. The United States is currently experiencing an opioid epidemic. In fact, more than 60,000 people have died in one year, demonstrating the severe nature of this problem.[31] Moreover, the price per gram of heroin in the United States has increased over time (see Figures 6.2 and 6.3). The Trump administration labeled this as an epidemic, declaring it a "national emergency." Today, opioids are the issue, but it remains to be seen what the drug of choice will be in the future as traffickers seek to diversify their revenue streams.

The United States has a co-responsibility to reduce its appetite for drugs, as it is the largest consumer in the world. Research indicates that rehabilitation, treatment, and education, when done properly, can be effective in reducing the demand for drugs.[32] However, combating demand cannot be addressed by one country alone; cooperation is required. The United Nations Office on Drugs and Crime (UNODC) highlights the need for shared responsibility in reducing demand:

> The most effective way of tackling the drug problem involves a comprehensive, balanced and coordinated approach, that addresses both supply control and demand reduction, which reinforce each other, together with the appropriate application of the principle of shared responsibility.

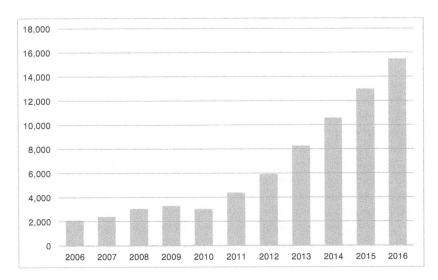

Figure 6.2 Heroin Deaths in the United States

Source: Created by authors with data from Drug Enforcement Administration (DEA), *2018 National Drug Threat Assessment* (Springfield, VA: DEA, 2018)

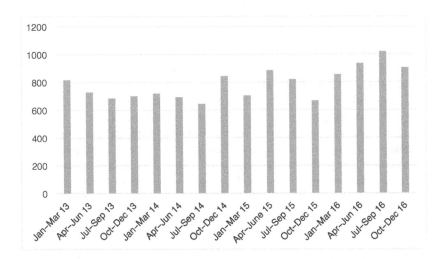

Figure 6.3 Domestic Heroin Purchases (Price per Gram)

Source: Created by authors with data from Drug Enforcement Administration (DEA), *2018 National Drug Threat Assessment* (Springfield, VA: DEA, 2018)

Extensive efforts are being carried out by Governments, international organizations, and non-governmental organizations, to suppress the illicit production, trafficking and distribution of drugs. Drug demand reduction programmes should be integrated to: promote cooperation amongst key actors; include a wide variety of appropriate interventions; promote health and social well-being amongst individuals, families and communities; and should also reduce the adverse consequences of drug abuse for the individual and for society at large.[33]

Experts contend that there must be cooperation between consuming, producing, and transit countries.[34]

If nothing is done to improve the situation in Latin American states (i.e, improve development, reduce corruption, and promote justice), then the security situation could become direr. Organized criminal groups will likely become wealthier and more powerful if nothing is done. These groups may begin to exert control over large swaths of territory and could have their influence spread into neighboring countries. Competing with the state, these networks might transform into states themselves, their leaders, into warlords. Furthermore, organized criminal networks will seek to expand influence and may begin working with other global non-state actors to enhance their position. We are already seeing this in Russia and China. Some scholars note that terrorist networks like Hezbollah, who may already have a small presence in the region, will continue to be an important factor to consider when analyzing regional security and stability.[35] Groups such as these will not only raise finances to fight their own wars but may target the United States. One could argue that it is in the best interests of the United States and its regional partners to take a proactive approach to Central and Latin America. Building walls to slow the flow of drugs and people into the United States is not enough. Rather, the United States must cooperate with its regional allies to address the root causes and at the same time reduce the demand for illicit commodities in the United States.

If weak and fragile states do nothing to strengthen their institutions, matters may degrade to the point of state failure. State failure is the worst case scenario, not just for the state in question, but also for neighboring states, as well as all countries in the international system. Failed states "provide opportunities for actors outside the government—whether religious fundamentalists, disaffected citizens, or merely opportunists seeking power—to attempt to seize the state apparatus by violent means."[36] When a state becomes the epicenter of such destabilizing activity, as Afghanistan was and continues to be, and as Iraq is today, the entire world suffers.[37]

Taking this perspective leads to the following conclusion: the route to success is through the reduction of corruption and the strengthening of economic development.[38] Studies show that "political mechanisms that increase political accountability, either by encouraging punishment of corrupt individuals or by reducing the informational problem related to government activities, tend to reduce the incidence of corruption."[39] The state is essential in promoting economic security and sustainability: "property rights to write contracts, bankruptcy laws and courts to enforce the contracts, financial market institutions to secure investment, governments to provide public goods and infrastructure."[40] Strong institutions will ultimately give people the confidence to invest in businesses. People will feel comfortable in that their work and profit will not be wasted on paying off politicians and police. Increased productivity brings increases in tax revenue that can then go into public goods and other infrastructure. All this is designed to promote investor confidence, potentially lowering unemployment, increasing economic growth and development. This may pull people away from illegitimate and illegal enterprises like narcotics trafficking and toward legitimate endeavors.[41] Yet this cannot be accomplished without first dealing with corruption, the cornerstone of state weakness and fragility.

This book understands the solution to be institutional strengthening of fragile states, not simply police crackdowns. In some instances, police crackdowns by themselves lead to violent reactions from entrenched and powerful cartels.[42] This may be the result of being a weak or fragile state in that non-state actors can be just as powerful as (or even more powerful than) the state itself.[43] As a result, a hardline approach may not be as productive as predicted.

Conclusion

The countries examined in this book have elements of state fragility, including high levels of corruption and impunity. Organized crime groups thrive in countries that are characterized by institutional weakness, as these organizations can survive by bribing judges, politicians, and police officers. Drug traffickers, gangs, and other criminal groups desire to continue their illicit activities and avoid being caught by the police and prosecuted by the judicial system. Those individuals who are incarcerated wish to control operations while behind prison bars. Thus, the more corrupt the state, the better for organized crime groups.

The best way to combat state fragility is to strengthen the state apparatus. This requires reforming institutions across the different branches of government (e.g., executive, legislative, and judiciary branches).[44] Transparency and accountability play a fundamental role in strengthening institutions. Corrupt politicians, judges, or police do not want transparency. Reporting mechanisms for citizens to report crimes are essential. However, the reporting mechanisms will not function if agencies do not follow up on such investigations. Unless institutions are reformed in the countries studied throughout this book, organized crime groups will continue to flourish.

Notes

1. For more, see Jonathan D. Rosen and Hanna S. Kassab, eds., *Fragile States in the Americas* (Lanham, MD: Lexington Books, 2016); J. Patrice McSherry, "Military power, impunity and state-society change in Latin America," *Canadian Journal of Political Science/Revue canadienne de science politique* 25, no. 3 (1992): pp. 463–488; Kimberley Thachuk, "Corruption and international security," *SAIS Review of International Affairs* 25, no. 1 (2005): pp. 143–152.

2. Daron Acemoglu and James Robinson, *Why Nations Fail: The Origins of Power, Prosperity and Poverty* (New York, NY: Crown Publishers, 2012), p. 50.

3. "Corruption and inequality: How populism misled people," *Corruption Perceptions Index*, 2017, www.transparency.org/news/feature/corruption_and_inequality_how_populists_mislead_people, accessed June 18, 2018.

4. Paul B. Stares, *Global Habit: The Drug Problem in a Borderless World* (Washington, DC: Brookings Institution, 1996), p. 6.

5. Jonathan D. Rosen and Hanna Samir Kassab, "Introduction," in *Fragile States in the Americas*, eds. Jonathan D. Rosen and Hanna S. Kassab (Lanham, MD: Lexington Books, 2016), p. xiii.

6. Ted Galen Carpenter, "Watch out, America: Mexico may be the next failed state," *CATO Institute*, January 29, 2015, www.cato.org/publications/commentary/watch-out-america-mexico-may-be-next-failed-state, accessed June 2018, p. 2.

7. Mark A. R. Kleiman, Jonathan P. Caulkins, and Angela Hawken, *Drugs and Drug Policy: What Everyone Needs to Know* (New York, NY: Oxford University Press, 2011), p. 16.

8. Daron Acemoglu and James Robinson, *Why Nations Fail: The Origins of Power, Prosperity and Poverty* (New York, NY: Crown Publishers, 2012), p. 76.

9. Hanna Samir Kassab, *Prioritization Theory and a Defensive Foreign Policy: Systemic Vulnerabilities in International Politics* (New York, NY: Palgrave, 2016), p. 31.

10. Henry Bruton, *Principles of Development Economics* (London: Prentice-Hall, 1965), pp. 2–3.

11. Álvaro Camacho Guizado and Andrés López Restrepo, "From smugglers to drug lords to traquetos: Changes in the Colombian illicit drug organizations," in *Peace, Democracy, and Human Rights in Colombia*, eds. Christopher Welna and Gustavo Gallón (Notre Dame: Notre Dame University Press, 2007).

12. Gautam Basu, "Concealment, corruption, and evasion: A transaction cost and case analysis of illicit supply chain activity," *Logistics, Information, and Service Economy* 7, no. 3 (2014): p. 210.

13. Douglass North, *Institutions, Institutional Change and Economic Performance* (Cambridge: Cambridge University Press, 1990), p. 4.

14. Maureen Meyer, *Mexico's Police: Many Reforms, Little Progress* (Washington, DC: WOLA, 2014), p. 2.

15. For more, see Kurt Gerhard Weyland, "The politics of corruption in Latin America," *Journal of Democracy* 9, no. 2 (1998): pp. 108–121; Stephen D. Morris, "Corruption in Latin America," *The Latin Americanist* 49, no. 2 (2006): pp. 5–16; Damarys Canache and Michael E. Allison, "Perceptions of political corruption in Latin American democracies," *Latin American Politics and Society* 47, no. 3 (2005): pp. 91–111.

16. Jonathan D. Rosen and Roberto Zepeda, *Organized Crime, Drug Trafficking, and Violence in Mexico: The Transition from Felipe Calderón to Enrique Peña Nieto* (Lanham, MD: Lexington Books, 2016); Roberto Zepeda Martínez and Jonathan D. Rosen, "Corrupción e inseguridad en México: consecuencias de una democracia imperfecta," Revista *AD UNIVERSA*, Año 4, Vol. 1 (diciembre 2014): pp. 60–85.

17. For more, see Adam Isacson, "Failing grades: Evaluating the results of plan Colombia," *Yale Journal of International Affairs* 1 (2005): p. 138.

18. For more, see Clarence I. Meeks III, "Illegal law enforcement: Aiding civil authorities in violation of the Posse Comitatus Act," *Military Law Review* 70 (1975): p. 83.

19. Peter Andreas, "The political economy of narco-corruption in Mexico," *Current History* 97 (1998): p. 160; Diane E. Davis, "Undermining the rule of law: Democratization and the dark side of police reform in Mexico," *Latin American Politics and Society* 48, no. 1 (2006): pp. 55–86.

20. Reuters Staff, "Military helps cut Honduras murder rate, but abuses spike," *Reuters*, July 9, 2015.

21. Mike LaSusa, "Military police occupy Honduras neighborhood after gang threat," *InSight Crime*, March 23, 2016, www.insightcrime.org/news/brief/military-police-occupy-honduras-neighborhood-after-gang-threat/, accessed June 18, 2018, p. 4.

22. Miguel García Sánchez, Jorge Daniel Montalvo, and Mitchell A. Seligson, *Cultura política de la democracia en Colombia, 2015: Actitudes democráticas en zonas de consolidación territorial* (Nashville, TN: Vanderbilt University, 2015).

23. Tim Johnson, "Oscar Naranjo, drug war hero in Colombia, tapped for post in Mexico," *Miami Herald*, June 15, 2012.

24. Mimi Yagoub, "Colombia police purges force in anti-corruption push," *InSight Crime*, May 13, 2016, www.insightcrime.org/news/brief/colombia-police-purges-force-in-anti-corruption-push/, accessed June 18, 2018, pp. 1–2; Óscar Andrés Sánchez A., "Purga en la Policía tendría efectos en el mediano plazo," *El Colombiano*, May 12, 2016.

25. Marten W. Brienen and Jonathan D. Rosen, eds., *New Approaches to Drug Policies: A Time for Change* (New York, NY: Palgrave Macmillan, August 2015); Jonathan D. Rosen and Hanna S. Kassab, eds., *Fragile States in the Americas* (Lanham, MD: Lexington Books, December 2016); Modesto Seara Vázquez, Alexander Müllenbach, and Lavard Skou Larsen, *Derecho internacional* público (Mexico City: Porrúa, 1971).

26. Patrick Corcoran, "Mexico's judicial reform, one year in: A mix of successes and defects," *InSight Crime*, August 8, 2017, www.insightcrime.org/news/analysis/mexico-s-judicial-reform-a-mix-of-successes-and-defects-one-year-in/, accessed June 18, 2018, p. 6.

27. Richard E. Messick, "Judicial reform and economic development: A survey of the issues," *The World Bank Research Observer* 14, no. 1 (1999): pp. 117–136; Edgardo Buscaglia, "Corruption and judicial reform in Latin America," *Policy Studies* 17, no. 4 (1996): pp. 273–285; Melinda Gann Hall, "State supreme courts in American democracy: Probing the myths of judicial reform," *American Political Science Review* 95, no. 2 (2001): pp. 315–330.

28. Peter DeShazo and Juan Enrique Vargas, *Judicial Reform in Latin America: An Assessment* (Washington, DC: CSIS, 2006), p. 15.

29. José Miguel Cruz, "Central American maras: From youth street gangs to transnational protection rackets," *Global Crime* 11, no. 4 (2010): pp. 379–398.

30. For more, see Bruce M. Bagley and Jonathan D. Rosen, eds., *Drug Trafficking, Organized Crime, and Violence in the Americas Today* (Gainesville, FL: University Press of Florida, 2015); Marten W. Brienen and Jonathan D. Rosen, eds., *New Approaches to Drug Policies: A Time for Change*.

31. Maya Salam, "The opioid epidemic: A crisis years in the making," *The New York Times*, October 26, 2017.

32. Bruce M. Bagley and Jonathan D. Rosen, eds., *Drug Trafficking, Organized Crime, and Violence in the Americas Today*.

33. "The United Nations approach to drug demand reduction," *UNODC*, www.unodc.org/ropan/en/DrugDemandReduction/drug-demand-reduction-introduction.html, accessed June 18, 2018, p. 1.

34. Roberto Zepeda and Jonathan D. Rosen, eds., *Cooperation and Drug Policies in the Americas: Trends in the Twenty-First Century* (Lanham, MD: Lexington Books, 2014).

35. For more on Hezbollah in Latin America, see Judith Palmer, "Hezbollah in Latin America: Should we be worried?" *Washington Report on the Hemisphere* 36, no. 11 (2016): p. 7.

36. Monika François and Inder Sud, "Promoting stability and development in fragile and failed states," *Development Policy Review* 24, no. 2 (2006): p. 143.
37. Quoted in Mujib Mashal, "Afghan Taliban awash in heroin cash, a troubling turn for war," *The New York Times*, October 29, 2017.
38. Hanna Samir Kassab, *Weak States, International Relations Theory: The Cases of Armenia, St. Kitts and Nevis, Lebanon and Cambodia* (New York, NY: Palgrave, 2015), p. 12.
39. Daniel Lederman, Norman V. Loayza, and Rodrigo R. Soares, "Accountability and corruption: Political institutions matter," *Economics & Politics* 17, no. 1 (2005): p. 1–2.
40. Gérard Roland, "Understanding Institutional Change: Fast-moving and slow-moving institutions," *Studies in Comparative International Development* 38, no. 4 (1990): p. 112.
41. Rafael de Hoyos, Halsey Rogers, and Miguel Székely, *Out of School and Out of Work: Risk and Opportunities for Latin America's Ninis* (Washington, DC: World Bank, 2016).
42. Richard Snyder and Angelica Duran-Martinez, "Does illegality breed violence? Drug trafficking and state-sponsored protection rackets," *Crime, Law and Social Change* 52, no. 3 (2009): p. 254.
43. Jonathan D. Rosen and Hanna Samir Kassab, "Introduction," in *Fragile States in the Americas*, eds. Jonathan D. Rosen and Hanna S. Kassab (Lanham, MD: Lexington Books, 2016), p. xiii.
44. Jonathan D. Rosen and Roberto Zepeda, *Organized Crime, Drug Trafficking, and Violence in Mexico: The Transition from Felipe Calderón to Enrique Peña Nieto.*

Works Cited

Acemoglu, Daron and James Robinson. *Why Nations Fail: The Origins of Power, Prosperity and Poverty*. New York, NY: Crown Publishers, 2012.

Andreas, Peter. "The political economy of narco-corruption in Mexico," *Current History* 97 (1998): p. 160.

Bagley, Bruce M. and Jonathan D. Rosen, eds. *Drug Trafficking, Organized Crime, and Violence in the Americas Today*. Gainesville, FL: University Press of Florida, 2015.

Basu, Gautam. "Concealment, corruption, and evasion: A transaction cost and case analysis of illicit supply chain activity," *Logistics, Information, and Service Economy* 7, no. 3 (2014): p. 210.

Brienen, Marten W. and Jonathan D. Rosen, eds. *New Approaches to Drug Policies: A Time for Change*. New York, NY: Palgrave Macmillan, August 2015.

Bruton, Henry. *Principles of Development Economics*. London, UK: Prentice-Hall, 1965.

Buscaglia, Edgardo. "Corruption and judicial reform in Latin America," *Policy Studies* 17, no. 4 (1996): pp. 273–285.

Camacho Guizado, Álvaro and Andrés López Restrepo. "From smugglers to drug lords to traquetos: Changes in the Colombian illicit drug organizations," in *Peace, Democracy, and Human Rights in Colombia*, eds. Christopher Welna and Gustavo Gallón. Notre Dame: Notre Dame University Press, 2007.

Canache, Damarys and Michael E. Allison. "Perceptions of political corruption in Latin American democracies," *Latin American Politics and Society* 47, no. 3 (2005): pp. 91–111.

Carpenter, Ted Galen. "Watch out, America: Mexico may be the next failed state," *CATO Institute*, January 29, 2015, www.cato.org/publications/commentary/watch-out-america-mexico-may-be-next-failed-state, accessed June 2018.

Corcoran, Patrick. "Mexico's judicial reform, one year in: A mix of successes and defects," *InSight Crime*, August 8, 2017, www.insightcrime.org/news/analysis/

mexico-s-judicial-reform-a-mix-of-successes-and-defects-one-year-in/, accessed June 18, 2018.

"Corruption and inequality: How populism misled people" *Corruption Perceptions Index*, 2017, www.transparency.org/news/feature/corruption_and_inequality_how_ populists_mislead_people, accessed June 18, 2018.

Cruz, José Miguel. "Central American maras: From youth street gangs to transnational protection rackets," *Global Crime* 11, no. 4 (2010): pp. 379–398.

Davis, Diane E. "Undermining the rule of law: Democratization and the dark side of police reform in Mexico," *Latin American Politics and Society* 48, no. 1 (2006): pp. 55–86.

DeShazo, Peter and Juan Enrique Vargas. *Judicial Reform in Latin America an Assessment*. Washington, DC: CSIS, 2006.

François, Monika and Inder Sud. "Promoting stability and development in fragile and failed states," *Development Policy Review* 24, no. 2 (2006): p. 143.

Gann Hall, Melinda. "State supreme courts in American democracy: Probing the myths of judicial reform," *American Political Science Review* 95, no. 2 (2001): pp. 315–330.

García Sánchez, Miguel, Jorge Daniel Montalvo, and Mitchell A. Seligson. *Cultura política de la democracia en Colombia, 2015: Actitudes democráticas en zonas de consolidación territorial*. Nashville, TN: Vanderbilt University, 2015.

Isacson, Adam. "Failing grades: Evaluating the results of plan Colombia," *Yale Journal of International Affairs* 1 (2005): p. 138.

Johnson, Tim. "Oscar Naranjo, drug war hero in Colombia, tapped for post in Mexico," *Miami Herald*, June 15, 2012.

Kassab, Hanna Samir. *Weak States, International Relations Theory: The Cases of Armenia, St. Kitts and Nevis, Lebanon and Cambodia*. New York, NY: Palgrave, 2015.

Kassab, Hanna Samir. *Prioritization Theory and a Defensive Foreign Policy: Systemic Vulnerabilities in International Politics*. New York, NY: Palgrave, 2016.

Kleiman, Mark A. R., Jonathan P. Caulkins, and Angela Hawken. *Drugs and Drug Policy: What Everyone Needs to Know*. New York, NY: Oxford University Press, 2011.

LaSusa, Mike. "Military police occupy Honduras neighborhood after gang threat," *InSight Crime*, March 23, 2016, www.insightcrime.org/news/brief/military-police-occupy-honduras-neighborhood-after-gang-threat/, accessed June 18, 2018.

Lederman, Daniel, Norman V. Loayza, and Rodrigo R. Soares. "Accountability and corruption: Political institutions matter," *Economics & Politics* 17, no. 1 (2005): p. 1–2.

Mashal, Mujib. "Afghan Taliban awash in heroin cash, a troubling turn for war," *The New York Times*, October 29, 2017.

McSherry, J. Patrice. "Military power, impunity and state-society change in Latin America," *Canadian Journal of Political Science/Revue canadienne de science politique* 25, no. 3 (1992): pp. 463–488.

Meeks III, Clarence I. "Illegal law enforcement: Aiding civil authorities in violation of the Posse Comitatus Act," *Military Law Rev* 70 (1975): p. 83.

Messick, Richard E. "Judicial reform and economic development: A survey of the issues," *The World Bank Research Observer* 14, no. 1 (1999): pp. 117–136.

Meyer, Maureen. *Mexico's Police: Many Reforms, Little Progress*. Washington, DC: WOLA, 2014.

Morris, Stephen D. "Corruption in Latin America," *The Latin Americanist* 49, no. 2 (2006): pp. 5–16.

North, Douglass. *Institutions, Institutional Change and Economic Performance*. Cambridge: Cambridge University Press, 1990.

Palmer, Judith. "Hezbollah in Latin America: Should we be worried?" *Washington Report on the Hemisphere* 36, no. 11 (2016): p. 7.

Rafael de Hoyos, Halsey Rogers, and Miguel Székely. *Out of School and Out of Work: Risk and Opportunities for Latin America's Ninis*. Washington, DC: World Bank, 2016.

Reuters, Staff. "Military helps cut Honduras murder rate, but abuses spike," *Reuters*, July 9, 2015.

Roland, Gérard. "Understanding Institutional Change: Fast-moving and slow-moving institutions," *Studies in Comparative International Development* 38, no. 4 (1990): p. 112.

Rosen, Jonathan D. and Hanna S. Kassab, eds. *Fragile States in the Americas*. Lanham, MD: Lexington Books, 2016.

Rosen, Jonathan D. and Hanna Samir Kassab. "Introduction," in *Fragile States in the Americas*, eds. Jonathan D. Rosen and Hanna S. Kassab. Lanham, MD: Lexington Books, 2016, p. xiii.

Rosen, Jonathan D. and Roberto Zepeda. *Organized Crime, Drug Trafficking, and Violence in Mexico: The Transition from Felipe Calderón to Enrique Peña Nieto*. Lanham, MD: Lexington Books, 2016.

Salam, Maya. "The opioid epidemic: A crisis years in the making," *The New York Times*, October 26, 2017.

Sánchez, A. Óscar Andrés. "Purga en la Policía tendría efectos en el mediano plazo," *El Colombiano*, May 12, 2016.

Seara Vázquez, Modesto, Alexander Müllenbach, and Lavard Skou Larsen. *Derecho internacional público*. Mexico City: Porrúa, 1971.

Snyder, Richard and Angelica Duran-Martinez. "Does illegality breed violence? Drug trafficking and state-sponsored protection rackets," *Crime, Law and Social Change* 52, no. 3 (2009): p. 254.

Stares, Paul B. *Global Habit: The Drug Problem in a Borderless World*. Washington, DC: Brookings Institution, 1996.

Thachuk, Kimberley. "Corruption and international security," *SAIS Review of International Affairs* 25, no. 1 (2005): pp. 143–152.

"The United Nations approach to drug demand reduction," *UNODC*, www.unodc.org/ropan/en/DrugDemandReduction/drug-demand-reduction-introduction.html, accessed June 18, 2018.

Weyland, Kurt Gerhard. "The politics of corruption in Latin America," *Journal of Democracy* 9, no. 2 (1998): pp. 108–121.

Yagoub, Mimi. "Colombia police purges force in anti-corruption push," *InSight Crime*, May 13, 2016, www.insightcrime.org/news/brief/colombia-police-purges-force-in-anti-corruption-push/, accessed June 18, 2018, pp. 1–2.

Zepeda Martínez, Roberto and Jonathan D. Rosen, eds. *Cooperation and Drug Policies in the Americas: Trends in the Twenty-First Century*. Lanham, MD: Lexington Books, 2014.

Zepeda Martínez, Roberto and Jonathan D. Rosen. "Corrupción e inseguridad en México: consecuencias de una democracia imperfecta," *Revista AD UNIVERSA*, Año 4, Vol. 1 (diciembre 2014): pp. 60–85.

Index